THE LOVECRAFT ANNUAL

Edited by S. T. Joshi   No. 9 (2015)

Contents

Abbreviations used in the text and notes:

AT   *The Ancient Track* (Hippocampus Press, 2013)
CE   *Collected Essays* (Hippocampus Press, 2004–06; 5 vols.)
CF   *Collected Fiction* (Hippocampus Press; 2015–16; 4 vols.)
LL   *Lovecraft's Library: A Catalogue*, 3rd rev. ed. (Hippocampus Press, 2012)
SL   *Selected Letters* (Arkham House, 1965–76; 5 vols.)

Published by Hippocampus Press, P.O. Box 641, New York, NY 10156
http://www.hippocampuspress.com

Cover illustration by Allen Koszowski. Hippocampus Press logo designed by Anastasia Damianakos. Cover design by Barbara Briggs Silbert.

Lovecraft Annual is published once a year, in Fall. Articles and letters should be sent to the editor, S. T. Joshi, ℅ Hippocampus Press, and must be accompanied by a self-addressed stamped envelope if return is desired. All reviews are assigned. Literary rights for articles and reviews will reside with *Lovecraft Annual* for one year after publication, whereupon they will revert to their respective authors. Payment is in contributor's copies.

ISSN 1935-6102
ISBN 978-1-61498-136-7

Letters to Marian F. Bonner

H. P. Lovecraft

Edited by David E. Schultz and S. T. Joshi

In March 1936, H. P. Lovecraft complained to correspondents of suffering from "the grippe"—an old-fashioned term for influenza. To one correspondent he wrote, "Following my own attack of grippe my aunt came down with an infinitely severer version of the same curst malady, so that since Feby. 17 I have had no time to be aught save a combined nurse, butler, & errand boy."[1] In fact, Lovecraft's bout of ill health likely was attributable to the undiagnosed cancer of the small intestine from which he died a year later. And as for his aunt, it is clear that she was no victim of the grippe either, for as we see in letters to a friend of his, Annie was hospitalized, having undergone "etherisation"—surely a necessary procedure preliminary to surgery. Lovecraft may have thought he had nothing more than the flu, but referring to his aunt's condition as "the grippe" was either a severe misperception on his part of what was troubling his aunt or a conscious attempt to dismiss it using a quaint euphemism; for his aunt had breast cancer and underwent a mastectomy at the age of seventy at the Jane Brown Hospital, followed by several weeks of recuperation at a local nursing home beginning 7 April, and ending with her return to 66 College on 21 May.

Annie E. P. Gamwell (1866–1941), Lovecraft's younger aunt, was the last of his close surviving relatives, as his grandparents, parents, other aunts and uncles, a cousin, and his elder aunt Lillian D. Clark (1856–1932) had perished some time ago. The recipient

---

1. HPL to R. H. Barlow, 11 March 1936; O *Fortunate Floridian: H. P. Lovecraft's Letters to R. H. Barlow*, ed. S. T. Joshi and David E. Schultz (Tampa, FL: University of Tampa Press, 2007), 320–21.

of the letters published here was a friend of Annie who lived just across the courtyard from Lovecraft and his aunt. She lived in a boarding-house—The Arsdale—at 55 Waterman Street, the street one block north of 66 College Street, where Lovecraft lived in the upper flat. Unlike the other houses along College, his residence was not at the sidewalk. Instead, it was set back from the street, well behind the adjacent property at 64 College, so that one needed to walk up a long sidewalk (which Lovecraft referred to as "Ely's Lane") to reach the house. Thus, Lovecraft's house was mid-block between Waterman Street to the north and College Street to the south.

At fifty-three, Marian[2] F[rederika] Bonner (1883–1952) was closer to Lovecraft's age than to his aunt's, but it is clear that her ties were primarily to Annie. Kenneth W. Faig, Jr. has pointed out that Bonner "spent her working career in the periodicals department of the Providence Public Library." This surely accounts for much of the discussion in Lovecraft's letters to her about his own library and that of the tongue-in-cheek K.A.T. fraternity. These letters commence immediately following Annie's surgery and become less frequent upon her return home from recovery. Initially, Lovecraft's sole reason for writing Bonner was to apprise her briefly of Annie's condition, but he continued to write, mostly about matters feline. It is clear from these letters that Lovecraft was more diligent in visiting his aunt than he had been in visiting his mother c. 1919–21. In those days, Lovecraft would visit his mother from time to time, but he would never enter the hospital, and saw his mother only on the hospital grounds.

Lovecraft is often thought to have been a recluse, and a dour one at that, but these letters show that is clearly not the case. True, he could have visited Bonner in person or spoken to her by telephone to convey news about his aunt, but it is also evident that Lovecraft, who enjoyed receiving letters himself, felt that others would enjoy chatty letters from him, especially about something of mutual interest to them. He manifestly relished it—

---

2. Note that Bonner's first name is spelled *Marian* or *Marion* in print. The envelopes that HPL addressed to her, which likely would indicate the preferred spelling, do not survive. Given that her mother's name was in fact "Marian" (as given on the stone marking her grave), it seems likely that the daughter's name was so spelled, and so we use that spelling here.

his earliest letters to Bonner were on his own personal stationery, and he wrote about the most mundane matters in his beloved eighteenth-century style. And although he was under considerable duress at the time because of financial difficulties, his growing correspondence, and the press of other work, he made time to write fairly long letters that he embellished with drawings—some hand-colored—of the felidae he loved so much. Furthermore, there is much humor in his account of how he sparred with his aunt when it came to washing dishes, how his handwriting could be deciphered if his correspondent would but purchase a small magnifier (from England!), and of how he bravely bore a bouquet of flowers some distance through the streets of Providence to the nursing home where his recuperating aunt might enjoy them.

Editors' Note

Lovecraft's letters to Marian F. Bonner reside at the John Hay Library of Brown University. R. H. Barlow, in going through Lovecraft's effects following his death, included Bonner and also her friend and neighbor Evelyn M. Staples on a list of known correspondents from whom letters might be obtained for transcription. Arkham House published extracts from some of the letters to Bonner. The letters to Staples, presumably similar in nature to those to Bonner, appear to be lost.

The editors wish to thank Kenneth W. Faig, Jr., Christopher Geissler of the John Hay Library, and Donovan K. Loucks for their assistance in preparing these letters for publication.

Abbreviations

ALS   autograph letter, signed
JHL   John Hay Library, Brown University (Providence, RI)
TLS   typed letter, signed

[1]   [ALS, JHL]

[H. P. LOVECRAFT
66 COLLEGE STREET
PROVIDENCE, R. I.]

March 22, 1936

Dear Miss Bonner:—

I called on my aunt at the hospital for the first time this afternoon, & she wished me to drop you a particular line of thanks for the many works of consideration extended—the pansies which arrived almost simultaneously with herself, the flowers arriving since then, & the bottle of eau de cologne, all of which were profoundly appreciated.

My aunt was in excellent spirits, & seemed to be making a fine recovery. She had just had an adequate duck dinner, & was completing the ice cream dessert when I arrived. Of course the whole experience is not a pleasant one—there has been pain (although the etherisation, conducted under modern conditions, was wholly free from unpleasantness & nausea), & there is still discomfort from the constant reclining in a fixed position; but everything is progressing according to schedule, & Dr. Kingman[1]—whom I called up the other day—considers the case very satisfactory. My aunt finds the Jane Brown Hospital extremely restful, in contrast with the R.I. Hospital where she was three years ago.[2] Before long she may be able to receive other callers than myself, & when that stage arrives you will certainly be at the head of the invitation list! Meanwhile she sends her most select regards—& her most enthusiastic thanks for the many cheering tributes.

Adding my own most cordial appreciation, I am

Very sincerely yours,

H. P. Lovecraft

P.S. I remained at the hospital for two hours, chatting on various subjects, & my aunt did not seem unduly fatigued. Her appearance is excellent—I would scarcely take her for a patient!

Notes

1. Lucius Collinwood Kingman (1878–1958) was a surgical specialist and later served as president of the Rhode Island Medical Society in 1940–41.
2. The Jane Brown building (1922) of Rhode Island Hospital is on the

grounds at 593 Eddy Street. In June 1933, shortly after moving with HPL to 66 College Street, AEPG fell and broke her ankle.

[2]   [ALS, JHL]

> [H. P. LOVECRAFT
> 66 COLLEGE STREET
> PROVIDENCE, R. I.]

March 26, 1936

Mifs M. F. Bonner,
> The Arsdale, 55, Waterman Str.,[1]
> Providence, (Brown Station), R.I., U.S.A.

Dear Madam:—

Unaccustomed though I am to elaborate attempts at self-exculpation, I am impelled to present at least a shadowy suggestion or instance or two in reply to the formidable charges (relative to the management of the microcosmic park) contained in your communication of present date.

I. A not wholly irrelevant question. Have you ever, by any chance, attempted to stop the present patient from doing anything she was determined to do?

II. An extremely homely & utilitarian semi-parallel. The defendant wishes that the prosecution might witness the perennial struggle (unabated during the period of malady, though then usually resulting in the defendant's victory) within the Garden House over the laborious honour of washing dishes and utensils after (or during) one of the defendant's meals. The present patient, being (baselessly, I assure you) dissatisfied with the defendant's technique, goes to the length of snatching articles from him before he can wash them—a procedure which he combats & occasionally circumvents only by darting suddenly through the bathroom door with the articles in question & washing them in the bowl while the present patient is still lurking watchfully by the kitchen sink. The defendant must sadly add, that even in this case the present patient often secures an ultimate technical victory by washing over again the articles thus washed. During the present patient's illness the defendant's apparent victories were doubtless caused less by his own skill than by said patient's absence from the immediate scene during the defendant's periods of nourishment.

In the present case the defendant would urge that the prosecution carefully consider Points I & II, correlating them both with each other & with the matter of the fractional forest. Whether or not the indictment is quashed, said defendant feels confident that these considerations would not be without influence before an adequate & impartial jury.

The defendant may add that he has twice visited the present patient since Sunday—on the afternoons of Tuesday, March 24th, & of today (Thursday, March 26th). He finds her condition improving, according to all authorities; although sleeplessness & discomfort still exist, while nervousness & worry over general affairs (signs, really, of convalescence) combine to make the days less than pleasant. She now sits up a short time each morning, & today was wheeled out to the sun-porch, where she enjoyed the unaccustomed view of the hospital's park-like grounds.

The present patient sends her best regards to the prosecution, & begs to say that the many cheering messages from that quarter have done much to lighten the tedium & oppression of these dismal days. She was also delighted to receive an encouraging floral tribute from the furry inhabitants of [#]55—Mrs. Spotty Perkins, John Perkins, Jun., & Gilbert John Murray Kynymond Elliot, 4th Earl of Minto.[2]

With this presentation of evidence & transcript of current information, the defence rests.

Accept, Madam, the renewed assurances of my high consideration.

Yr oblig'd ob[dt] Serv[t].,
H. P. Lovecraft

Notes

1. The Arsdale at 53–55 Waterman Street was later renamed the Hopkins House of Brown University (for Chancellor Stephen Hopkins) and used as a student dormitory. It was later razed.

2. Adjacent to HPL's residence was a shed next to the neighboring boarding-house (where AEPG frequently took her meals), with flat roof that provided a place for the local cats to sun. HPL made friends with the cats, luring some to his study with catnip and allowing them to sleep in

the Morris chair or even play on his desk. Since HPL lived on Brown University's "fraternity row," he named the group of felines the Kappa Alpha Tau (K.A.T.). HPL mentions several of the cats as now living at Bonner's residence. See HPL to Edward H. Cole (28 January 1936; ms., JHL): "Local chapter of Kappa Alpha Tau sadly depleted through removal to another neighbourhood of black & white President & tiger Vice-President (brothers)—together with their human family. But black John Perkins sticks around—& the people at the boarding house have decided to keep his little brother, Gilbert John Murray Kynymond Elliot, 4th Earl of Minto." The cat Gilbert etc. was "named by an old lady at the boarding-house who spends her summers in New-Brunswick" (HPL to Helen V. Sully, 18 May 1936; ms, JHL). The woman is Evelyn M. Staples. See letter 3, n. 1. The 4th Earl of Minto (1845–1914) was governor-general of Canada (1898–1904) and viceroy and governor-general of India (1905–10).

[3]   [ALS, JHL]

H. P. LOVECRAFT
66 COLLEGE STREET
PROVIDENCE, R. I.

March 31, 1936

Dear Miss Bonner:—

At last the Hermit of Lockwood St.[1] becomes accessible! When I telephoned this noon my aunt said that she would very much appreciate a call from you—& from Miss Staples,[2] if you can persuade that gentle ailurophile to accompany you—*tomorrow morning* (Wednesday, April 1st—but the invitation is *not* an April Fool stunt!) around 11 o'clock. You will, I imagine, be the first non-blood-kinsfolk to be invited to invade her sanctum—an honour which I trust you will duly appreciate!

Please do not regard the invitation as quasi-compulsory—like a summons to a royal audience—if you have other plans for tomorrow. It is merely that the patient would appreciate seeing you if you find it entirely convenient to drop around.

With best wishes, & much appreciation of the cheer which your messages have afforded the patient,

Yr obt hble Servt

H. P. Lovecraft

Notes

1. AEPG was recovering at the Jane Brown Hospital at 44 Lockwood Street, about 1.5 miles from 66 College.

2. Evelyn M. Staples (1860–1938), born in Barrington, RI, had lived for a time in New Brunswick, Canada. She settled in Providence and taught at the Charles Street School (291 Charles Street) no later than 1910. By 1930, she was residing at 55 Waterman Street, in the same boarding-house as Marian F. Bonner. She continued to live there through 1938.

[4]   [TLS, JHL]

> The Garden House,
> #1, Ely's Court,
> over-against John Hay Library,
> 66, College Street,
> Providence, R.I., U.S.A.,
> 1st April, 1936.

Miss M. F. Bonner,
> The Arsdale,
> 55, Waterman Str. (East Side Station),
> Providence, R.I., U.S.A.,

Dear Miss Bonner:—

Being in receipt of your enquiry and correction of recent date, I take pleasure in attending to the various topics in order of presentation.

First, regarding the term by which the undersigned's aunt was described. Observation of said aunt's coiffure this morning has doubtless apprised you of the erroneousness of the *Haircut* interpretation. To this I may add that the actual word was *Hermit*—a designation often applied to persons in extreme seclusion, as the individual referred to has been up to this morning. The word is an interesting one, being derived (through the French *hermite*) from the Latin *eremita*, meaning a religious recluse; this term in turn being a transliteration of the Greek ἐρημίτης—which itself comes from the word ἐρῆμος, meaning a desert or solitude, and perhaps alluding to the desert environment of the typical early anchorite. Further and less elementary information could probably be gleaned in the appropriate department of the Providence Public Library. The word *eremite* represents the same etymology in purer form.

Second, regarding the term by which your kindly and delightful fellow-inhabitant of The Arsdale was described. The word was *ailurophile*, and signifies one who, like myself, possesses an extreme fondness for the feline species. It is, of course, derived from the Greek αἴλουρος, a cat—this term meaning literally "wag-tail", from αἰόλος, quick-moving or changeable (cf. Αἴολος—Lat. Aeolus—the God of the Winds), and ὀυρά, tail. (If it be objected that the felidae are not habitual tail-waggers, except in anger or disapproval, I respectfully refer you to Mr. John Perkins of The Arsdale, whose eloquent caudal appendage is in a constant state of gentle vivacity even when he is most contentedly rounding out a catnip gorge.) I cannot guarantee the presence of this word in Webster (I have no edition later than 1890, and this gives only the word *ailuroidea*, a zoölogical term signifying the general catlike group of carnivora), but it has in the last twelve years been greatly popularised by the amiable and innocuous Professor William Lyon Phelps in his "As I Like It" column of *Scribners* (vide periodical room, P.P.L.);[1] this eminent Victorian being himself enthusiastically ailurophilic.[2] The coinage of the word follows the most regular laws of philology—αἴλουρος, cat, and φιλέω, I love. Whether any singular word αἰλουρόφιλος exists in Greek to signify "cat-lover" I am frankly ignorant. It is not, however, in the tattered unabridged Liddell and Scott[3] which I inherited from my uncle. But if it did not exist in the classic Attic speech, this surely signifies a grave oversight on the part of the ancients. Professor Phelps' employment of this word took my attention most keenly when I first noticed it in 1924, since I had myself, through independent coinage, been habitually using it for years. Incidentally, I may remark that the word αἴλουρος figures in the name of the *Kappa Alpha Tau* fraternity of sleek old Toms which meets on the shed roof in the ex-Randall yard across the garden from my west windows.[4] Whilst the superficial tend to give a commonplace phonetic interpretation to the initials K.A.T., I always correct this error by informing them that the name really signifies Κομψῶν Αἰλουρῶν Τάξις— i.e., a band or company of elegant or well-drest felidae. The dense ignorance of the majority is surprising and discouraging!

Third. The magnifier enclosed in my recent epistle was there by intention, not by mistake. I was acting upon a recent suggestion that such devices are necessary in decoding my ciphers, and shall probably include them in all outgoing non-typed mail. Most certainly, it was meant for permanent retention. I regret most profoundly that it did not prove more efficacious in identifying *hermit* and *ailurophile,* and would suggest that a more powerful instrument be employed. Enclosed is an advertisement of an instrument which can scarcely fail to give satisfaction, and which may be obtained for the low price of only £6, 15s. from Messrs. James Swift & Son, 81, Tottenham Court Rd., London. With double nosepiece and extra eyepiece (15s. as quoted) and 0.1″ oil immersion objective (£5), this device is guaranteed to unriddle even my postcards.

Fourth. I am extremely grateful for the correction of my humiliating error regarding the postal affiliations of The Arsdale. I had fancied that the village pust-office sarved all edifices belonging to the university corporation, but I now perceive my mistake with the utmost embarrassment.

Fifth. In writing fiction I employ a script similar in size to that in my epistles (as distinguished from postcards).

Sixth. I trust that the legibility of the present communication is above reproach. I have just cleaned the type of this venerable junk-pile (purchased July 6, 1906, as a rebuilt machine), and believe the ribbon still retains some pigment. I regret profoundly the absence of Greek letters from the keyboard, which perforce throws me back now and then upon the sputtering Parker.

In conclusion, I may add that my aunt enjoyed most profoundly the visit from you and Miss Staples this morning—a visit whose encouraging influence was perceptible when I called this afternoon. She appreciated particularly the floral tribute, which so admirably blended the elements of aesthetic appeal and salubrious nutrition.

With profoundest apologies for past cacographical offences,
    Believe me, Madam,
            Yr most oblig'd & obdt Servt,

                    /a/ H. P. Lovecraft
                    /t/ (H. P. LOVECRAFT)

Notes

1. I.e., the Providence Public Library.
2 William Lyon Phelps (1865–1943) was an American author, critic, and scholar. He taught at Yale for forty-one years before retiring in 1933. Some of his articles from *Scribner's Magazine* were gathered in *As I Like It* (1924).
3. Henry George Liddell (1811–1898) and Robert Scott (1811–1887), *A Greek-English Lexicon* (1843; *LL* 533). Still the standard Greek-English lexicon.
4. The Samuel N. Gerard house at 58 College, once owned by R. F. Randall. The Randalls had a black and white cat whom Lovecraft referred to as President Peter Randall, Esq. of the Kappa Alpha Tau, and a tiger-striped brother he called Stephen. When the Randall family moved, the cats did as well. Other members of the "fraternity" included a tiger, Vice-President Count Magnus Osterberg (whom Stephen Randall succeeded as vice-president), Peter Randall's successor, President Johnny Perkins (who would come to call on HPL), his brothers Vice-President Gilbert John Murray Kynymond Elliott, Earl of Minto, and Little Sam Perkins, and their mother, Mrs. Spotty Perkins. Lovecraft could see the cats sunning themselves on the adjacent shed roof.

[5]   [TLS, JHL]

PRESIDENT,
JOHN PERKINS, JUN.
58, WATERMAN ST.

ΚΟΝΤΩΝ ΑΙΛΟΥΡΩΝ ΤΑΞΙΣ

SECRETARY,
THE RT. HON., THE
FOURTH EARL OF MINTO,
55, WATERMAN ST.

COLLEGE HILL CHAPTER, PROVIDENCE
EXECUTIVE OFFICES
1, ELY'S COURT & ADJACENT SHEDS
AND FENCES.

April 4, ... 1936 ....

Dear Miss Bonner:—
            The K. A. T. Executive Office is in receipt of your recent communication, and takes pleasure in replying to various points contained therein.
    First: there *is* a word *hermitess*, which has been employed by no less illustrious a writer than the late Samuel T. Coleridge. It is, however, relatively rare; the preferred usage being to let *hermit* cover both genders—like the word *poet*, whose scope includes both sexes despite the parallel existence of the word *poetess*.
    Second: The K.A.T. Educational Board extends no academic demerits for failure to identify *ailurophile*, since knowledge of the

word is necessarily largely accidental. The Board is itself only a very intermittent follower of Grandma Phelps's[1] cheerful and well-bred column—and the word in question would not have stuck in its consciousness save that it happened to be the first printed occurrence of a coinage which the Board had devised on its own account during the first decade of the century.

Third: this Board disclaims all imputation of being a collector of "firsts". Indeed, no one could despise mere editions *as editions* more than said Board. We accumulate volumes for what is recorded in them—not for the date somebody happened to print them. Of all obtainable editions of a book, we would choose not the first but the last—which had the benefit of all the additions and revisions the author chose to make. In many cases bibliophily and literature are not merely unrelated but actually antagonistic— and I am among the keenest appreciators of Mr. Addison's 158th *Tatler* (for Thursday, April 13, 1710), wherein he gently ridicules the title-page pedantry of Tom Folio the Book Broker.[2] The Board acknowledges with gratitude your invitation to inspect the attic shelves of the Arsdale, and hopes to be able to do so at no distant date. The Hoppin volume referred to, we imagine, is "Recollections of Auton House".[3] In our executive offices we have the original (and probably only edition) of Greene's "Old Grimes" (Sidney S. Rider, 1867) with *illustrations* by Augustus Hoppin.[4]

Fourth: the ex-hermit or hermitess of Lockwood Street (whom we visited yesterday afternoon) retains the pleasantest recollections of your call of 1st inst., and wishes to extend particular thanks for cards received since then—notably the ichthyic specimen of yesterday. Nerve-shock has undoubtedly played a part in her case, but I think the tension is now greatly relaxing. I shall make renewed observations tomorrow.

Fifth: this board has not perused Mr. Walpole's "Inquisitor"[5]— having been too congested with other business when the volume lay on the centre-table of the adjoining parlour. Indeed, we have virtually abandoned any attempt at contemporaneousness in our literary knowledge. Our correlated reading extends, perhaps, up to the middle 1920's. Some time we hope to compile from adequate sources a list of the really significant volumes issued since 1925—a list which would include such new figures as Thomas Wolfe, and the sociological novelists like Albert Halper[6]—and thus touch the high spots without wading through the underbrush.

Sixth: the Board probably will take in Professor Edman's lecture—the last of a notable series, of which the performances of Profs. Savery and Rothschild seem to have been the most brilliant to date.[7]

Seventh: congratulations on your debut in King Lear. As Regan you will be able to present some very unctuous hypocrisy. In my youth I was very fond of heavy and villainous parts, Richard III being beyond comparison my favourite.

Eighth: Anent the art of vessel-cleansing. No—most emphatically—accumulation is the *precise and antipodal reverse* of my lifelong policy. On the contrary, I cannot endure dealing with more than one item at a time, or using any medium save running water direct from the faucet. As fast as one vessel or implement is used, I cleanse it for re-use—never having in the house any soiled item except that from which—or with which—I am taking nourishment. Thus I use but one plate, one fork, one knife, one spoon, one cup, one saucer, and so on . . . . . washing and reëmploying as needed. This I considered the only civilised policy in the absence of a proper staff of servants—for a sink full of used and engreased objects is anathema to me. As once remarked, my policy is not uniformly endorsed at #66—but I nevertheless persist in it as far as possible. Thus, while appreciating in the extreme the philanthropick offer of yourself and the Chief Ailurophile to coöperate in an Augean-Stable ordeal, I am happy to state that the nonexistence of any accumulation makes it needless for the Board to impose on your joint generosity. At this moment—and indeed at all moments save during meals—there is not a soiled dish or article of cutlery in the upper half of the Garden House!

Ninth: We extend congratulations on your first pedestrian tour as a Field Naturalist—though we ourselves would not relish the Great Outdoors quite so early in the Season. 80 to 90 Fahrenheit is our optimum range, and below 70 we find progress distinctly uncomfortable. When we are not able to escape to more genial climes, Mid-May marks the opening of our river-bank and Quinsnicket season.

Tenth: the Board presumes you have duly ordered the "Discovery" microscope from Messrs. Swift & Son—but since the order is probably not yet filled, we are dictating the present bulletin to our staff of typists.

With the season's compliments we beg to subscribe ourselves

Most faithfully yours,

The Board of Education, Kappa Alpha Tau.

Per   /a/ H P Lovecraft /t/ (H. P. Lovecraft),
3d Assistant Under-Secretary.

Notes

1. HPL once described Phelps's speeches as "bland," hence the epithet used.
2. See Joseph Addison (1672–1719), *The Tatler and The Guardian*, ed. George Washington Greene (Philadelphia: J. B. Lippincott Co., 1876 or 1878; *LL* 8).
3. Augustus Hoppin (1828–1896), *Recollections of Auton House: A Book for Children* (Boston: Houghton Mifflin, 1881). But see letter 6, n. 4.
4. Albert Gorton Greene, *Old Grimes* (Providence: S. S. Rider & Brother, 1867; *LL* 374).
5. Hugh Walpole (1884–1941), *The Inquisitor* (Garden City, NY: Doubleday, Doran, 1935), a novel.
6. Albert Halper (1904–1984), novelist and playwright, author of *Union Square* (1933), *Foundry* (1934), and *On the Shore* (1934) among others.
7. For Edman, see letter 7, n. 7. William Briggs Savery (1875–1945) was a professor of philosophy at the University of Washington (1902–45) and a follower of George Santayana, William James, and John Dewey. Rothschild is unidentified.

[6]   [ALS, JHL]

1, Ely's Court, Providence,
April 9, 1936

Dear Mifs Bonner:—

In acknowledging your bulletin of the 7th we wish to append the following bits of information concerning the current patient.

(a) We delivered to her on the 5th inst. the vernal boughs entrusted to us for that purpose—carrying them boldly through the following public thoroughfares: College, Benefit, Transit, South Main, Cent, Point, Eddy, & Lockwood Sts. No small boys jeered at us, being probably impressed with the punitive possibilities of our aesthetic burthen. The patient was properly delighted, & wished me to apprise you of that fact.

(b) On Tuesday, April 7, at 4 p.m., the patient left the gashouse district by motor to complete her convalescence at Dorcus Convalescent Home,[1] 32, Blackstone Blvd. (cor Irving Ave.) (Tel. PL 3485), an extremely prepossessing private retreat whose domestic atmosphere & favourable situation ought to aid greatly in promoting rapid recovery. After a trial of a ground-floor room (which proved too noisy) the patient is now settled in a really delightful second-floor room at the front of the house, with a door leading out upon a screened private porch which commands a fine view of the boulevard. The edifice is a relique of the 1890's, but makes up in comfort what it lacks in taste. The patient, though missing the detailed & instantaneous service provided by the hospital, is getting to like it better & better—& indeed finds the cuisine even superior to Aunt Jane Brown's. When I called yesterday afternoon she seemed in fine shape indeed, & ate her dinner at a table while seated on the edge of the bed. She continues to welcome callers—the best hour being in the morning at any time after 10, & the second-best being in the afternoon betwixt 3 & 4. The mid-day period is devoted to a siesta—a habit she ought to continue after her return to the Garden House.

The K.A.T. Educational Board is pleased to note your stand on purely technical bibliophily, & takes pleasure in getting ahead of the P.P.L. in the matter of No. 158 of *The Tatler*. Despite non-membership in the K.A.T., no inhabitant of our President's home ought to be wholly deprived of our library privileges—& besides, if we recall aright, at least one representative of the rival institution has been notably generous in extending the latter's facilities to relatives of one of our under-secretaries. Hence, with unparalleled magnanimity, we have gone to the prodigious trouble of reaching up to Shelf vii, Case D, & extracting the volume in question—which we herewith proffer as a loan, albeit without any of our rival's chronological restrictions. No fines for overdueness in case you are tempted to peruse more than the single account of Tom Folio. We regret exceedingly that this tome includes only Mr. Addison's contributions to the *Tatler* & *Guardian*. Some time we hope to acquire complete sets of both papers (we have *Spectator, Rambler, World,* & *Looker-On* complete, & possess an odd volume of the *Idler*),[2] since the essays of Sir Richard Steele are not less fascinating than those of his celebrated contemporary. One of the objects of our infant reading was an illustrated (by Hugh Thomson) book of Addison–Steele selections called "Days With Sir Roger de Coverley" (still on our shelves),[3] which probably did much toward giving us an 18th-century bias.

Your correction regarding the identity of the Hoppin item is accepted with gratitude & belated recognition. To be sure A E P G let me see it—& I now recall it well ... the annals of the whiskered Victorian beset by hay-fever, who tried everything once, including aëronautics![4] My memory needs jogging now—it isn't what it was back in the 90's! This volume is certainly a rare embodiment of its age, & is worth guarding as an heirloom. I would surely never part with my "Old Grimes"—which was given me by my late elder aunt some years ago after an extremely clever renovation by a local bookbinder (W. E. Horton,[5] 681 Westminster St.); it having been nearly ruined by mould whilst in storage. I was then staying in Brooklyn, N.Y., & acknowledged the gift in some lines whose anticlimactic spirit was suggested by the text itself:

Old *Theobald** for an elder Scene
  This garish Age is dropping;
The Verſes are by *A. G. Greene*,
  Cuts by *Auguſtus Hoppin.*

To lovelier Scenes it leads his Feet,
  By *Seekonk's* ſhady Rill;
For fixing up the Leaves ſo neat
  There must be quite a Bill!

His Gratitude no common Song
  With fitting Grace may found;
The Book, tho' muſty, still is ſtrong,
  And very well rebound.

Thus ceaſing, left with ſoaring Aims
  His thankful Throat ſhall burſt,
He vows that *Horton* well reclaims
  What *Rider* publiſh'd firſt![6]

My mother used to *sing* "Old Grimes" to me 40 years ago, to the tune of "Auld Lang Syne". Regarding early Rhodinsularia in general—the K.A.T. library also has Job Durfee's epic "What Cheer", & his son Tom's "The Village Picnic & Other Poems"[7]—both written in the still-standing colonial house at the southward corner of Benefit & Jenckes Sts.[8]

Regarding the difference betwixt "mystery" & "fantastic" fiction, as these terms are commonly used—I believe that by the former only *detective* tales & their close congeners are usually meant. Some striking event or situation of unknown cause, but with a natural explanation deductively reached, is the usual so-called "mystery" pattern. On the other hand *fantastic* fiction involves the impossible & incredible, admitting supernatural causation of every sort. It is, in its purest form, simply *the projection or crystallisation of a certain type of human mood*. Its truth is not to objective events, but only to human emotions. In this genre the greatest masters—in addition to Poe—are Algernon Blackwood, Lord Dunsany, Arthur Machen, Montague Rhodes James, Walter de la Mare, William Hope Hodgson, & to some extent the present incumbent of Lord Minto's erstwhile vice-regal sect at Ottawa.[9] Many of the finest specimens, though, are the work of writers who do not specialise in this field—for example, "The Turn of the Screw" by Henry James, & "The King in Yellow" by the late popular hack Robert W. Chambers.

As for *towers*—they do form a delectably appropriate setting for seclusive scribblers of supernatural shockers, though their harmony with the architecture of the Garden House is distinctly

---

*a pseudonym of mine, based on the "hero" of Pope's "Dunciad".

doubtful. The only typical turriform structures of the Georgian age are *windmills* & *steeples*. I might emulate Henry Ford & import a windmill from Cape Cod or Aquidneck to set up in the garden beyond Ely's Court—& if I do so I shall certainly secure an owl or raven. Whether I could *keep* the latter would depend on how well he might get along with the K.A.T. boys.

Many thanks for the tip anent last Monday's *Time*. I'll try to get a look at it. If you like *words*, I presume you've read Trench's now venerable classic on the subject.[10]

With the hope that your "Discovery" microscope has arrived in time to untangle the foregoing hieroglyphs, I remain

      Yr most ob^t h^ble Servt

      H P Lovecraft

Notes

1. Emma K. Dorcus was the proprietress of The Cedars convalescent home.

2. HPL refers to some of the famous periodical essayists of the eighteenth century: Joseph Addison (1672–1919), Sir Richard Steele (1672–1729), et al., *The Spectator* (1711–14); Samuel Johnson (1709–1784), *The Rambler* (1750–52); Edward Moore (1712–1757) et al., *The World* (1753–57); William Roberts (1767–1849), *The Looker-On* (1792–94); Samuel Johnson, *The Idler* (1758–60). HPL had two different editions of *The Spectator* (Edinburgh: A. Lawrie, 1804 [8 vols.], *LL* 9; London: J. M. Dent; New York: E. P. Dutton (Everyman's Library), [1930–34] [4 vols.], *LL* 10), along with a volume of selections edited by Thomas Arnold (Oxford: Clarendon Press, 1891; *LL* 7). He had the complete *Rambler*, ed. Alexander Chalmers (Philadelphia: E. Earlie, 1812 [4 vols.]; *LL* 484 and Vol. 1 of *Idler* (Philadelphia: Printed by Tesson & Lee for S. F. Bradford & J. Conrad, 1803 [2 vols.]; *LL* 480). In the multi-volume series *The British Essayists*, ed. Alexander Chalmers (Boston: Little, Brown, 1855–57 [38 vols.]; *LL* 119), HPL had Vols. 22–24 (*The World*) and 35–37 (*The Looker-On*), both published in 1856.

3. Joseph Addison and Sir Richard Steele, *Days with Sir Roger de Coverley*, Illustrated by Hugh Thomson [1860–1920] (London: Macmillan, 1886).

4. *Hay Fever* (Boston: J. R. Osgood & Co., 1873).

5. Walter Eugene Horton (1854–1938) worked as a bookbinder in Providence as early 1878.

6. Published in *AT* as "[On *Old Grimes* by Albert Gorton Greene]."

7. Job Durfee (1790–1847), *What Cheer; or, Roger Williams in Banishment: A Poem*, rev. ed. by Thomas Durfee (Providence: Preston & Rounds, 1896; *LL* 285); Thomas Durfee (1826–1901), *The Village Picnic*

and Other Poems (Providence: George H. Whitney, 1872; *LL* 286).

8. See *The Case of Charles Dexter Ward:* "Farther and farther down that almost perpendicular hill he would venture, each time reaching older and quainter levels of the ancient city. He would hesitate gingerly down vertical Jenckes Street with its bank walls and colonial gables to the shady Benefit Street corner, where before him was a wooden antique with an Ionic-pilastered pair of doorways, and beside him a prehistoric gambrel-roofer with a bit of primal farmyard remaining, and the great Judge Durfee house with its fallen vestiges of Georgian grandeur."

9. John Buchan (1875–1940), 1st Baron Tweedsmuir, whose *The Runagates Club* and other weird works HPL admired. He was the last governor-general of Canada (1935–40).

10. See letter 7, n. 3.

[7]   [ALS, JHL][1]

April 17, 1936

Dear Mifs Bonner:—

Sight of the patient, up, dressed, around, & alert is surely a heartening thing—& the homelike atmosphere of the Dorcus promotes the effect. I may add with pleasure that on Tuesday the 14th—when there was a bit of sun—she took her first *outdoor walk*, looking up Slater Ave. & reorienting herself to the outside world. She will probably be home next week—an event welcomed equally by the K.A.T. & by herself.

The fraternity is greatly flattered by your commendation of its second issue of stationery, though it entertains no extravagant illusions concerning the artistic value of the designs. So far as drawing goes, we consider the drawing of regular pay a far rarer & less easily attainable feat in this age! We are, however, glad that Pres. Perkins & the chief Ailurophile were given an opportunity to inspect the work.

We duly appreciate the distinction betwixt *fines* & *charges* (as betwixt *penalties* & *sanctions,* or betwixt *barber-shops* & *tonsorial laboratories*), but are happy to repeat that our library imposes neither. Mr. Addison is at your complete disposal for an indefinite period, & I can lend you more of him if you like—including a set of his miscellaneous works (poems—the play "Cato", &c.) published in 1774.[2] He surely did have ideas as well as style, & a perusal of all his essays will disclose more than one apparently modern notion! I surely regret the loss of your paternal library, & wish you could have managed to retain it. Some volumes have been eliminated from the books I have inherited, but there is a certain nucleus to which I adhere more tenaciously than to any other possessions. Durfee's poems ("Village Picnic" &c) & Trench's "Study of Words"[3] are at your disposal at any time. The latter is something of a classic—& the Garden House contains at least two copies, one in the K.A.T. library & the other in the patient's. You must indeed examine the bibliotheca some time, for it may contain many an item worth borrowing. Not but what its marble rival next door—or its granite rival a square down the hill[4]—or very possibly the P.P.L.—could parallel a good many of its items—but we at least allow the unique privilege of overdueness without *charges.*

Let me thank you most abundantly for the "Bekes"—to use our local colloquialism (based on the sketchy phonetic value of the signatory initials) for the diurnal columnar essays of Bertrand Kelton Hart, Esq.[5] I always peruse these with extreme pleasure when they are passed down to me—& I, in turn, pass them along to a learned friend of mine in the distant metropolis of Milwaukee. He—a teacher of English in the West Division High School—uses many of them as a basis of classroom exercises, saves many in a scrap book, & constantly carries a pocketful for reading in odd moments. He has come, after many years, to measure distance by "Bekes". Thus the trolley trip from his home downtown is 2 Bekes. The train ride from Milwaukee to Chicago is 10 Bekes, &c. He is coming east next summer, & I expect to see him in person after many years. When he does I shall ask him the distance in Bekes from Milwaukee to Providence. I shall use my judgment about letting the patient read this batch—or rather, I guess I'll use *her* judgment. Since she recently looked over 3 weeks of N.Y. Times Supplements, & is now perusing Santayana's "Last Puritan",[6] I fancy a mere month of Bekes might not be very formidable. But she shall herself be the arbiter of that point.

That cutting on *locality words* is highly interesting. I have noticed marked local differences of phrase, vocabulary, & speech-rhythm in different parts of the country—& sometimes within relatively narrow limits. Popular versions of quotations vary locally. In the Middle West Burke's famous phrase "chip of the old Block" (applied to the younger Pitt) is commonly rendered "chip *off* the old Block", &c. In New York any ordinary large cheese of the old-time non-tinfoil sort is called "*store* cheese" by dealers. &c. &c. Rhode Island is the most conservative of all the states of the Union in retaining original usages. Nowhere else in America does "Intelligence Office" still signify an exchange for the securing of domestic servants ... & we alone habitually pronounce correctly such names as Greenwich, Warwick, & Olney. Even in Massachusetts one repeatedly hears *War-wick*, *Öl-ney*, &c.

The address of Prof. Edman was very well editorialised—despite the proofreader's determination to place a superfluous *r* in the speaker's name. I enjoyed the event, even though half-frozen by the auditorium's defective heating. Other recent addresses of interest were those of Prof. Robinson on late archaic Greek art, & of Prof. Taylor on the Mayan ruins.[7]

Why did I traverse *Cent St.* in reaching Aunt Jane's from here? Atmosphere? Not at all. The reason is extremely prosaic. It is the *shortest cut* from S. Main to the Point St. Bridge for the southbound pedestrian! This I soon learned in 1933, during my first period of habitual travel to South Providence.[8] Congratulations on your hardihood in public hat transportation. I, too, have conveyed grotesque loads in my day—yet am none the worse for it.

Aye, it is indeed lonely without ex-President Peter Randall—& his tiger brother Stephen, who so closely resembled the late Count Magnus Osterberg. Even now I occasionally forget their departure, & look expectantly at the clubhouse roof to see if any of my old friends are there. Old Peter was always like me—never visible in cold weather! He, by the way, was the first living being I ever saw in these ancient gardens, when exploring them three years ago with a view to future tenancy. In those days he fled at my approach—but in time he came to know & tolerate the other

old gent, & would purr & roll over when Grandpa drew nigh . . .
still imbued with some sportive recollection of his long-vanished
kittenhood. And *what* a kitten he must have been, with that
white spot at the tip of his tail!

You surely ought to see the ancient Durfee house at Benefit &
Jenckes—fallen though it is from its once high estate. That east-
ward-running blind alley is surely fascinating—as is, indeed, the
entire street. I wish it might be reclaimed as John St. was a decade
or so ago—or as, at an earlier period, Pinckney St. in Boston was.
Yes—& Stoll's Alley & parts of Church St. in Charleston. One of
the issues of *The Netopian* (late publication of R.I. Hospital Trust
Co.) had an excellent illustrated article on Benefit St.—which our
library has at your disposal if you wish to consult it.[9]

Pray congratulate Pres. Perkins upon his delineation of the 3d
Asst. Under-Secretary. He remembers more of my history than
you do, for when I was the approximate age of the portrait I actually *did* wear glasses continuously (I wear 'em *now* for continuous
middle-distance gazing, as at an illustrated lecture or theatrical
performance). It was only about a decade ago that I discovered I
could leave them off without acquiring (as formerly) headache &
dizziness—& I promptly took advantage of that discovery, since
the confounded things always were a nuisance. In these latter days
my sight isn't what it used to be, & I keep fearing I'll have to go
back to continuous four-eyedness. But I'll stave it off as long as I
can! Oh, yes—& tell Mr. Perkins that I always heed the admoni-
tion subjoined to the portrait.

I am now starting out for 32 Blackstone, & will duly convey your
regards to the patient. Incidentally, if you noticed the architecture
of her present habitat (I prefer *not* to notice the architecture of Victorian structures), you will realise that she is now living in the next
room to a *tower* even though not in the stately Norman turret itself.
Around 1890 American architects thought there was nothing
smarter to do than to put into small wooden houses the lines which
were meant to belong to monumental stone chateaux—& to mix &
debase those lines until only a keen & tolerant observer could recognise the lineage! Fortunately this seigneurial pile is a merely
temporary residence—for, as previously mentioned, a few days
will bring the objective realisation of your recent dream.

Extending the most appropriately urbane purrs,
I have the Honour to fubfcribe my felf,
Madam,
Your moft oblig'd, moft ob^t Servt.

Notes

1. The images on this "stationery" were designed by R. H. Barlow.

2. HPL refers to *The Miscellaneous Works, in Verse and Prose, of the Right Honourable Joseph Addison*, with Some Account of the Life and Writings of the Author, by Mr. [Thomas] Tickell (Dublin: Printed for T. Walker, 1773 [3 vols.]; *LL* 5).

3. Thomas Durfee (1826–1901), *The Village Picnic and Other Poems* (Providence, RI: George H. Whitney, 1872; *LL* 284); Richard Chevenix Trench (1807–1886), *On the Study of Words: Five Lectures* (London: John W. Parker & Son, 1851; *LL* 892).

4. The marble edifice is the John Hay Library, the granite the Providence Athanaeum at 251 Benefit Street.

5. Bertrand Kelton Hart (1892–1941), was literary editor of the *Providence Journal* and author of the column, "The Sideshow." A "beke" (B+K+H) connotes the length of time it took to read one of Hart's columns. Hart's widow, Philomena Hart, edited and published *The Sideshow of B. K. Hart: A Selection from Columns Written for the Providence Journal, 1929–1941* (Providence, RI: Roger Williams Press, E. A. Johnson Co., [1941]).

6. George Santayana (1863–1950), *The Last Puritan: A Memoir in the Form of a Novel* (1935).

7. Irwin Edman (1896–1954), professor of philosophy at Columbia and author of many books on philosophy; Charles A. Robinson, Jr. (1900–1965), professor of classics at Brown and author of numerous books on Greek history; Norman Wilde Taylor (1892–?), author of "Amid Maya Ruins" (*Women and Missions*, May 1931).

8. See letter 1, n. 2.

9. *Netopian* 10, No. 7 (January 1930) contained "Looking Backward through the Years on Benefit Street" (7, 10–11) and "On Benefit Street, Providence, May Be Found Some of Rhode Island's Most Characteristic Colonial Architecture" (8–9).

Providence Locations Discussed by H. P. Lovecraft and Marian F. Bonner

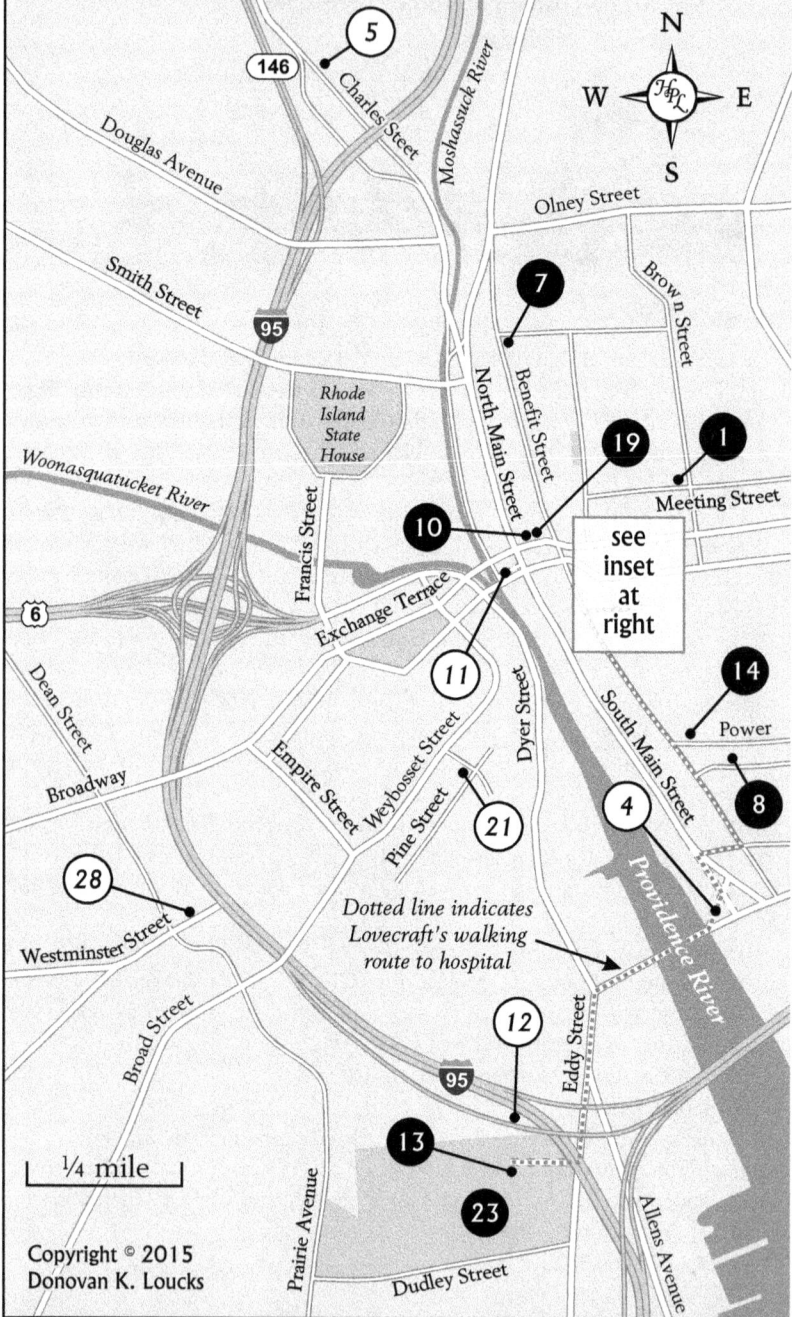

146

5

Charles Street

Douglas Avenue

Moshassuck River

Olney Street

N

W ⟨HPL⟩ E

S

Smith Street

95

Brown Street

7

Benefit Street

North Main Street

Rhode Island State House

Woonasquatucket River

19

1

Meeting Street

10

see inset at right

6

Francis Street

Exchange Terrace

11

14

Power

8

Dean Street

Empire Street

Weybosset Street

Dyer Street

South Main Street

4

Providence River

Broadway

Pine Street

21

28

Westminster Street

Dotted line indicates Lovecraft's walking route to hospital

12

Eddy Street

Broad Street

95

13

23

Prairie Avenue

Dudley Street

Allens Avenue

¼ mile

Copyright © 2015
Donovan K. Loucks

1. 156 Meeting Street
2. *496 Benefit Street*
3. *The Arsdale*
4. *Cent Street*
5. *Charles Street Grammar School*
6. *Dorcus Convalescent Home*
7. Durfee House
8. Edward Carrington House
9. *Ely's Court*
10. Fleur-de-Lys Building
11. *Friend Street*
12. *Gasometer*
13. Jane Brown Building
14. John Brown House
15. John Hay Library
16. List Art Building
17. *Lovecraft's Birthplace*
18. Lovecraft's Home
19. Providence Art Club
20. Providence Athenaeum
21. *Providence Opera House*
22. *Randall House*
23. Rhode Island State Hospital
24. *Robinson House*
25. Samuel N. Gerard House
26. *Slater Ave. Grammar School*
27. *Vacant Stable*
28. *W. E. Horton, Bookbinder*

Italics, white circles, and dashed lines indicate nonextant sites.

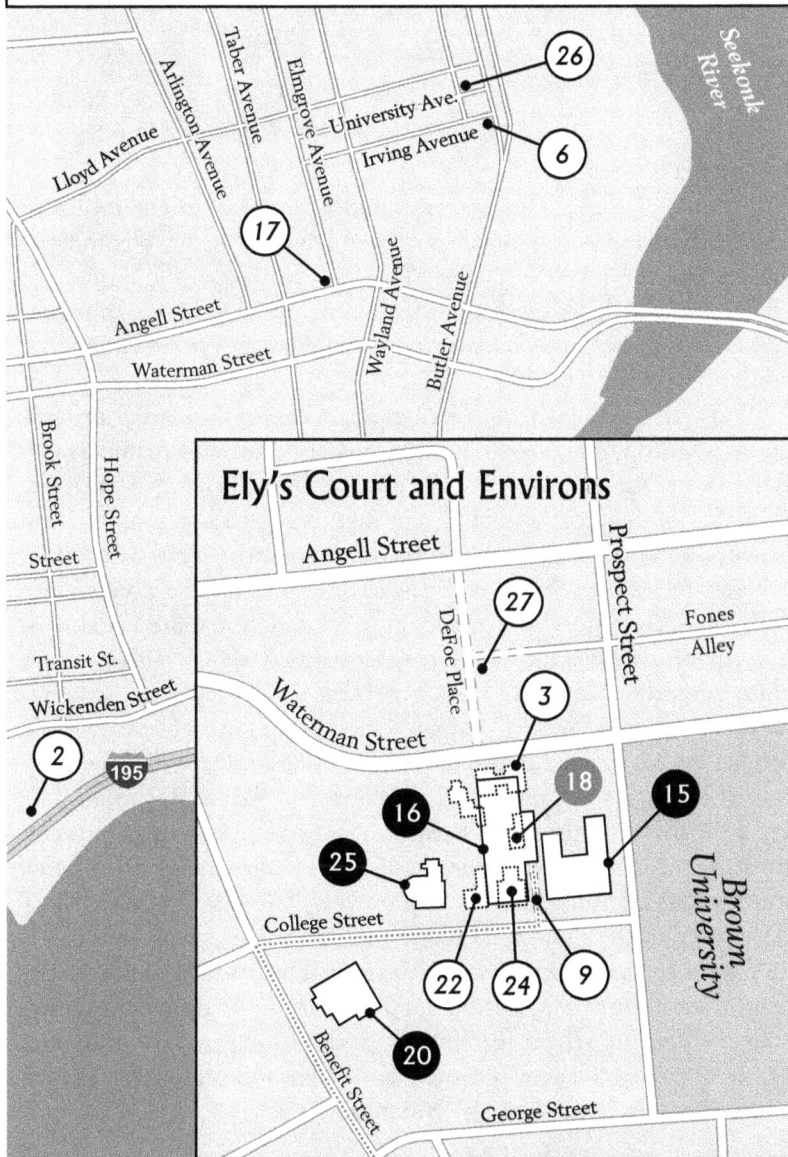

Ely's Court and Environs

[8]   [ALS, JHL]

Dear Miſs Bonner:—

       The fraternity indeed rejoices at the return of the Garden House's long-absent chatelaine, & will welcome the time when the recent ordeal shall have retreated to the domain of the fabulous & half-forgotten. Meanwhile it reiterates its appreciation of the part played by your cheering messages in sustaining the spirits of the ex-patient.

Turning to recent topics in logical order—pray extend my sincerest gratitude to Pres. Perkins for his appointment of me as Official Limner of the local K.A.T. chapter. I shall proceed with the initial task—the portraits of all the members—just as soon as I can induce the latter (including the restless executive himself) to grant me suitable sittings. The list of suggested poses has been very carefully filed, & is most profoundly appreciated. Some are capable of very diverse treatment—thus *cat-a-comb* may signify either something like the Canal St. Station of the B.M.T. subway in New-York, or some process like that which my Florida friend Barlow applies to his Persian companions Cyrus & Darius when their acquisitive interest in entomology seems excessive. Regarding our letter-head #3—this same Barlow, rather than the local limner, must be held responsible for its pictorial designs; the latter being impressions of linoleum cuts fashioned by his skilful young hands. As you infer, the right-hand panel consists of hieroglyphs interpretable only by members of the fraternity. The *lettering* involves the resurrection from my autobiographical museum of two rubber-stamp alphabets which formed my pride & joy some 40 years ago. Many of my earlier works—such as "Wilkes's Explorations" (1902), "Ross's Explorations" (1902), "Antarctic Atlas" (1903), & "Astronomy" (1903),[1] have title-pages printed from these old reliable devices, & I never could bear to discard them. To the best of my knowledge, the recent letter-head forms the first impressions made from these alphabets since the year 1904. In order to anticipate questions regarding the awkward outlines of the K, let me state that this letter was perforce formed by the superimposition of I upon the western half of X . . . a makeshift necessitated by the regrettable loss of K from the font at some unknown period. (cf. the humorously-intended sketch of Poe,* entitled "X-ing a Paragrab")[2] Incidentally—whilst in the disclaiming business—let me state with sorrowful candour that I am *not* the designer of my bookplate. Would that I *could* draw like that! The artist in this case is my young friend Wilfred B. Talman, Esq., of Spring Valley, N.Y. (who, by the way, has studied here at Brown & the School of Design)—now assistant editor of a group of four trade papers (does the P.P.L. handle such things as *The Texaco Star* &c.?) for the olefic Texas Co., & having an office on the 18th floor of Manhattan's Chrysler Bldg.

Turning to the next point: (a) I have used exclamation-points several times during a long life. (b) *confounded* is by no means a strong word for me to use once I am involved in a really vigorous argument. Under suitable provocation, the K.A.T. vocabulary is the very reverse of lacteal . . . as strange felidae & canidae used to discover when they rudely invaded the fence-top isolation of the late Count Magnus Osterberg.

Regarding the possible transmission of my recent 'Beke' remarks to that sprightly essayist himself—I'm sure I have no possible objection . . . nor do I think that Maurice Winter Moe, Esq., of Milwaukee, would object in the least to the identification of the scene of his labours. The outline of your Bekeward note seems eminently adequate—the signature supplying the needed touch of sprightliness. Incidentally, the eruditic Zythopolitan[3] himself—in contributing to R. H. L.'s (formerly B. L. T.'s) "Line o' Type" in the *Chicago Tribune*[4]—signs with the compact trisyllable *Mawimo*. Such is the brevity of human memory—among the busy—that

*whilst we think of it, pray convey our thanks to your colleague Mr. Sherman, whose thoughtful postal regarding the article in *Am. Lit.* was duly received & hope to act upon.

Beke is not likely to identify Mawimo from the present allusion, though as a matter of fact he has heard directly from him. Back in 1929–31 I exchanged a few letters with Beke myself, in the course of which I mentioned Moe's interest. Later—during a period when Beke was discussing folk balladry *in extenso*—Mawimo sent him several specimens current in pioneer Wisconsin, though those were neither printed nor acknowledged. By this time Beke has doubtless forgotten both Moe & myself. For a while, though, I was one of The Sideshow's prominently noticed freaks—as you may gather from the accompanying cuttings[5] (all of which please return some time). These yellowed parchments of yesteryear speak for themselves—telling of how I butted into a discussion of weird fiction, & how (in connexion with my tale "The Call of Cthulhu") a really amazing coincidence developed.[6] My aunt was very grateful for the recent bunch of Bekes, all of which she devoured with avidity. She informs me that your adventurous pedestrian organisation will invade the bibliotaph's aestival country-seat during the ensuing months—a report indeed confirmed by his own 'colyum'.

As to the manner in which I used to rant & rave through such passages as

"What! fhall th' afpiring Blood of *Lancafter*
Sink in the Ground? I thought it wou'd have mounted!
See how my Sword weeps for the poor King's Death!
O, may fuch purple Tears be alway fhed
From thofe that wifh the downfall of our Houfe!
If any Spark of Life be yet remaining,
Down, down to Hell, and fay I fent thee thither!"[7]

... I believe I dwelt more upon the metrical form than the moderns are accustomed to encourage. I was a heavy tragedian of the old school, & verse was verse so far as I was concerned. I was not insensible of the demands of the meaning, yet the *rhythm* would never leave my subconsciousness. Not that I made a real pause after each line (Lancaster, shed, &c), but that I realised the pause myself so fully as to make a microscopic difference in the rendering. I also gave the pronoun *my* its old-fashion'd value "me" or "mih" when it did not call especial attention to the quality of

possession—as recommended in Walker's (18th cent.) Rhetorical
Grammar.[8] Thus in the above, I would ironically & leeringly whine

"See how *mih* Sword weeps for the poor King's death!"

Ah, me—tragedy isn't what it was when I was young! Nowadays
we hear young whippersnappers preaching quiet, realistic technique, & frowning on the vigorous, orotund delivery that Booth,
Barrett,[9] & I used to sling from the stage of Forbes' Theatre, Swarts
Hall, Harrington's Opera House, & the Providence Opera House!

> "Hence, babbling Dreams! Ye threaten here in vain!
> Confcience, avaunt—*Richard's* himfelf again!
> Hark! the fhrill Trumpet founds—to Horfe, away!
> My* Soul's in Arms, and eager for the Fray!"[10]

I am astonished to hear that the newer generations in Rhode-
Island are forgetting the proper pronunciation of *Warwick*—but I
suppose I would encounter the error if I saw more of the public.
In my day, a person who would say *War-wick* would be likely to
say *Gay'-no* Street—or *West-min-i-ster*—or *Ellumgrove Ave*. But alas

> —"Dociles imitandis
>   Turpibus et pravis omnes sumus."[11]

Possibly I mentioned that one of the features of a revision job I
am doing is the compilation of a list of 100 or more words commonly mispronounced.[12] A little reflection revealed many score
more than could possibly be used! My own guide to pronunciation is generally Stormonth—the dictionary used by my father.[13]

My aunt pointed out your old home yesterday, when we took
a walk to see the Carrington house.[14] That locality is a favourite of
mine, & I share your rejoicing in its restoration during the past
decade. No part of Providence is more delightful & unspoiled, nor
could one guess from the immediate environment that a large city
stretched around that idyllic village scene. The Carrington estate is
extremely fascinating. We went into the inner courtyard—quaint
& cobblestoned—where I had never been before. It is a veritable

---

*mih

world apart, surviving from the great maritime age. I am eager for the public opening of the house as a museum—which really ought to be speeded up in order to coincide with the tercentenary celebration.[15]

Yes—my general ocular trouble is short sight, coupled with a muscular maladjustment in the left eye. I hope fervently that I shall not again be driven into the full-time wearing of spectacles.

Under separate cover—or rather, under no cover at all—I am lending the two volumes recently mentioned . . . Trench on the Study of Words, & Tom Durfee's "Village Picnic". No hurry about return—& no fi—er—*charges* in case of retention beyond some theoretical time limit. ¶ Extending the most respectful Compliments, I am, Madam,

Your moft ob[t] hble Servt—

H P Lovecraft—ed Afst Under-Sec K.A.T.

Notes

1. HPL refers to some of his early scientific works. The first three are small treatises; they are non-extant. *Astronomy* (sometimes combined with *The Monthly Almanack*) was a monthly magazine of which seven issues survive (Aug. 1903–Feb. 1904).

2. Clarence Edgar Sherman (1887–1974), who succeeded William E. Foster as head librarian of the Providence Public Library in 1930, after Foster had served in that position for fifty-three years.

3. Denizen of "Zythopolis," HPL's coined Greek word for "Beer-town," or Milwaukee.

4. "A Line O' Type or Two" was a popular column in the *Chicago Tribune*, edited by Bert Leston Taylor (1866–1921) until his death, followed by Richard Henry Little (1869–1946).

5. B. K. Hart, "The Sideshow," *Providence Journal*. The clippings HPL provided are unknown, but likely are of the following columns: 101, No. 280 (23 November 1929): 2; 101, No. 281 (25 November 1929): 2; 101, No. 286 (30 November 1929): 10.

6. Hart had read HPL's "The Call of Cthulhu" in *Beware After Dark!*, finding

that he had once occupied the Fleur-de-Lys building at 7 Thomas Street in Providence, where the artist Henry Anthony Wilcox lived in the story.

7. Shakespeare, *3 Henry VI* 5.6.61–67.

8. John Walker (1732–1807), *A Rhetorical Grammar; or, Course of Lessons in Elocution* <1785> (1st American ed. Boston: J. T. Buckingham, 1814; *LL* 915).

9 HPL refers to the celebrated stage actors Edwin Booth (1833–1893) and Lawrence Barrett (1838–1891).

10. The text derives from the 1699 adaptation of Shakespeare's *Richard III* by Colley Cibber (1671–1757), at the end of Act 5, Scene 5.

11. Juvenal, *Satires* 14.40–41: We are all inclined toward imitating base and wicked things.

12. Anne Tillery Renshaw, *Well Bred Speech: A Brief Intensive Aid for English Students* (Washington, DC: Standard Press, 1936).

13. James Stormonth (1824–1882), *A Dictionary of the English Language*, The Pronunciation Carefully Revised by the Rev. P. H. Help <1871> (New York: Harper & Brothers, 1885; *LL* 850).

14. Edward Carrington House (1810; 1812), 66 Williams Street. John Corliss built the original two-story part of the house in 1810. In 1936, Margarethe Dwight, a descendant of Carrington, gave the house and many of its furnishings to the Museum of Art, Rhode Island School of Design, as a museum showing the influence of the China trade in New England. It was sold to private owners in 1961.

15. HPL refers to the tercentenary of the founding of Rhode Island (1636–1936).

[9]   [ALS, JHL]

The Garden House,
1, Ely's Court,
Providence-Plantations
4th May, 1936

Dear Miss Bonner:—

        The K.A.T. takes pleasure in acknowledging yrs. of 1st inst. with enclosures, as well as the safe return of archaic Bekes (thanks for repair material thoughtfully enclosed) & of Tho: Durfee's "Village Picnic". We likewise appreciate the marked article in the *Atlantic* on the exclamatory style[1]—an article of added interest by reason of our having met Mr. Devoe (then a somewhat affected youth with important-looking rudimentary side-whiskers) in New-York in the year 1928.

We rejoice that the early Bekes proved of interest, but regret to say that the K.A.T. anthology of horrors still remains unedited. As for a bibliography—we do indeed keep a record of such *stories* as we think good enough to remember, but of nothing else—since all our verse & other minor mewings may at once be classed as negligible. We would, indeed, be well-nigh willing to pay blackmail to keep such miscellany out of the sight of the keenly critical. Every now & then we go over our list of tales & strike out such as we are no longer willing to recognise. The last deletion left some 47 in the catalogue, but about ten of these will probably succumb very shortly to the growing critical severity of the author's old age. We strive never to forget the sound advice given by Mr. Q. H. Flaccus a couple of millennia ago—

> "Vir bonus et prudens versus reprobandet inertes;
>   Culpebit duros; incomptis allinet atrum
>   Transverso calamo signum . . . "[2]

No—our macabre metrical reply to Beke's spectral threat is not to be found in the rival institution across the fence . . . indeed, we are one of the few American poets *not* represented* in the justly celebrated Harris Collection.[3] Regarding your projected epistle to Beke—we really see no reason why it should not be sent. Beke probably recalls neither Mawimo nor ourself—& even if he did, he would be unlikely to connect the idea of Bekes as a linear unit with two nebulous figures of the dim past. In these sunset years we have about given up the habit of bombarding 'colyums' with communications; so that unless the contemplated note goes forward, the

---

*except, perhaps, by junk in magazines which the collection has.

public is likely never to learn of the metric system's potential success. Regarding the columnar announcement of your coming pilgrimage—permit me to reverse the order of donation & enclose the item you overlooked. We appreciate most heartily the invitation to accompany the erstwhile patient & your genial band on the Joyeuse Garde[4] expedition, & trust that nothing (unless some miracle sends us Charlestonward or Floridaward) may prevent us from accepting. No—the K.A.T. has never been there (although last week we were driven along the so-called "Drift Road" near Westport Point & told that Joyeuse Garde lay at some undetermined point betwixt the highway & the sea), nor has it ever met Beke in person. As to the tale of mine referred to by Beke but not named—I can't exactly place the reference, but if you mean the praise so charitably given in the column discussing De la Mare's anthology,[5] I must confess that I don't know what tale drew it forth. I really have not the least idea how many things of mine Beke has read—but I doubt if he can have seen many. Under separate cover, as per request, is "The Outsider" (in an issue of W T)—which can be returned at your leisure. I don't think much of this early attempt, for it is deplorably melodramatic & mechanical—but it happened to please the youth who drew up one of the lists for Beke.* This youth (August W. Derleth), by the way, is now making headway as a serious author—getting ahead of the old gentleman whom he once so kindly commended! Concerning the spontaneity of Bekes, ancient & modern—I fancy the 1929–30 specimens had a fresh vitality & enthusiasm, & a certain authenticity of substance, which isn't so often met with in 1935–6. No fountain can be perennially inexhaustible; & if Beke's sprightliness & anecdotage seem now & then a little forced & unctuous in recent years, I can say only that he is, at his worst, a darned sight cleverer than I could ever be at my best!

Does the K.A.T. Library have a Dept. of Fantasy? (I don't know of any word on the order of "Americana" or "Shakespeariana" which quite covers the broad field including supernatural horror-fiction and its penumbra[.]) Yes—in a measure, it does. Not so much a deliberate collection as a spontaneous growth—but enough to catalogue, anyhow. It is, indeed, the only section of John Hay's com-

---

*I'll wager Beke has never seen the story himself. If he had, he wouldn't think much of it.

petitor which *is* catalogued*—this listing being for the benefit of distant members of the "weird fiction gang" who wish to borrow spectral volumes not obtainable in their home-town bibliothecae. Enclosed is a copy of the list[6]—any item on which is at your disposal if your interest & curiosity run in this direction. You will recognise many titles as standard classics—"Udolpho", "The Monk", "Melmoth", &c. Regarding our own attempts—there is no single rule of composition. Some are 'dashed off', some are mentally planned ahead, & some involve endless correction & pen-chewing. The more laboured they are, the worse they generally turn out to be. No—we are never scared of the dark *now*, though we used to be prior to 1895 or '96. Our grandfather cured us of this tendency by daring us (when our years numbered approximately 5) to walk through certain chains of dark rooms in the fairly capacious old home at 454 Angell. Little by little our hardihood increased—& by the time we graduated from the fully-inhabited 2nd floor to the merely servant-&-store-&-guest-room-occupied 3*d* floor, we were reasonably hard-boiled so far as the Amorphous Entities of Shadow were concerned. *Actual nightmares*, though, were another story. We still have 1 or 2 per year—though even the worst is pallid beside the real 1896 product. I invented the name of NIGHT-GAUNTS for the Things I dreamed of in '96 & '97.[7]

Concerning old Providence street-names—we are likely to blunder as badly as the average sap, though in the '90's we were an assiduous devotee to contemporary Sampson-Murdock & Pabodie products.[8] Assuredly, we are far from formidable—& indeed, were a list of the books we *ain't* read to be compiled, we would lose whatever residual aura of grim authoritativeness may still cluster around our pompous facade! ¶ We used to like "Swiss F. R.", though hopelessly overawed by the unfailing competence of the castaways. At one time we had the much inferior sequel "Willis the Pilot"—but this seems to have disappeared from the shelves in the course of repeated eliminations.[9] ¶ I shall surely welcome the temporary accessibility of 'the most elegant private mansion on this continent'.[10]

Yr. most oblig'd & obt. Servt

---

*That is, catalogued *now*. Between 1903 & 1911 I tried to maintain a *general* catalogue of my library.

Yr. most oblig'd & obt. Servt
    H. P. Lovecraft—
        3d Asst. Under-Secy.—K.A.T.

P.S. The list of words frequently mispronounced is part of a school text-book—"Well Bred English"—which I am revising & expanding for the author. If I ever get it done, it will probably be published in the autumn or winter. I picked up a fine acquisition for the list the other night at that Edman lecture—when a man behind me said *sŏn'-o-rous*. It occurred to me that I had heard this before from reasonably educated persons—hence I set it down as sufficiently typical. A correspondent has just suggested *ev-i-dent'-ly*—but I'm not sure how typical this is. Another part of the job is a list of 50 current *stock phrases* to be avoided.

[P.]P.S. The idea of a course in Franklin is surely interesting, although there was always something a bit bourgeois & tradesmanlike about the thrifty sage. I've never read Mather's "Essays to do Good", although I have an hereditary copy of his famous "Magnalia Christi Americana" printed in 1703. I've also read his "Wonders of the Invisible World"—which, as well as the Magnalia, has some fair source-material for weird tales.[11] My "Unnamable" was founded on a passage in the Magnalia. ¶ Have never seen Byron's verses on Pitcairn's Island[12]—such not being in the family copy.

Notes

The coat of arms that HPL has drawn is based on his own, which had instead of cats' heads three foxes' heads.

1. Alan Taylor Devoe, "The Exclamation Point Style," *Atlantic Monthly* 157, No. 5 (May 1936): 581–82.
2. Horace (Q. Horatius Flaccus, 65–8 B.C.E.), *Ars Poetica* 445–47: "A friendly Critic, when dull Lines move slow, / Or harshly rude, will his Resentment show; / Will mark the blotted Pages, and efface / What is not polish'd to its highest Grace" (tr. Philip Francis).
3. The Harris Collection of American Poetry and Plays at the John Hay Library, one of the world's greatest collections of such material.
4. "Joyeuse Garde" was Bertrand K. Hart's home at 787 Pine Hill Road, built in 1820 and also known as Buttonwood Farm, in the town of Westport, MA. The John Hay Library of Brown University possesses a hand-

drawn Christmas card by Hart depicting his house, with verses beginning
"From Joyeuse Garde, now waiting snow . . .". The reason he adopted the
epithet for his home is not known, but the Chateau de Joyeuse Garde is a
ruined castle in Brittany associated with the Arthurian legend.

5. In discussing *They Walk Again: An Anthology of Ghost Stories* (1931),
ed. Colin de la Mare (son of Walter), Hart concluded, "What has become
of my mentor in these matters, up in Barnes street? I want his verdict on
the wisdom and probity of this selection." "The Sideshow," *Providence
Journal* (10 November 1931): 14.

6. "Weird &c. Items in Library of H. P. Lovecraft" (printed in *LL*). Other
lists of approximately the same sort appear in letters to Robert Bloch,
Clark Ashton Smith, and others.

7. Mentioned in *The Dream-Quest of Unknown Kadath* (1926–27) and
Fungi from Yuggoth (1929–30).

8. Sampson-Murdock publisher of the standard Providence city directories. C. A. Pabodie & Son published maps.

9. Johann David Wyss (1743–1818), *Der schweitzerische Robinson* (1812),
first translated into English as *The Family Robinson Crusoe* (1816) and
subsequently titled *The Swiss Family Robinson* (1824f.). *Willis the Pilot: A
Sequel to The Swiss Family Robinson; or, Adventures of an Emigrant Family Wreck* (1858), may not be by Wyss.

10. John Quincy Adams's description of the John Brown House at 52
Power St. HPL visited the house in June 1936.

11. Cotton Mather (1663–1728), *Essays to Do Good* (Boston: Lincoln &
Edmands, 1808); *Magnalia Christi Americana* (London: Printed for T.
Parkhurst, 1702; *LL* 598); *The Wonders of the Invisible World* (Boston:
Printed by Benj. Harris for Sam. Phillips, 1693).

12. "The Island" (1823).

[10]   [ALS, JHL]

Κ ομ Ψ Ω Ν
Α ι λ ο Υ Ρ Ω Ν
Τ Α Ξ Ι Σ
Εἰς τὴν Βιβλιοθήκην

May 22, 1936

Dear Mifs Bonner:—

              Permit me to acknowledge with utmost gratitude, on behalf of the Historical MS. Dept. of the K.A.T. Library, the Providence street notes so kindly transcribed. These settled a long-standing controversy in the 3d. Asst. Under-Secretary's household (& in said 3d A.U.S.'s favour) regarding the inclusion of *S. Angell St.* in the line of the original *Angell.* The limited length of Thayer St., the location of the "North Pumps", the former name of the avenue on whose Angell St. corner I was born, the date of Prospect Alley's naming—all these things proved of the keenest interest. But the library regrets to say that its staff has so far been unable to identify *Friend St.* Could it be *Hope?* I cannot be sure at the moment when the latter was named, or whether its entire length always bore the same name. Part of it was always a path or road, originally forming (with Meeting, Angell, & S. Angell) the Indian route from the bay to the Seekonk—& also forming the rear boundary of the settlers' long, thin home lots.

Another failure of our sadly inefficient staff relates to the often-referred-to poem of Mrs. Whitman on the busts atop the John Brown gates in Power St. Our edition of Mrs. W's poems—a posthumous one issued in the 1890's & said to be the fullest single collection in print[1]—contains nothing of this kind, & we have at the moment no clue to its discovery. When the coming of a little leisure permits me to enquire at other libraries, we may be able to solve the mystery. But at present we are stumped.

Adverting to matters described as "amazing"—we may say that our non-personal-acquaintance with B.K.H. is merely a typical example of our traditional policy of unobtrusiveness. The canidae bark & fawn & slobber over eminent persons on every possible occasion—but we felidae keep to our policy of non-encroachment, & continue to walk our fence-tops independently & unexcitedly until we have some definite & specific reason for exchanging purrs with the King Toms of the neighbouring fences. Certain young friends of ours[2] have written to dignitaries like H. G. Wells, Machen, Dunsany, &c., & have spent good postage mailing copies of their first books (usually printed at their own expense) to Santayana, the late Mr. Kipling, the late George Sterling, H. L. Mencken, & other high lights—including the book departments of all the leading newspapers & magazines. Not so the members of the Kappa Alpha Tau. We appreciate the great, but we are sceptical of their possible interest in our crude attempts. It is wiser, we think, to keep our minds on those attempts themselves. Time enough to know the great when our work speaks for itself & spontaneously attracts their notice . . . & if it never does that, we are just as well off in our merciful obscurity.

No—weeding out poor work is not a very painful process. Far more painful is the ordeal of beholding a stilted, bombastic piece of junk & being forced to admit that one wrote it oneself. Now & then the magazine *Weird Tales* drags out some early atrocity which I have long since repudiated, & reprints it for the benefit of a gaping yokelry. I can't stop them—for they own the copyright. But in such cases I thank the dark gods Nyarlathotep & Yog-Sothoth that relatively few civilised persons ever see *Weird Tales!*

The modernity—or, rather, the timelessness—of Mr. Flaccus is assuredly a striking phenomenon. It is not a matter of chance that he has been more quoted, parodied, & imitated in all ages than any other poet of antiquity. Though he dealt much in surfaces—thus appealing more to the urbane than to the intense—he had that *curiosa felicitas* which instinctively prompted him to choose such surfaces as are most universal, & most persistent amidst mutations & metamorphoses. That first satire against misers is assuredly as timely in 1936 as in B.C. 36—for both ages represent an economic crisis in which the concentration of wealth has produced an impasse requiring new & drastic remedies & a readjustment of perspective & ideology.

Congratulations are due you for your recent dramatic achievements, & I trust that critics hailed your Regan with suitable respect. Poor old Lear! The elder gals gave him a raw deal, but one cannot refrain from thinking that he was a bit naive to expect them to live up to their protestations.

The library list came safely back—& any of the items on it are at your disposal if they seem to promise interest. Many thanks for the additional orthoëpic boners—*tex-tyle* & *ăvvyation*—both of which I have appreciatively entered on the list. Someone else recently suggested *e-quit'-a-ble* & *con'-trast* (as a verb)—but I am in doubt as to the *typical* nature of these slips. Regarding *sŏn'-o-rous*—I have not been able to find any authority for it, either in Stormonth or in the columns of variant pronunciations prefixed to my 1890 Webster.

Other dictionaries might yield different results. At any rate, this pronunciation seems to possess a wide unofficial currency.

Stock phrases are hackneyed or "bromidic" expressions . . . "wend one's way", "the psychological moment", "all Nature rejoices", "easier said than done", "trip the light fantastic", "wee, small hours", &c. &c. &c. Their elimination is one of the first necessities of a good style. No—the term does not signify syntactically *incorrect* phrases. I presume the meaning is that such expressions are cheap, common, ready-made devices always kept in *stock* for the use of the unoriginal & the unimaginative.

I duly conveyed your sympathy to the dental victim—but perhaps she has had a chance to apprise you that her ordeal has not as yet been unduly formidable. Her activity increases. We have been to see the Old Providence pictures by Henry J. Peck at the Art Club, & have walked around the more southerly portions of the ancient hill in quest of the scenes of some of them. Peck catches the spirit of Old Providence as cleverly & consistency [*sic*] as any artist I can think of, & I have been an admirer of his work since his first exhibition in 1928.[3]

[Marginal note:] Many thanks for Bekes enclosed. My elder aunt was a Trollope devotee. I shall probably read "Honey in the Horn"[4] in 1946 if living.

The K.A.T. president & vice-president seem to bear up well despite the absence of the Chief Ailourophile—indeed, they are sometimes so lively in their garden gambols that it's rather hard for an old man to catch them! They both paid me a visit not long since—indeed, I wish they might decide to adopt #66 as one of their major clubhouses!

As for the *casual* mention of Florida*—we have learned with the years to regard all things casually. One is then less disappointed when they fail to materialise . . . as the spoken-of Florida trip will probably fail. In my youth I regarded a journey to the end of the Dyer Ave. car line (I recall the white cars that exchanged the grip for horses at the foot of the hill—& the transformation of those cars to electric power & dark green hue in 1894. The old open horse cars were spliced together—1½ of them making one

---

*from which, if we ever reach it, we shall surely send a typically overcrowded card.

of the rebuilt open cars numbered from 101 to 115 & used on Dyer Ave. & Plainfield St. routes. The closed cars of '94 on these lines were new—first a series numbered from 7 or 8 to the late teens & having no iron posts from dasher to hood, & then [these being transferred to Governor & Brook Sts.] a series with iron posts numbered from the late 20's through the 30's. All this equipment remained in use till the opening of the tunnel in Aug. 1914) as an event. In middle age a ride to East Greenwich or Buttonwoods or Taunton seemed about the same ... as did a trip to Boston. By 1922 or 23 it took a trip to New Hampshire or New York to impart a sense of adventurous exploration. And now I never feel really started till I have reached Washington or Newport, Vt., or some such place. As I go southward, Olneyville & New York coalesce into a single (& not very favourable) impression, & Philadelphia is what Cranston Print Works used to be. Richmond is like Buttonwoods, & Charleston or Florida is like the end of the old Sea View line ... through Narragansett Pier & Peacedale & Wakefield. Alas that the economics of transportation have called a halt to this progressive expansion of orbit & ideas! ¶ With renew'd expressions of gratitude for the street list &c., Yr most obt Servt

    H P Lovecraft

Notes

The epigram in the drawing means "In the library."

1. Sarah Helen Power Whitman (1803–1878), *Poems* (Providence: Preston & Rounds, 2nd ed. 1894; *LL* 949). HPL refers to the poem "A Bunch of Grapes," which can be found in Whitman's *Poems* (Boston: Houghton, Osgood & Co., 1879), 178–80.
2. HPL has in mind in particular August Derleth and R. H. Barlow.
3. Henry J. Peck (1880–1964) published *Glimpses of Providence: From Crayon Drawings, with Notes* ([Warren, RI: Henry J. Peck, n.d.]). HPL once met Peck in person.
4. H. L. Davis, *Honey in the Horn* (New York & London: Harper & Bros., 1935).

[11]   [ALS, JHL]

June 9, 1936

Dear Mifs Bonner:—

From an edifice with well-nigh 130 years to its credit, the K.A.T. commiseratingly returns the greetings from your painfully modernistic abode! It must seem strange to inhabit such a mushroom growth of merely 75 years' standing . . . . though come to think of it, our librarian did not until 1933 have the pleasure of tenanting anything of pre–Civil-war date. Some inhabitants of the Garden House allude nostalgically to such late-19th-century gadgets as card-&-weight windows—though the present writer is not among these. For our part, we yearned for small-paned & archaic windows over a period of more than 40 years—hence, having at last achieved them, we profess ourselves satisfied! As for waxed floors—our one regret is that the southwest study at 1, Ely's Court is encumbered with an intensive hardwood surface, as contrasted with the wide boards we prefer. However—everyone to his taste . . . & I presume Victorian structures at least afford warmth & shelter! The absence of horological chimes must be a genuine deprivation—though I assume that the loss is not complete. But despite all possible objections, I presume that 156 has many advantages over the declining Arsdale.[1] The only reason the higher officials of the K.A.T. remain at the latter is that it affords convenient access to the clubhouse & its roof. I regret that the quadrupedal population at 156 is of a merely canine variety.

And speaking of regrets—the K.A.T. yowls dolefully over the

dispensation of fate whereby the 13th lives up to its infelicitous reputation. For as the Parcae would have it, events have made it impossible for us to be represented in the coming Joyeuse Garde invasion! On Saturday last we received word that the first of our many expected visiting delegations of the summer had lit upon the following week-end for its advent—so that the long-awaited Ides must perforce be dedicated to the sundry rounds of historic & antiquarian sightseeing expected by the pilgrims. This is not the Milwaukee pedagogue who measures distance in Bekes (he is expected in August), but a pair of brothers (one of N.Y. & the other just on from the home town of St. Paul to join him) in the weird-fictional & (in the case of the Twin City one) weird art line.[2] Their itinerary virtually precluding any change of dates, I must relinquish purely local activities in order to play the perfect (or approximately so) host! Alas for the irreconcilabilities of schedules independently conceived ... . & let my appreciation of the Joyeuse Garde invitation be no less abundantly manifest because of this unforeseen plan-wrecker! To make matters worse, the Quondam Patient also has doubts of her ability to be on hand—not that she has to entertain my guests, but that she is anxious not to overtax her newly regained strength with trips of any degree of strenuousness. However—she'll speak of that herself if she has not already done so. Eheu!

As for the K.A.T. policy toward celebrities—we could name quite a few contemporaries who share it. So far as our long recollection goes, we have been actually introduced to only one celebrity of the first rank [except the magician Houdini, for whom we did some revision work in 1924–6 . . . but he was an idol of the crowd rather than one of the solid achievers of the age]—this being the late astronomer Percival Lowell, who lectured here in 1907. We didn't butt in on him—but having arrived early at Sayles Hall, we were espied amidst the prematurely gathered handful by Prof. Upton; who, knowing our devotion to celestial science, most considerately hailed me & made us known to the eminent Martian discoverer. Dr. Lowell no doubt remembered our existence fully five minutes after his courteous handshake.[3]

Yes—a K.A.T. delegation visited the Tercentenary House on the Mall (which is *not* a good specimen of early R.I. architecture, but rather of a northeastern Massachusetts type) on May 18, but found no state maps (of the sort described in the "These Plantations" column of the Bulletin) available. If the maps *are* now ready, we shall have to send another delegation for a supply . . . to outfit the library as well as to present to visitors. According to J. Earl Clauson, the tercentenary map is quite a work of art & antiquarian scholarship combined—shewing small rural roads (the only kind worth traversing) as well as the ugly motor highways.

How do we pronounce *ate?* Well—as a matter of personal usage, especially before strangers, we employ the conventionally ultramodern *ayt*—which also seems to have been customary in the family for two generations behind us. *But*—let me assure you that the *ĕt* sound was not only deemed perfectly correct up to a relatively recent date, but was recorded by Stormonth as the *only* permissible pronunciation . . . this in the 3d quarter of the 19th century! A learned friend of ours, born in 1870 & the son of a Baptist clergyman & academy principal in Massachusetts & New Hampshire,[4] habitually says *ĕt*—& with an apparent bland unconsciousness that anybody says anything else. The ultra-modern Webster of 1890[5] lists *ĕt* as "obsolescent & colloquial"—but old Noah always was a radical! Incidentally—one might add that the past & participial form pronounced ĕt is not properly *spelled* "ate". It is spelled *eat*—thus in the lacteal Mr. Tennyson

> —   "The island princes overbold
> Have *eat* our substance."[6]

And more—even the now comically regarded *"het"* (= heăt) for *heated* was correct in Elizabethan times. Shakespeare says "the iron, though *heat* red hot".[7] My teacher in the Slater Ave. Primary & Grammar School 38 to 33 years ago used to say "het"—she (Abbie A. Hathaway, a daughter of the contractor heading the Waterman St. firm of Hathaway & Douglas) having probably been born in the 1840's. It was certainly a common New England ruralism up to the Civil War period. Stormonth, however, does not sanction it. Hervey Allan, in his life of Poe entitled "Israfel",[8] makes some interesting speculations as to the type of pronunciation prevalent in various American cities in the 1830's & 1840's.

The Georgia poet Chivers (a favourite object of study with our neighbour Prof. Damon)[9] rhymed *Yuba* with *ruby*—thus affording a clue as to the handling of a final *ă* a century ago even in circles of considerable cultivation. [short final ă was probably *y*—as "Ezry", "Elviry", &c., whilst long ā was just that—in the English sense—as "Americay", "Floriday", &c.]

Many thanks for the extremely apt verses quoted from the Library Journal. We are going to exhibit these, in a spirit of respectful reprobation, to a couple of all-too-bibliophilic (as distinct from literary) acquaintances!

Once more wishing you a congenial settlement in your up-to-date quarters—& reiterating regret at the development which precludes Joyeuse Garde*—

I have the honour to remain
        Yr most oblig'd obt Servt
            H. P. Lovecraft—Lib'n K.A.T.

Notes

1. See letter 12 regarding Bonner's change of address.
2. I.e., Howard Wandrei the artist and Donald Wandrei the writer. It does not appear as if they actually visited HPL at this time.
3. HPL refers to the noted astronomer Percival Lowell (1855–1916) and to Winslow Upton (1853–1914), astronomer and professor at Brown University. See HPL to Rheinhart Kleiner, 19 February 1916: "As to celebrities—one experience of mine had to do with . . . Percival Lowell. . . He lectured in this city in 1907, when I was writing for the *Tribune*, and Prof. Upton of Brown introduced me to him before the lecture in Sayles' Hall. . . I never had, have not, & never will have the slightest belief in Lowell's speculations; & when I met him I had just been attacking his theories in my astronomical articles with my characteristically merciless language. With the egotism of my 17 years, I feared that Lowell had read what I had written! I tried to be as noncommittal as possible in speaking, and fortunately discovered that the eminent observer was more disposed to ask me about my telescope, studies, &c., than to discuss Mars. Prof. Upton soon led him away to the platform, & I congratulated myself that a disaster had been averted!" *Letters to Rheinhart Kleiner*, ed. S. T. Joshi and David E. Schultz (New York: Hippocampus Press, 2005), 32.
4. I.e., James F. Morton.

---

*the excursion to which I surely hope will—for those who can make it—be pleasant & weather-favoured!

5. Noah Webster (1758–1834), *Webster's International Dictionary of the English Language* (Springfield, MA: G. & C. Merriam, 1891; *LL* 932).
6. Alfred, Lord Tennyson (1809–1892), "Song of the Lotos-Eaters," ll. 75–76.
7. Shakespeare, *King John* 4.1.61.
8. Hervey Allen (1889–1949), *Israfel: The Life and Times of Edgar Allan Poe* (New York: George H. Doran Co., 1927 [2 vols.]; *LL* 18).
9. S[amuel] Foster Damon (1893–1971), Harvard graduate who since 1927 was a professor in the English department at Brown University. He was also for many years the curator of the Harris Collection of American Poetry and Plays at the John Hay Library. He accepted HPL's papers from R. H. Barlow. Damon also wrote the biography *Thomas Holley Chivers: Friend of Poe with Selections from His Poems: A Strange Chapter in American Literary History* (New York: Harper & Brothers, 1930).

[12]   [ANS, JHL]

[June 19, 1936]

Mifs M. F. Bonner,
        156, Gaol-Lane,¹ Profpect-Hill,
            near yᵉ Beacon-Pole,
                Providence, in Rᵈ: Ifland.

The Providence Chapter of the Kappa Alpha Tau desires to exprefs to Mifs Bonner its most sincere appreciation of her message of sympathy regarding the recent dual bereavement; a paralysing blow which has necefsitated the complete reorganisation of the Chapter, & has left the garden oasis in a state of unrelieved desolation.

The Chapter also transmits the appreciative acknowledgments of Mr. & Mrs. John Perkins, Sr., parents of our late officers. Mrs. Perkins has just returned from her pedagogical duties at Brown University, where she acted as an Afsistant Profefsor in the Department of Psychology.²

19ᵗʰ June.   Per the 3ᵈ Afst. Under-Secretary

Notes

1. Bonner had moved to 156 Meeting Street (formerly Gaol-Lane).
2. See HPL to R. H. Barlow, 13 June 1936: "I have lost my best friends—& the local chapter of the Kappa Alpha Tau staggers under a crushing blow. This week both Mr. John Perkins (black—b. Feby. 14, 1935) & the

Earl of Minto (black & white—b. Oct. '35) succumbed to some malady which is afflicting all the felidae of the neighbourhood—a thing which may be an obscure epidemic, yet which may be the malign activities of some contemptible poisoner. The sad end of the brothers seemed connected with some digestive disorder, & recalled the equally sad fate of their bygone brother—little Sam Perkins (May–Sept. '34)—of whom you have heard. If this *is* the work of some wretched neo-Borgia, I hope to hell somebody feeds him a poison a thousandfold more painful than that which he has subtly supplied his innocent furry victims!" O *Fortunate Floridian* 345.

[13]   [ALS, JHL]

EXECUTIVE COMMITTEE
K · A · T ·
ELY'S COURT AND DE FOE PLACE,
PROVIDENCE,
R. I.

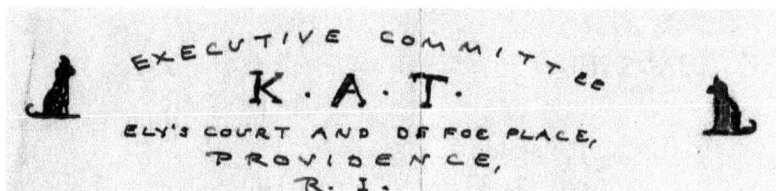

November 23, 1936

Mifs Marian Bonner,
    156, Gaol-Lane, Providence,

Dear Madam:—

            Replying to your enquiry of 22nd inst. regarding the posthumous action of the Kappa Alpha Tau on the recent tragical heroism of Senhora Caterina Almedia of 496, Back-Street, we beg to inform you that a memorial fund was collected at our last meeting (in the vacant stable at Prospect Alley & De Foe Place), to be used in providing a dozen catnip mice apiece for the surviving children of the deceased—Senhorita Inkspot Almedia, Senhor Manuel Almedia, & Senhor Rodrigo Braganza Almedia. A memorial of this practical nature was deemed advisable, insomuch as the symbolic & decorative side was so well covered by our human colleagues of the N.Y. Anti-Vivisection Society. We have also extended invitations to the young Senhoras Almedia to become members of our sadly depleted chapter upon their attainment of their majority, & to Senhorita Inkspot to become affiliated with the Ladies' Auxiliary.

With appreciation of your interest in the activities of our organisation, we beg to remain
Most faithfully yours,
The Executive Committee, Providence Chapter,
Κομψῶν Αἰλουρων Τάξις

Per: Thomas Broadbeam-Blackman, Pres't[1]
[elected at Sabbat of Oct. 31 to succeed Mr. John Perkins, Sr. Mr. Perkins' non-attendance at recent meetings militated against him, & prejudice concerning Mr. Broadbeam-Blackman's dour temperament & bluff mannerisms was easily overcome.]

Dan'l Defoe Vice-Pres't   White Stubtail Congdon, Secy
  Mrs. Spotty Perkins,   H. P. Lovecraft, Librarian &
  Pres. Ladies' Auxiliary   3[d] Asst. Under-Secy.

Notes

1. HPL mentions this cat and those named below only in letters to Bonner.

[14]   [ALS, JHL]

Providence Chapter   Kappa Alpha Tau

1, Ely's Court,

Dec'r. 7.... 1936....

Mifs M. F. Bonner,
  156 Gaol-Lane, Profpect-Hill,
    N[r.] the Beacon-Pole.

Dear Madam:—
                The K.A.T. authorities, pausing for a moment from their grateful contemplation of newly acquired almanacks, wish to acknowledge with appreciation the message from Pres. Emerson Thoreau Cornell of the Framingham Chapter, in the

Province of the Maſsachsetts-Bay, as kindly transmitted through
you. We are keenly interested in his clever & original lounging-
place, & in his sportive gambols with his diminutive testudinate
friend. The latter, we are certain, must feel honoured at his choice
as boon companion of the snowy & scholarly Pres. Cornell; whilst
the strenuousness of the sport cannot but form a salutory influence in combating the natural sluggishness of the reptilian disposi-
tion. Messages from Pres. Cornell will always be welcome—& he
may rest assured that the picture enclosed in his letter (a view of
us when confronted by a long revision job or a volume of Victorian fiction) does *not* represent our attitude in hearing from him.

Nor does it typify our sentiments toward the Hon. James
O'Flaherty McCarthy,[1] at whose delicatessen (even in the ould
days phwin it was a branch av Riley's) we have purchased many a
pound of cheese & many a slice of veal loaf. Mr. McCarthy's rough
exterior would not weigh against him with us—for is not our new
chapter president, Thos· Broadbeam-Blackburn, Esq., a bit brusque
& negligent of the amenities? I am sure that Mr. McCarthy would
be a welcome addition to any K.A.T. enterprise! Larng loives to
'im intoirely!

We have indeed seen the new *Harpers* (thanks, I believe, to
the Chief Ailurophile) & perused "The House of the Laburnums",[2]
which is a clever bit of spectral horror though by no means original in plot. The idea of ghosts of *future* events is a fairly old one, &
has had notable exemplars as far back as Wilkie Collins's "Dream
Woman".[3] A later specimen with the same general idea is W. F.
Harvey's "August Heat" (1910), to be found in the first "Omnibus
of Crime".[4] This Downes story is notable chiefly for the atmosphere—& I rather fancy that *Harpers* (normally unsympathetic
toward the weird) took it more because of the author's established status than because of any particular intrinsic merit. However, it is undeniably pretty good as the milder sort of spectral
fiction goes.

As orally expressed before, we rejoice that you have located
"The Witch-Cult in Western Europe"[5] & have thereby become
familiar with Sabbats, Estbats, Covens, & all the other attributes of
the festering horror which brooded over mediaeval & renaissance
Europe & perhaps over colonial Salem. And we apologise that our

nominated guide Sir Walter failed to mention Sabbats at all—as he really should have done, since the term was well-known from constant repetition at witch-trials long before the actuality of any subterraneous cult was suspected.

Pray consider all the facilities of our Chapter, including the bibliothecal, perennially at your service, & accept our renewed expressions of gratitude for the additions to the almanack department of our archives.

Madam,

Yr moft oblig'd & ob^t Servt$^{s.}$
K.A.T., Providence Chapter

per:

T. Broadbeam-Blackburn, Pres't.

Dan'l Defoe, Vice-Prefident

H. P. Lovecraft, Lib'n & 3d Afst. Under-Secy.

Notes

1. Probably James F. McCarthy (1906–?). "O'Flaherty" is HPL's joke.
2. Mollie Panter-Downes, "The House of the Laburnums," *Harpers* 174, No. 1 (December 1936): 42–45; rpt. *The Ash-Tree Press Annual Macabre 1997*, ed. Jack Adrian (Ashcroft, BC: Ash-Tree Press 1997). Panter-Downes (1906–1997) was a British writer and author of the bestselling novel *The Shoreless Sea* (1923).
3. Wilkie Collins (1824–1889), "The Dream Woman," first published in *Temple Bar* (Nov.–Dec. 1874) and collected in Collins's *The Frozen Deep and Other Stories* (1874).
4. Dorothy L. Sayers (1893–1957), ed., *The Omnibus of Crime* <1928> (Garden City, NY: Garden City Publishing Co., 1931; *LL* 762). The story first appeared in Harvey's *Midnight House and Other Tales* (1910).
5. Margaret A. Murray (1863–1963), *The Witch-Cult in Western Europe* (Oxford: Clarendon Press, 1921).

Miscellaneous Impressions of H.P.L.

Marian F. Bonner

When Mrs. Phillips Gamwell, Howard Phillips Lovecraft's aunt, re-turned to Providence from Cambridge, Massachusetts, she and H.P.L. took an apartment on College Street near my dwelling. I had heard of Mrs. Gamwell before, so it was not long before I was visit-ing her, thusly bringing about my acquaintance with her nephew.

What stands out in my acquaintance with H.P.L. was his whimsical humor, his love of the past, and his love of cats, not to speak of the avidity with which he read any scrap of writing on Edgar Allan Poe, his ideal.

It was very fitting that Mr. Lovecraft lived his last years in a house said to be built about 1815. His study, where he worked the entire night, looked out onto the yard of a fraternity which con-tained a shed, an ideal "club-room" for the neighborhood cats. He soon had a K.A.T. fraternity, and in letters wove whimsical yarns along this vein. Some of his letters to me were decorated in pen and ink, and bore a letterhead of cat's faces.

Whenever I told him of any cat in downtown Providence, sug-gesting election into above fraternity, he almost always knew of it. Possibly these endeavors of mine earned me the election into the "Fraternity" as an honorary member, "with complimentary purrs." At one time he wrote in a brochure on cats, which he presented to me, that the said brochure was "not yet published." The latter is now in the possession of the John Hay Library of Brown University.

His handwriting was not easy to read, as he used, among other things, the old-fashioned long "s." Realizing his weakness he would often compare his manuscripts very carefully with the type.

When I lived on Meeting Street, he once sent me a postal di-rected to "Gaol Lane," its former name. He was delighted that I received it promptly without correction. Evidently one Providence Post Office official knew his Rhode Island history!

His aunt once told me of the meals he would pick up at various unearthly hours, perhaps at a diner. He abused his digestion horribly according to her reports. His use of sugar in his favorite beverage, coffee, was enormous.

At Christmastime, I would get his help to "smuggle in" my present to his aunt. I can clearly remember the three of us sitting around their tiny Christmas tree.

Mr. Lovecraft could sing, though I heard him sing but once. He possessed a clear, light voice.

He once told me a walk to Roger Williams Park* was nothing to him, and that there he could sit on a bench and work at his writings, entirely oblivious to the passing crowd. If you saw him on the street, he never saw you. As he shot by, you realized that his body was there, but his thoughts were elsewhere.

It seems there is a postal law enabling one to write on most of the address side of a picture postcard. Mr. Lovecraft took a fiendish delight in covering every bit of a postal that he could with the message. He was the despair of the postal authorities. Those postals were crazy-looking things!

He told me that it was his custom to read aloud the plays of Shakespeare with his mother. The more cruel the part, the better he liked it, and would shout it out to be heard by the neighbors. I have had neighbors tell me of his "quarrels," but I know that it was only Shakespeare being read.

I know how much store Mrs. Gamwell set by him, and how much she missed him after his death.

[First published in *Rhode Island on Lovecraft*, ed. Donald M. Grant and Thomas P. Hadley (Providence, RI: Grant-Hadley, 1945), 23–24.]

---

*A distance of about 3.5 miles from 66 College. *Ed.*

Can You Direct Me to Ely Court?: Some Notes on 66 College Street

Kenneth W. Faig, Jr.

In Memory of Alice Rachel Sheppard (1870–1961)
and Mary Spink (1877–1968)

H. P. Lovecraft had only a cramped single room with alcove when he lived at 10 Barnes Street from 1926 to 1933. His elder aunt Lillian D. (Phillips) Clark (1856–1932) had a room on the floor above, and Lovecraft usually spent an hour every evening with his aunt. After she died in 1932, Lovecraft and his younger aunt Annie E. (Phillips) Gamwell (1866–1941), then residing on Slater Avenue, decided to seek common quarters. As luck would have it, they found a wonderful flat on the second floor of 66 College Street, tucked just behind Brown University's John Hay Library.

Lovecraft claimed that his new home was of colonial origin and cited several architectural features to support his contention. The rear wing, down three steps from the main part of the building, had wide colonial floorboards. Lovecraft's aunt had her quarters in this wing. His own study looked out from the southwest windows of the main part of the structure. The photographs that Robert H. Barlow took of Lovecraft's study when he came to Providence to organize his mentor's papers in 1937, first reproduced in *Marginalia* (Arkham House, 1944), speak to the sensibilities that guided Lovecraft when he furnished his study. Many family heirlooms, in storage since the dissolution of the 454 Angell Street household following the death of Whipple V. Phillips in 1904, were able once more to be displayed. Lovecraft purchased new bookcases the better to accommodate his growing collection. Beginning in 1933, he and his aunt even had a decorated Christmas tree during the holiday season. In a word, Lovecraft and his aunt were delighted to find themselves in a genuinely old building perched atop the "antient hill" overlooking downtown Providence.

The author's final years at 66 College brought challenges as well as blessings. Only a few weeks after taking up residence there on 15 May 1933, Mrs. Gamwell slipped on the stairs and broke her ankle. After being hospitalized, she recovered in a nursing home. But once she returned to 66 College, many support tasks devolved upon her nephew. Then in the spring of 1936, Mrs. Gamwell was hospitalized once more, this time for removal of a cancerous right breast. Once again, she spent a period of nursing home recovery and then returned to 66 College Street, where her nephew was once again pressed into service to provide necessary help. In the end, it was Lovecraft himself who fell ill, dying of cancer of the small intestine on 15 March 1937. His aunt survived him by nearly four years, dying on 29 January 1941.

The house at 66 College Street was removed to 65 Prospect Street in 1959 and continues to be one of the "must-sees" for Lovecraftian visitors to Providence. The Providence Preservation Society (PPS) plaque for the house does not agree with Lovecraft's contention that the house was of colonial origin: it dates the house to c. 1825 and names the first owner as Samuel B. Mumford. Lovecraft claimed that he could discern the "Garden House" on the famous 1809 Providence theatre curtain now owned by the Rhode Island Historical Society and kept at its Aldrich House headquarters at 110 Benevolent Street. Samuel Brenton Mumford, the first owner of the house according to PPS, was born in Providence on 12 September 1796, the son of Joseph Mumford and Mary Carr. He became a prosperous commission merchant, with offices at 19 South Main in 1826, 7 South Water in 1844, and 9 South Water in 1847. He married Louisa G. Dexter, the daughter of Benjamin G. Dexter, in Providence on 9 February 1818. Perhaps he and his new bride moved into the so-called Garden House, set back a considerable distance from College Street, soon after their wedding. The 1826 Providence directory stated his home address as Angell Street.

Samuel Brenton Mumford died on 27 February 1849. He was survived by his widow Louisa for more than a quarter-century. The widow Louisa D. Mumford was listed at 25 Waterman Street in the

1853 Providence directory. When she applied for a passport to travel to Cuba in 1864, she stated her date of birth as 2 January 1801;
perhaps she was shaving a few years, since her age at death was
recorded as seventy-eight when she died on 12 February 1876. She
had been listed at 45 College Street in the 1871–73 Providence directories. Then, in 1875–76, she was listed at 151 Benefit St. Samuel Brenton Mumford and his wife Louisa (Dexter) Mumford are
buried in the North Burial Ground in Providence. The heirs of S. B.
Mumford still owned the Garden House and the lot on which it
stood when the 1875 Providence atlas was published. Perhaps they
only disposed of the property after Mumford's widow died in 1876.

The 1899 Providence *House Directory and Family Address
Book* provides a hint to us concerning 66 College Street: the addresses on the north side of College St. immediately west of Prospect St. are listed as follows (see end of paper for directory
abbreviations):

64	Sheldon, F. J., Mr. & Mrs., h.
	Sheldon, Frank A., ins. agt., b.
68	Pegram, John C., Jr., physician, h.
70	Bowen, Cordelia J., widow, h.
	Bowen, E. G., Miss, teacher, h.
	Bowen, Frank, hardware, etc., b.

Note there is no house listed at 66 College Street. The mystery is
solved by a separate listing for College Court:

1	Cushing, Kate P., tchr., rms.
	Cushing, Rebecca R., Mrs., tchr., r.
	Dart, Willard C., publisher, rms.
	Peck, Robert H., draughtsman, h.
	Whipple, Inez, Miss, rms.

The directory indicates that College Court runs [northward]
from College in Ward 1. In the 1875 Providence atlas,[1] a walkway

---

1. Plate N on Historic Mapworks. See:

http://www.historicmapworks.com/Map/US/32343/Plate+N/Providence+187
5+Vol+1+Wards+1+-+2+-+3++East+Providence/Rhode+Island/

separates the President's House[2] of Brown University from the residence of W. H. and C. J. Bowen on the north side of College Street. To the north of these two residences, on Waterman Street, are the homes of S. K. Parsons (abutting the Bowen residence on College Street) and of J. W. C. Ely, abutting the President's House. To the west of the W. H. and C. J. Bowen residence, is property owned by the "Heirs of S. B. Mumford," stretching all the way north to Waterman St. The Garden House, set back a considerable distance from the north side of College Street, occupies this property. The two joined buildings on Waterman St. that eventually became The Paxton (and then The Arsdale), also owned by the Mumford heirs, abut the Garden House property to the north. The Bowen residence was removed as part of the construction of the John Hay Library in 1910. The President's House was moved further down College St. and was demolished as part of an expansion of the Rhode Island School of Design in 1936.

In the 1918 Providence atlas,[3] a wall separates the John Hay Library from the setback Garden House and the residence of C. H. Robertson to the west on the north side of College Street. The residences of R. Ely and S. K. Parsons abut the John Hay Library to the north on Waterman St. Behind the Garden House and the Robertson residence on Waterman Street is The Paxton, a boarding house later known as The Arsdale.[4]

College Court pops up from time to time in the Providence directories after the Mumford era. In 1847, Frank Thompson ran an

---

2. According to Martha Mitchell's *Encyclopedia Brunoniana*, Brown University's second President's House was dedicated on the corner of Prospect and College Streets In 1840. It was last occupied by Brown's president in 1898. Brown's third President's House was dedicated at 180 Hope Street in 1901. It was replaced by the current President's House (originally built in 1922) at 55 Power Street in 1947.

3. Map 19 scan 4 on Rootsweb. See: http://www.rootsweb.ancestry.com/~rigenweb/maps/1918prov/1918Providence19-2a.jpg

4. HPL's friends Marian Bonner (1883–1952) and Evelyn M. Staples (1860–1938) resided at The Arsdale (55 Waterman Street) in the mid-1930s. They owned several of the cats who loved to sun themselves on the shed behind the Garden House. Helen V. Sully stayed at The Arsdale when she visited in 1933, and Robert H. Barlow stayed there when he visited for over a month in 1936. HPL and his aunt customarily took their holiday meals at The Arsdale.

eatery and oyster saloon at South College Court and at the Mansion House.[5] In 1865, Anthony Dougherty, partner in the firm of Haywood & Dougherty at 9 Market Square, resided in College Court By 1880, 1 College Court had clearly been cut up into apartments:

> Bowers, Mrs. Lloyd, bds.
> Fish, Sarah, Miss, h.
> Holden, John, farmer, h.
> Jenckes, Thomas, bds.
> Manton, Mary, Mrs., bds.

The 1884 directory listed the residence of Mrs. Leon Chappotin at 1 College Court; and the 1887 directory listed the residence of Mrs. Sarah Rodman at the same address. The five residents of 1 College Court in 1899 were already listed above.

My belief is that the reassignment of 1 College Court as 66 College Street dates to about 1905. In 1906, we find three residents listed at 66 College Street:

> Peck, Robert H., draughtsman, City Engineer's Office, h.
> Price, Albert G., foreman, 157 Orange, 3rd floor, h.
> Roxbury, Harriet E., teacher, State Normal School, h.

The residences that formerly stood at numbers 68 and 70 College Street were eventually removed or demolished for the construction of the John Hay Library, which was dedicated on 11 November 1910.

However, College Court was not the only name for the lane leading back to the Garden House before the number 66 College was assigned in 1905. The 1901 directory contained the following listings for "1 Ely Ct.":

Crahan, Morris, prop. Crahan Engraving Co., 193 Westminster, h. 1 Ely Court & at Edgewood

---

5. I am not sure that "South College Court" corresponded to "College Court." Edgar Allan Poe had stayed at the Mansion House (formerly the Golden Ball Inn) on Benefit Street when he was courting Sarah Helen Whitman (1803–1878) in 1848. By the twentieth century, the Mansion House had become a cheap rooming house and was demolished in 1941.

Dart, Willard C. (Dart & Bigelow[6]), 35 Westminster, rm. 3, rms. 1 Ely Ct.

The 1913 and 1923 Providence directories listed Ely Court running from 64 College in Ward 1. The 1917 street directory listed the following addresses on the north side of College Street approaching Prospect Street:

64	Forbes, Anna R. H., Mrs.
	Hayes, Frederick, lawyer, b.
	Ely Ct. begins
000	cor Prospect, John Hay Library

Then, in the 1948 directory, there is an apparent final reference to Ely Court: the listing of streets indicates that Ely Court runs "from College northerly [in] Ward 1."

When H. P. Lovecraft corresponded with Marian Bonner as third assistant secretary on behalf of the Kappa Alpha Tau feline fraternity in 1936, he gave the fraternity's address, as #1, Ely's Court. Whether Ely Court or Ely's Court was ever an official postal address or a public way remains to be determined.[7] It seems that College Court was the more common usage for the lane back to the Garden House during the period 1850–99. The name Ely Court clearly seems to lead back to the Ely family who resided on the southwest corner of Waterman and Prospect (36 Prospect Street) both in 1875 and in 1918.

James Winchell Coleman Ely was born in Vermont in October 1820,[8] the son of Rev. Richard M. Ely (b. 10 Feb. 1795; d. 10 May

6. Dart & Bigelow were translators and correspondents, fluent in English, French, German, and Spanish.

7. In 2015, a private walkway (probably Brown University property) ran between the John Hay Library and the List Art Building from College Street to Waterman Street. There is a seating area on lawn of the List Art Building on the Waterman St. side. Several stairways allow the walkway to ascend from College Street to Waterman Street. I am not sure that it is fair to say that this walkway replicates the path of the former Ely Court. However, it is doubtless as good a proxy as we are likely to have for now.

8. The 1900 U.S. census recorded that James W. C. Ely was born in October 1821, but his Swan Point Cemetery record gives his year of birth as 1820.

1861, Cavendish, Windsor County, Vermont) and his wife Lora.
He had a younger brother, Francis W. Ely, born eight years later in
Springfield, Vermont, who married Sarah E. Hill on 4 April 1859,
in Cavendish, Windsor County, Vermont. James Ely became a
physician, while his younger brother Francis Ely became an engi-
neer. James Ely married Susan Backus, the daughter of Thomas
and Almira (——) Backus, born in Connecticut in September
1824. By 1850, we find the following household in Providence:

> Joseph Cady, age 76, born CT
> Susan Cady, age 73, born VT
> James W. C. Ely, age 29, physician, born VT
> Susan B. Ely, age 25, born CT
> Joseph C. Ely, age 1, born RI
> Mary A. McLane, age 19, born Ireland
> Ann Tierney, age 25, born Ireland

By 1860, James W. C. Ely had his own household in Providence:

> James W. C. Ely, age 39, born VT
> Susan B. Ely, age 35, born CT
> Joseph C. Ely, age 11, born RI
> Edward F. Ely, age 2, born RI
> Joseph Cady, age 89, born CT
> Ann Tierney, age 32, born Ireland

By 1870 the household consisted of:

> James W. C. Ely, age 49, born VT, physician
> Susan B. Ely, age 45, born CT, housekeeper
> Joseph C. Ely, age 21, born RI, student
> Edward F. Ely, age 12, born RI, at school
> Ann Tierney, age 50, born Ireland, servant

Joseph Cady Ely (b. 24 March 1849, Providence, R.I.; d. 21 June
1897, Providence, R.I.) and Edward Francis Ely (b. 12 February
1858, Providence, R.I.; d. 1920, Providence, R.I.) were the sons of
James W. C. and Susan (Backus) Ely. Joseph C. Ely was an attor-
ney and married Alice Peck (b. November 1854, Massachusetts; d.
14 December 1924, Providence, R.I.). Edward F. Ely was a partner

in the firm of Hoppin & Ely, architects and remained single. The 1880 census enumerated James W. C. Ely, his wife Susan, their son Edward F., and two servants at 36 Prospect St.[9] The 1900 census enumerated James W. C. Ely, Susan (Backus) Ely, and their son Edward F. Ely and two servants at 36 Prospect St. The same census recorded Alice P. Ely, widow of James C. Ely, and her daughter Ruth Ely (b. 3 May 1881, Providence, R.I.; d. June 1973) at 94 Waterman Street. In 1903, James W. C. Ely and his son Edward F. Ely still resided at 36 Prospect Street; James still kept his doctor's office at 61 Waterman, and the firm of Hoppin & Ely, architects, was located at 32 Westminster Street. In the same year, Alice (Peck) Ely, widow of Joseph C. Ely, was residing at 94 Waterman Street.

James W. C. Ely and his wife Susan (Backus) Ely were both long-lived. James died in Providence on 6 May 1906, age eighty-five, and his widow Susan followed him in death on 23 December 1909, also age eighty-five. In 1910 and 1915, their son Edward F. Ely lived at 36 Prospect Street with two servants. In 1920, Alice Ely, widow of Joseph C. Ely, and her daughter Ruth Ely lived at 94 Waterman Street with two servants. Ruth Ely obtained a passport for European travel on 11 December 1923—a photograph accompanied her passport application. Ruth Ely remained single and was still living at 94 Waterman Street (with two servants) in 1940.[10] The whole extended Ely family—James W. C. Ely (1820–1906), Susan (Backus) Ely (1824–1909), Edward Francis Ely (1858–1920), Joseph C. Ely (1849–1897), Alice (Peck) Ely (1854–1924), and Ruth Ely (1881–1973)—are buried in Swan Point Cemetery in Providence.

The Ely family left such an imprint on the immediate neighborhood that Ely Court (once known as College Court) appeared in Providence directories as late 1948, twelve years after Lovecraft corresponded with Marian Bonner. From 1905 until its removal to 65 Prospect Street in 1959, the Garden House bore 66 College

9. 36 Prospect Street, on the southwest corner of Waterman and Prospect Streets, is still standing in 2015.

10. 94 Waterman Street, on the north side of Waterman Street between Brown Street and Thayer Street, is still standing in 2015.

Street as its postal address. I will pass by most of the tenants from
1905 until 1941: we already know two of them, Annie E. (Phillips)
Gamwell in 1933–41 and H. P. Lovecraft in 1933–37. They occupied the second-floor flat. The 1928–42 tenant of the first-floor
flat, Alice Rachel Sheppard, deserves to be better known to Love-
craftians than she is. Alice Rachel Sheppard was born in Phoenix,
Warwick, R.I., on 10 September 1870 to Rev. Theodore William
Sheppard (b. 2 December 1833, New Jersey; d. 16 December 1892,
R.I.) and his wife Jane (Porter) Sheppard (b. 9 August 1833, Roch-
ester, N.Y.; d. 9 March 1915, Providence, R.I.).[11] Her father was
the son of Nathan Sheppard and Rachel Cook,[12] who married in
Cumberland County, New Jersey, on 7 April 1814. In 1850, Theo-
dore Sheppard, age fifteen, was apparently apprenticed to James
A. Welden as a tailor in Bridgeton, Cumberland County, New Jersey.[13] The 1880 census recorded the following family in Warwick,
R.I.: Theodore W. Sheppard, age forty-six, born New Jersey of
New Jersey–born parents, clergyman; Jane P. Sheppard, age forty-
six, wife, born New York of New Hampshire–born father and
New York–born mother; William C. Sheppard, age thirteen, son,
born New Hampshire of New Jersey–born father and New York–
born mother; and Alice R. Sheppard, daughter, age nine, born

---

11. The death certificate of Alice Rachel Sheppard's brother William Carey
Sheppard gives the names of his parents as Theodore W. Sheppard and Jane P.
Richardson. I follow the Find-A-Grave record from Greenwood Cemetery in
Coventry, R.I., in giving her mother's maiden name as Jane Porter.

12. Perhaps the Rachel Sheppard who died in Bowentown, N.J., of dropsy on 28
July 1849.

13. This fact leads me to believe that he probably did not belong to the following
Fairfield, Cumberland County, N.J., family (all born N.J.) in 1850: Nathan Sheppard, age 53, farmer; Sarah Sheppard, age 54; William Sheppard, age 19, farmer;
Cornelia Sheppard, age 17; Benjamin Sheppard, age 15; and Joseph Sheppard, age
10. This Nathan Sheppard (b. 26 July 1796, N.J.; d. 9 March 1855, Fairfield
Township, Cumberland County, N.J.) married Sarah B. Rose (b. 7 March 1794; d.
3 July 1879) on 19 March 1817 in Cumberland County, N.J. They are buried in
Old Stone Church Cemetery, Fairfield, Cumberland County, N.J. Alternative
dates of b. 12 December 1797, N.J., d. 11 January 1881, Cumberland, N.J. are also
found for Sarah B. (Rose) Sheppard. Her son William Rose Sheppard (b. 22 September 1831, Cedarville, Cumberland County, N.J.; d. 12 March 1879, Cape May,
N.J.) became a physician.

Rhode Island of New Jersey–born father and New York–born mother. Rev. Theodore W. Sheppard served as pastor of the Mt. Vernon Christian Society in Foster, R.I., from 1889 until his death in 1892.[14] His son Rev. William Carey Sheppard (b. 1866 New Hampshire; d. 14 January 1909, Plaistow, Rockingham, N.H.) was also a clergyman.[15]

Alice Rachel Sheppard had a distinguished career as a language teacher. She graduated from Boston University with an A.B. degree in 1892. She was a member of Kappa Kappa Gamma sorority, and was president of the Gamma Delta chapter, as well as vice president of her class, in her senior year in 1891–92. She was also assistant editor of the student magazines *Beacon* and *Hub* and a member of the Philological Society. She specialized in the German language and pursued her studies in Göttingen in 1899. She returned to Providence, where she obtained her A.M. degree from Brown University in 1900.[16] She was living with her widowed mother Jane (Porter) Sheppard at 38 Congdon Street and teaching at Classical High School in 1901. She studied in Berlin in 1902–03 and returned to become head of the German Department at Classical High School in Providence. She went on to serve as director of the New England Modern Language Association in 1912–15 and as president of the Rhode Island chapter of the Association of Collegiate Alumnae in 1914–16.[17]

---

14. The new church was dedicated on 29 August 1889. Rev. Theodore W. Sheppard preached the dedication sermon, and Rev. George W. Kennedy (1824–1900) offered the dedication prayer. Thereafter, Rev. Sheppard preached three Sundays per month at Mt. Vernon Christian Society until his death in 1892.

15. William Carey Sheppard married Annie Nye Peaslee (1866–1952), the daughter of Ruben Peaslee (1810–1875) and Harriet —— (1823–1893) on 28 December 1889, in Haverhill, Mass. They had children William Theodore Sheppard (1891–1907), Katherine Sheppard (1897–1984), Edson Peaslee Sheppard Sr. (1900–1978), and Harriel Rachel Sheppard (1909–1925). William Carey Sheppard, his wife, his son William Theodore Sheppard, and his daughters Katherine and Harriet Rachel Sheppard are buried with his sister Alice Rachel Sheppard and their parents in Greenwood Cemetery, Coventry, R.I.

16. *Liber Brunensis* for 1899 listed her as a master of arts candidate in fine arts and German.

17. Most of this biographical information concerning Miss Sheppard derives from

In 1908–09, Miss Sheppard took her seventy-four-year-old widowed mother Jane (Porter) Sheppard along with her while she taught a term at Fontainebleau in France. She continued to live at 38 Congdon Street after the death of her mother in 1915, and still lived there as late as 1924. Then, in 1928, she took up residence at 66 College Street, where she remained through 1942. In the 1930s, she took annual trips to Europe, returning to New York City from Bremen on the *Europa* on 7 September 1932; from Bremen on the *Columbus* on 5 September 1933; from Hamburg on the *Hamburg* on 7 September 1934; and from Naples on the *Comte di Savoia* on 7 September 1935. She told her upstairs neighbor H. P. Lovecraft of the darkening situation in Germany under the Nazi dictatorship, and he began to modify his views based on her intelligence. After Lovecraft died, Miss Sheppard returned to New York City from one further European trip on 21 December 1938, having sailed from Trieste on the *Roma*.

Alice Rachel Sheppard was still living at 66 College St. in 1942, after Annie Gamwell had died on 29 January 1941. She had probably retired from teaching at Classical High School by the mid-1930s. She survived her friend Annie Gamwell by more than twenty years. The 1947–49 Providence directories listed her at 40 Benevolent Street. The 1953–60 Providence directories listed her at 389 Angell Street. She died on 2 July 1961, at the age of ninety, and was buried with her parents and her brother William Carey Sheppard in Greenwood Cemetery in Coventry, R.I.

One more resident of 66 College Street with a tangential connection with H. P. Lovecraft remains: Mary Spink, who lived at 66 College from 1938 to 1947. She was a friend of Mrs. Gamwell, rather than of her nephew, who had died in 1937. Mary Spink had been born in Providence on 19 July 1877, the daughter of Judge Joseph Edwin Spink (1842–1910) and Emma Elizabeth Hudson (1848–1937). The 1900 census enumerated the following household (all born R.I.) at 150 South Angell Street in Providence: Joseph Spink (head), born July 1842, married 1873/74, municipal court judge; Emma R. Spink (wife), born January 1848, eight children borne, five living; Mary Spink (daughter), born July 1877, single; Alice G. Spink (daughter), born September 1879, single; Hope Spink (daughter), born July 1884, single; Martha E. Spink (daughter), born May 1887; and Agatha Spink (daughter), born May 1891, single. (Irish-born servant Julia A. Sullivan, born April 1875, was also in the household.) The family resided at the same address in 1910. All five surviving daughters remained single and members of their parents' household. Joseph Spink was now a probate judge. Daughter Alice G. Spink worked as assistant manager of a settlement house. Niece Dorothy E. Newton, age thirteen, born 1892/93 RI, had replaced servant Julia A. Sullivan.

Mary Spink had in the meantime obtained her A.B. degree from Wellesley College in 1899. She followed with an A.M. degree from Brown University in 1902. Perhaps she and Miss Sheppard were fellow graduate students at Brown. After the death of Judge Spink in 1910, Mary Spink lived with her widowed mother at 84 Cushing Street in Providence. In 1920, Emma Spink's niece Dorothy Newton, age twenty-three, single, born 1892/93 in Massachusetts of R.I.-born father and N.H.-born mother, was residing with them and working as a government typist. Neither Emma Spink nor her daughter Mary Spink were then employed. By 1924, however, Mary Spink had become a notary public. She had probably already begun her longtime career as a title research clerk at Title Guarantee Co. of Rhode Island at 66 South Main. She continued to be listed at 84 Cushing Street until she removed to 230 Brown Street in 1936–37. Then, in 1938, she took up residence at 66 College Street, where she remained through 1947. She evidently became friends with Annie E. (Phillips) Gamwell, for in 1940 she compiled a rough catalogue of H. P. Lovecraft's library, which forms the basis for most of the listings in S. T. Joshi's *Lovecraft's Library*. After leaving 66 College Street, she lived at 34 Jenckes Street from 1949 onward. She continued to work for Title Guarantee Co. of Rhode Island through at least 1956. The 1964 Providence directory continued to list her at 34 Jenckes Street, but finally added the notation "retd." She died in December 1968, age ninety-one.

In 1940, Mrs. Gamwell's niece Helen M. Morrish, age fifty-five, a Canadian-born practical nurse, resided with Mrs. Gamwell in the second-story flat at 66 College Street. But by the mid-1940s,

Brown University, which owned 66 College Street, began to rent the premises mainly to junior faculty and other staff members. Mary B. Gilson (1945–46) and Mary Spink (1938–47) may have been the last renters without direct Brown University connections. (Of course, Miss Spink was an alumna.) Assistant professor Juan Lopez-Morillas and his wife Frances M. were tenants in 1944–47. Assistant professor Edward J. Brown and his wife Catherine were tenants in 1952–57. The Browns must have liked the Garden House; they were still residing there in 1957, after Edward J. Brown had been promoted to full professor. Carroll Rikert, Jr., controller of accounts for Brown University, and his wife Jane W. were tenants in 1953–54. Assistant professor Gene B. Carpenter and his wife Elizabeth C. were tenants in 1956. Assistant professor William Deminoff and his wife Elizabeth were also tenants in 1956. Research associate Cornelius Haas was a tenant in 1957. He was the final tenant I found before the removal of the Garden House from 66 College Street to 65 Prospect Street in 1959.

One famous owner of the property at 65 Prospect Street was John C. A. Watkins (1912–2000), who served with distinction in World War II, joined the *Providence Journal* in 1950, and served as its publisher from 1954 to 1979, its CEO until 1983, and its chairman until 1985. He married (1) Helen Danforth (1922–2014), but they divorced and she married (2) Patrick B. Buchanan. John C. A. Watkins took the actress Jane Watkins (1915/16–1989) as his second wife in 1960. In more recent years, Edward R. Feller, M.D., Clinical Professor of Medicine at Brown University, a gastroenterologist and internist, has been owner of 65 Prospect Street.[18] The "Garden House" at 65 Prospect Street is still maintained as beautifully as H. P. Lovecraft and Annie E. (Phillips) Gamwell

---

18. The magnificent mansion of Thomas Lloyd Halsey (1751–1838)—reportedly haunted by a piano-playing ghost in HPL's time—is only a few blocks north at 140 Prospect St. Halsey himself is buried in St. John's Churchyard, where HPL loved to take visitors to Providence. He and his wife are buried immediately west of the church building and have tall monuments. The Cathedral of St. John was closed by the Episcopal Diocese in 2012 because of rising maintenance costs and declining attendance. In 2014, the diocese announced its interest in partnering with the State of Rhode Island to re-open the former cathedral as a museum dedicated to the slave trade.

might have wished. Brown University's starkly modern List Art Building now occupies the site where the Garden House once stood. I do not know whether mail addressed to 1 College Court or 1 Ely Court would reach Brown's art department.

Many questions relating to the Garden House remain. The question of its dating should be considered in greater depth. Is it possible that the rear "ell" represents an older building to which the main part of the Garden House was later attached? The 1918 Providence atlas shows the immediate locale of the Garden House in much the same state as H. P. Lovecraft may have known it in 1933–37. The 1918 atlas shows an outbuilding adjoining the western property line of The Paxton (and the residence of I. Tucker). This outbuilding or shed would have been visible from the southwestern windows of Lovecraft's study, because of the setback of #66 from the north side of College Street. The 1918 atlas map shows clearly how deeply recessed the Garden House was from College Street. Nevertheless, questions about the detailed layout of the Garden House property doubtless remain. One wonders what delightful plantings may have earned the house its name. The history of all the wonderful cats who convened as the Kappa Alpha Tau fraternity on the shed rooftop also remains to be written. It could doubtlessly be reconstructed based on Lovecraft's letters to Miss Bonner and others.

It would be interesting to have more details concerning succession of ownership of the Garden House. At what time subsequent to 1875 was the property sold by the Mumford heirs? Could there have been owners before Samuel Brenton Mumford and his wife Louisa G. (Dexter) Mumford? Do the Colonial Dames of Rhode Island have photographs of the Garden House during the 1920s? Snapshots of Annie E. (Phillips) Gamwell and of H. P. Lovecraft in the doorway of the Garden House are the only known published exterior photographs from the 1930s, while Robert H. Barlow's photographs from 1937 are the only known published interior photographs from the same period. One can only go so far with Internet research.[19] The next stage of progress on the Garden

---

19. Sanborn fire maps of Providence RI are available on the Internet, but only on a proprietary pay-for-use basis.

House will require hands-on research using Providence resources.

Clark Ashton Smith expressed the wish that Lovecraft's study at 66 College St.—including all the books, paintings, furniture and mementos—might be preserved as a museum. The sad reality was that the only asset considered worthy of inclusion in the inventory of the author's estate was a $500 mortgage on a Providence quarry, which was not finally paid off until 1957, at which time Horace B. Knowles & Sons was probably paid the remaining unpaid balance due for the author's 1937 funeral.[20] Lovecraft's library—despite its 1940 cataloging by Mary Spink—was not sold until after the death of Annie E. (Phillips) Gamwell in 1941. I do not know how much the sale of the books to H. Douglass Dana raised for her estate. Fortunately, young Robert H. Barlow traveled to Providence shortly after the death of his mentor and assured the preservation of the author's manuscripts at the neighboring John Hay Library with the cooperation of Professor S. Foster Damon. Out of consideration for the privacy of the grieving Annie Gamwell, Barlow stayed at the downtown YMCA rather than at The Arsdale. The beauty of 65 Prospect Street (formerly 66 College Street) remains. We can share the joy of Annie E. (Phillips) Gamwell and H. P. Lovecraft in their final home. I hope it will remain a focus for Lovecraftian visitors to Providence for decades—if not for centuries—to come. Showing private property owners the same courtesy that Robert H. Barlow showed to Annie Gamwell in 1937 will help to assure the preservation of 65 Prospect St. and the other Lovecraft shrines of Providence.

I hope this essay has shed some light on the house where H. P. Lovecraft spent the last four years of his life. Alice Rachel Sheppard (1870–1961) and Mary Spink (1877–1968) were both well-educated ladies who deserve more than mere footnotes in the story of H. P. Lovecraft's life and posthumous literary reputation. I hope this essay has paid some justifiable tribute to their memory. It is more difficult to summon up the shades of figures more remotely involved in the history of the Garden House at 66 College Street—perhaps Samuel Brenton Mumford, Louisa G. (Dexter)

20. An excellent consideration of HPL's literary estate, including reproductions of many documents, is posted on the Internet (http://www.aetherial.net/lovecraft/index.html) by Chris J. Karr under the title "The Black Seas of Copyright."

Mumford, James Winchell Coleman Ely, Susan (Backus) Ely, and all the others who resided in the immediate locale will be difficult to rescue from the shadows. We can only hope that the other residents found as much happiness in living in the Garden House as did H. P. Lovecraft and his aunt.

Directory Abbreviations:
h. = house
r. = resides
bds. = boards
rms. = rooms
retd. = retired

Works Cited

Joshi, S. T. *Lovecraft's Library: A Catalogue*. New York: Hippocampus Press, 3rd ed. 2012.

Matthews, Margery I.; Benson, Virginia I.; and Wilson, Arthur E. *Churches of Foster: A History of Religious Life in Rural Rhode Island*. Foster, RI: North Foster Baptist Church, 1978.

Mitchell, Martha. *Encyclopedia Brunoniana*. Providence, RI: Brown University Library, 1993. Online at: http://www.brown.edu/Administration/News_Bureau/Databases/Encyclopedia/search.php?serial=P0390

Wolf, Raymond A. *Foster*. Charleston, SC: Arcadia Publishing, 2012.

Note: Vital statistics quoted in this article can be confirmed using FamilySearch (LDS) and Ancestry.

66 College Street

David E. Schultz

When H. P. Lovecraft and his aunt Annie E. P. Gamwell began to feel the financial pinch, they moved to 66 College Street to share the upper flat. Not only did they reduce the cost of rent by living in the same household, Lovecraft had far more living space than he had at 10 Barnes Street, where he paid $40 a month for only a room and an alcove. It is clear from his many surviving letters from May 1933 that Lovecraft was absolutely delighted with the place.

> The consolation is that this place is the upper part of a *real colonial house*—the first I shall ever have lived in, despite my lifelong admiration of such. The edifice, yellow & wooden, & (though of a New England type) suggesting houses you may have seen in Georgetown, Alexandria, Fredericksburg, & other old places, is on the crest of Providence's ancient hill in a quaint grassy court just off College St.—behind & next to the John Hay Library of Brown University, about half a mile south of 10 Barnes St. The fine colonial doorway is like my bookplate come to life. In the rear is a picturesque village-like garden at a higher level than the front of the house. The upper flat we have taken contains 5 rooms besides bath & kitchenette nook on the main (2nd) floor, plus 2 attic storerooms—one of which is so attractive that I wish I could have it for an extra den! My quarters—a large study & a small bedroom—will be on the south side, with my working table under a west window offering a splendid view of the lower town's outspread roofs & of the mystical sunsets that flame behind them. The interior is as fascinating as the exterior—with colonial fireplaces, mantels, & chimney cupboards, curving Georgian staircase, wide floor-boards, old-fashioned latches, small-paned windows, six-panel doors, rear wing with floor at a different level (3 steps down), quaint attic

stairs, &c.—just like the old houses open as museums. After admiring such all my life, I find something magical & dreamlike in the idea of *living in one*. . . . All this doesn't sound much like an *economy* measure, but it is just that. The whole thing costs only what I've been paying for one room & alcove alone at 10 Barnes St. Steam heat & hot water are piped from the adjacent college library. The house is owned by the university.[1]

The new residence delighted Lovecraft so much that he sketched the appearance of the house in letters to numerous correspondents (see Figures 2 through 4 for examples), drawing particular attention to the monitor roof and the fanlight carving over the front door (as in Figure 5). For the most part, the drawings are very similar, but some features vary from letter to letter, and because of this, it is difficult to determine what he is attempting to depict. For example, it is not certain what the vertical pole-like structures are in front of the house as depicted in Figure 2. Bollards? Hitching posts for horses? The poles for the clotheslines as shown in Figure 8? In Figure 3, the poles appear again, but only on the right side of the picture. The lines to the left seem almost to be a fence, but that cannot be. In both figures, there seems to be a fence or wall or some other structure on the right of the picture, presumably at some distance behind the steps to the porch. There is no equivalent structure on the left side of the picture. However, Figure 4 has such structures on both sides of the house, but not the poles in the front.

Figures 6 and 7 show that the wall that separates the John Hay Library from the houses stands fairly close to Lovecraft's house, and yet it is not represented in the sketches.

Lovecraft believed that the Samuel B. Mumford house dated to c. 1800; it was actually built c. 1825. Henry Bowen, who served as Rhode Island Secretary of State from 1819 to 1849, sold the property to Mumford in 1823. Henry was the son of Jabez Bowen, an American shipper, politician, militia colonel during the American Revolutionary War, deputy governor of Rhode Island, and chief justice of the Rhode Island Supreme Court. And also a character in Lovecraft's

1. HPL to R. H. Barlow, 14 May 1933; *O Fortunate Floridian*, ed. S. T. Joshi and David E. Schultz (Tampa, FL: University of Tampa Press, 2007), 61–62. This account of the new residence is typical.

The Case of Charles Dexter Ward. He owned and sold much of the property along College Street, which he had acquired in 1782. Mumford died in 1849. The house was being taxed to his heirs as late as 1854. A George H. Brown occupied the house from 1880 until 1892. In 1897, the house was still taxed to Mumford. In 1909, one Katherine G. Welling (relation unknown) sold the house to C. H. Robinson, who also owned the house at 64 College.

The house was somewhat oddly situated, at least in 1933 when Lovecraft and his aunt took up residence there. It stood mid-block, behind 64 College to the south (which directly abutted the street) and behind a boarding house to the north at 53–55 Waterman. Describing this situation to a correspondent, Lovecraft wrote, "About College St.—no, it is not this thoroughfare, but the little court or alley opening off it & having #66 at its rear, which was once called 'Ely's Lane'. I enclose an illustrative diagram. [See Figure 1] The old names of College St. are Presbyterian Lane, Rosemary Lane, & Hanover St. Ely's Lane was so-called because it abutted on the property of the Ely family."

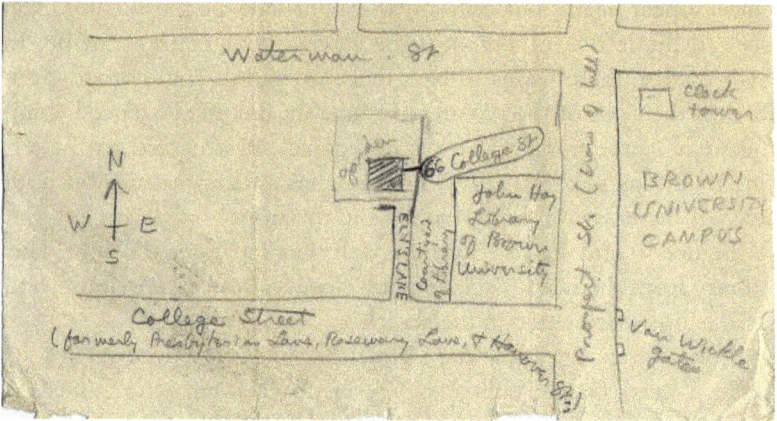

Figure 1: Sketch of layout at 66 College Street by H. P. Lovecraft, enclosed in a letter to Duane W. Rimel, June 1, 1934. (Courtesy of Brown University, John Hay Library.)

The Samuel B. Mumford house may have been one of the earliest houses to be built on College Street. The Truman Beckwith house (42 College) at the base of the hill was constructed in 1826, about the time the Mumford house was built; the William J. King house (48 College) was constructed c. 1846, and the Whipple–

Slater house (54 College) was constructed c. 1838 and remodeled c. 1867. These three houses were owned by prosperous cotton merchants. The Reuben F. Randall house at 58 College and the C. H. Robinson house at 64 College are non-extant, as they were razed to make room for the Albert and Vera List Art Building (1969–71). The Mumford house was moved in 1959 to 65 Prospect Street, where it stands at the corner of Meeting Street, across the street from the First Church of Christ, Scientist (1906), "the colossal Roman bulk . . . whose proud copper dome is the dominating feature of the Providence skyline."[2]

A record of the Providence Preservation Society has an interesting entry:

1853   Whereas Henry Bowen has conceded to Samuel B. Mumford a lot of land on College Street whereas it is agreed that no building whatever (except necessary fences) shall be erected with[in] 20′ of the N/ly line of said College Street...128.232 (Original agreement in 1823.)

The back of the house constructed at 64 College, as seen in Figure 8, seems to fulfill that stipulation.

At the time Lovecraft lived on College Street, many of the surrounding houses on both College and Waterman Streets were fraternity houses, and so Lovecraft lived on what was known as "fraternity row." Though the Mumford house was owned by the university, it was rented as a duplex and not for student housing. Fraternity houses located near Lovecraft's residence included:

48 College, Zeta Phi fraternity
54 College, Samuel N. Gerard House, Alpha Delta Phi fraternity
58 College, Reuben F. Randall House, Alpha Omega Tau fraternity
64 College Street, C. H. Robinson House, Phi Delta Theta fraternity
57 Waterman, Lambda Chi Alpha fraternity

Lovecraft extended the collegial spirit to his own house, calling it the headquarters of the Kappa Alpha Tau fraternity.

In Lovecraft's day, the residence of Marian Bonner, his aunt's friend and his correspondent late in his life, was known as The

2. HPL to Frank Belknap Long, 1 May 1926; ms., John Hay Library.

Arsdale. It was a boarding-house, apparently the same as the place
known years before as The Paxton. After Lovecraft's time, The
Arsdale was also used for student housing, called Hopkins House
(named for Chancellor Stephen Hopkins). It is no longer extant.

The advertisement below is from the Providence *Evening News*
(12 December 1910), p. 7:

> **THE PAXTON.** 53 Waterman street.
> Rooms and Table Board.

The same name is given to the establishment as late as 1919 in the
Providence Business Directory (p. 807). A plat map of the area of
1918 also labels the H-
shaped building The Pax-
ton. (See inset. Note that
the Mumford house just
below it in the plat map
is not labeled, and that it
appears to straddle two
lots.) The Paxton, be-
cause of its shape, probably had two addresses.
Lovecraft addressed his
letters to Marian Bonner
to 55 Waterman, but Martha Mitchell's *Encyclopedia Brunoniana*[3]
gives the address for The Arsdale as 53 Waterman.

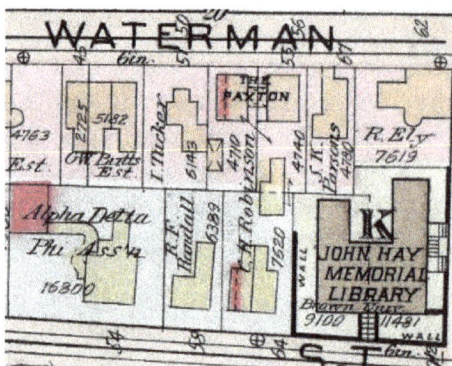

Lovecraft himself was no stranger to The Arsdale. Aside from
being able to see it every day from his flat, he and his aunt had occasion to take meals there. Helen Sully said that Lovecraft arranged for her to stay at the boarding-house across the yard from
66 College when she visited him in 1933. Presumably, Lovecraft
may have found lodging for other visitors who came from out of
town. In 1936, when R. H. Barlow came from Florida to visit, he
took a room at the boarding-house from 28 July to 1 September.
Thanks to Barlow, his mentor's papers now reside at the John Hay
Library, which had been a close neighbor in the last years of his life.

---

3. http://www.brown.edu/Administration/News_Bureau/Databases/Encyclopedia/
search.php?serial=F0270

Figure 2: To Robert Bloch, late May 1933.[4]

Figure 3: To Carl F. Strauch, 31 May 1933[5]

Figures 4 and 5: To August Derleth, sometime between 3 and 8 May 1933, showing the front of 66 College, and also a close-up view of the front door.[6]

---

4. *Letters to Robert Bloch and Others*, ed. David E. Schultz and S. T. Joshi (New York: Hippocampus Press, 2015), 31.

5. "Letters to Carl Ferdinand Strauch," ed. S. T. Joshi and David E. Schultz, *Lovecraft Annual* No. 4 (2010): 140.

6. *Essential Solitude: The Letters of H. P. Lovecraft and August Derleth*, ed. David E. Schultz and S. T. Joshi (New York: Hippocampus Press, 2008), 564 and 569.

Figure 6: Looking north toward Lovecraft's dwelling from the courtyard behind the wall separating the John Hay Library property from 1 Ely Court. The higher portion of the wall in the foreground is near the sidewalk parallel to College Street, as seen in Figure 9. The height of the wall is more readily apparent in that figure. Lovecraft and his aunt Annie Gamwell occupied the second floor of the house. The windows to Lovecraft's study, which faced west, cannot be seen from this angle. The other side of the wall in the foreground can be seen in Figure 9.

Figure 7: A closer view of the front door to 66 College. As above, the photo is taken from the library's side of the separating fence. In this view, it is more readily apparent that the basement, like that of the Shunned House on Benefit Street, is at ground level and that one must ascend a flight of stairs to reach the first floor.

Figure 8: A view of Lovecraft's dwelling (left) with his study windows clearly visible in the near corner of the upper story. The leftmost window faces west, affording the view Lovecraft so often described of flaming sunsets. The a south face of the building is parallel to College Street. The house at 64 College is very close by.

Figure 9: 64 College, obscuring Lovecraft's house behind it. Ely's Court is the narrow path between the house and the adjacent John Hay Library. The slope of the sidewalk is evidence that College Hill is indeed steep. *Brown Alumni Monthly* 20, No. 8 (March 1920): front cover. The caption refers to it as "House at 64–66 College Street."

Figure 10: Image of 64 College. The letters of the Phi Delta Theta fraternity can be seen on the canopy.

Figure 11: In this view of 64 College, taken from the southeast, the library is not seen, but 66 College is to the far right. It is clear that Lovecraft's house was set back quite far from College Street, and that Ely's Court was wide enough for a car to pass.

Figure 12: The house at 57 Waterman (no longer extant), home of the Lambda Chi Alpha fraternity, next door to The Arsdale, the boarding-house where Marian Bonner lived at 55 Waterman. *Brown Alumni Monthly* 37, No. 4 (November 1936): 97.

Acknowledgments

This brief article is the outgrowth of discussions with Donovan K. Loucks about the map he prepared to accompany H. P. Lovecraft's letters to his neighbor Marian F. Bonner. Donovan had shared with me images of photos he had seen in the Lovecraft collection at the John Hay Library, and he obtained scans of other images for this article with the assistance of Christopher Geissler and Ray Butti of the John Hay Library. Donovan apprised me of the Mary A. Gowdey Library of House Histories of the Providence Preservation Society (source of the document in the appendix) and also the online *Encyclopedia Brunoniana*. And he identified many of the fraternity houses in the vicinity of Lovecraft's house. All photos not credited to other publications are courtesy of the John Hay Library of Brown University.

Appendix

PROVIDENCE PRESERVATION SOCIETY
Records of   Plat 12
#66 College Street.....Wood   Lot 220

#45 in 1854   #47 in 1880   #68 in 1885

1823   Henry Bowen sells for $720 to Samuel B Mumford "a certain
        lot of land["] on the N/ly side of College Street bounded
        S/ly by College Street 60'; W by John Whipple 130'; N by
        Nathan Waterman 60';...being the same lot that was de-
        vised by the late Jabez Bowen Esq to his son Horatio G
        Bowen and by him conveyed to said Henry....47/46

1823   Henry Bowen for $20 to Samuel B Mumford 10' of land on
        the N side of College Street adjoining the W/ly bound of
        grantee's land...47/131 Subject to an agreement...(see
        178.232... 1853)

1827   Policy Record: Samuel Mumford—N side College St wood
        — 24 × 36'—2 stories hi front & rear. Add. 16 × 20' 1½ sto-
        ries high—woodhouse adjng 16' sq—occ. for a DH

1828   The Samuel Mumfords lived here and until 1844. Mr. Mum-
        ford was a commercial merchant of Browne and Van
        Slyck...Prov Dir

1853   Whereas Henry Bowen has conveyed to Samuel B Mumford
        a lot of land on College Street whereas it is agreed that no
        building whatever (except necessary fences) shall be erected
        with[in] 20' of the N/ly line of said College Street...128.232
        (Original agreement in 1823)

1854   Property is taxed to Samuel B Mumford Heirs...William
        Bailey Trustee for William B. Greene, Newport and Richard
        W G Welling N Y u/w of Samuel B Mumford...

1880   George H Browne lived here and until 1892...(Browne &
        Van Slyck). Prov Dir

1897   Property taxed to Samuel B Mumford.

1909   Katherine G Welling et al sells this property to C H Robin-
        son...it being the same conveyed to me u/w (by deed)
        Samuel B Mumford. Subject to terms of agreement in a bond
        from S B Mumford to Henry Bowen in 1823.502/23 9

        Moved to #65 PROSPECT Street Sept 1959

The Thing (Flung Daily) on the Doorstep: Lovecraft in the Antipodean Press, 1803–2007

Brendan Whyte

I. *Lovecraft as Surname*

Lovecraft is an unusual name. Its meaning seems obvious: the craft or art of making love (whether this be simple wooing or, since the mid-twentieth century, the act of sexual intercourse itself). However, the noun "craft" has more subtle shades of meaning than the commonest current one of skill or art (e.g., handicraft, stagecraft). The primal meaning of craft, derived from "Kraft" in the old Germanic languages,[1] is strength, power, or force. From this base meaning, the word has engendered various other meanings in English: occult art or magic; human skill or art, as opposed to nature; an artifice or device, especially a magical one; a deceitful action or trick; the skill or art used to deceive or defraud; or scholarship, a branch of learning, or science (*Shorter Oxford English Dictionary*, 5th ed. 2002, 1.545).

Therefore the surname Lovecraft not only implies the superficial "art of making love," which has both originally innocent and more recent euphemistically obscene implications, but also hints at the more sinister and even occult connotations of the knowledge, art, or ability to arouse feelings of love by cunning or deceitful means. For a writer who has caused so many to enjoy stories of cosmic terrors and "what man was not meant to know," the cognomen is by no means inapt.[2] One could ask whether

---

1. "Love" is also derived from the old Germanic *lubo*.
2. Not to mention the pathetic irony of it given the cause of death of HPL's father.

HPL's[3] stories would have been as successful, or his cult status so high, if he had been named H. P. Lovelace, H. P. Flower, or H. P. Jones.

Lovecraft is unusual in another sense: that of frequency of occurrence. Despite its obvious modern English meaning, it is a surprisingly rare surname. As of November 2014, the online residential telephone directory for the whole of Australia[4] (population 23.7 million) listed only a single subscriber—in South Australia—with the name, while the business directory[5] listed a single company: film producers Lovecraft 21C Productions Pty. Ltd., in Sydney, NSW. For New Zealand (population 4.5 million), the online directory[6] has no residential or business subscribers named Lovecraft.

All Australian citizens over the age of eighteen are legally required to enroll to vote, thus electoral rolls capture virtually all the adult citizen population. As of June 2009, there were 13,892,562 enrolled electors in 150 Commonwealth electoral divisions (electorates). The 2009 rolls contain a total of six Lovecrafts: five at four addresses in two divisions in South Australia, and one in Sydney, NSW. In New Zealand, where enrollment is not compulsory, as of 30 November 2014, the 3,138,486 enrolled voters (92.55% of the estimated eligible population) included no Lovecrafts.[7]

It is therefore unsurprising that the name Lovecraft conjures up a single image, that of a particular early twentieth-century New England author. There simply are not very many other people of the name.

II. *Lovecraft as Search-Term*

The development of the Internet, and of scanning and optical character recognition (OCR) technologies since the late twentieth century, have allowed historical paper archives to be made not only accessible to a researcher anywhere on the planet, but also

---

3. To avoid confusion between lovecraft the word, Lovecraft the surname, and H. P. Lovecraft the author, the latter is referred to throughout as HPL.

4. www.whitepages.com.au, compiled by Sensis for Telstra.

5. www.yellowpages.com.au

6. www.whitepages.co.nz, covering residential, business and government listings.

7. www.elections.gov.nz and e-mail from Rex Arrell, Manager corporate services, Electoral Commission, Wellington, 4 Dec. 2014.

word-searchable. Given HPL's contributions to various New England newspapers from the first decade of the twentieth century,
the rest of the present paper asks whether, and in what contexts,
his name appears in Australian and New Zealand newspapers
(both of which countries appear in his stories, particularly "The
Call of Cthulhu" and "The Shadow out of Time").

Australia's historic newspapers are being digitized as part of
the "Trove" project, hosted by the National Library of Australia,
while the New Zealand National Library hosts "Papers Past."[8] Both
allow searching by keyword, title, date, and state or region, while
Trove's OCRed text is correctable by crowdsourcing.

Trove's coverage begins with the *Sydney Gazette and New
South Wales Advertiser* of 5 March 1803 (a mere fifteen years after
the first white settlers—the convicts on the First Fleet—arrived
on the continent) and covers an ever-increasing range of defunct
and continuing papers for the nineteenth and first half of the
twentieth century. Coverage drops abruptly after 1954, due to
copyright law.[9] Nevertheless, some copyright owners have allowed later issues of their titles to be digitised, in particular the
federal capital's *Canberra Times* (hereafter *CT*), but the most recent paper available is the November 2007 issue of *Woroni*, also
from Canberra, the Australian National University's student union
paper. Papers Past currently includes 92 titles, of which the earliest is the *New Zealand Gazette* for 21 August 1839. No papers
have been digitized beyond 31 December 1945, even though New
Zealand copyright lasts only fifty years.

As of the end of November 2014, a keyword search for "Lovecraft" returned 352 results in Trove's newspapers,[10] and a mere 3 in

8. http://trove.nla.gov.au/newspaper and http://paperspast.natlib.govt.nz/

9. Until 2005, copyright in newspapers was 50 years in Australia. In 2005 a US-
Australia "free trade" agreement required Australia to extend its copyright period
to 70 years for non-government publications. Therefore the 1955 papers, due to
enter the public domain at the end of 2005, now remain in copyright until 2025.

10. The state-wise breakdown is NSW 289, ACT 36, SA 8, WA 7, Tas 6, Vic 3,
Qld 2, national 1 (i.e., *Australian Women's Weekly*). NSW is predominant because that state is the original and most populous settlement in the country, and
Sydney always has been the continent's largest city. The surprising second place
for the ACT is due to the post-1954 digitization of the *CT* and *Woroni*. Victoria's

Papers Past (none of which refer to HPL or local Lovecrafts). Beginning with the earliest, dated 20 August 1834, the vast majority of the first 276 Australian results refer to Joshua Lovecraft, tailor and draper of Sydney, up to the time of his death, aged sixty-two or sixty-three, on 16 August 1866, and even into 1869 with regard to his estate, managed by his executor William Lovecraft in London. Most of the references to Joshua Lovecraft are his own frequent business advertisements, along with mention of consignments for him in shipping import lists, Masonic and social news, real estate advertisements, and several public notices. Other Lovecrafts include one or more Misses Lovecraft, one being a Miss Mary Lovecraft, who appear about thirty times between 1837 to 1851, predominantly in shipping arrivals and departures; a Mr. W. & Mrs. S. Lovecraft appear thrice in shipping lists in 1860, bound for Sydney from Plymouth on *La Hogue,* in company with Mr. Charles Scott and his five sisters. In 1866, Joshua Lovecraft was executor to Charles Scott before his own death. The Mr. W. Lovecraft appears to be a very young William John Lovecraft, nephew to Charles Scott, and whose death, age twenty-five, on 24 September 1869, attracted three newspaper notices.

After 1869, the only press references to Lovecraft as an Australian surname are two, twenty-four years apart, to Great War veteran Felix Lovecraft Marriott—his second Christian name most likely his mother's maiden name—whose marriage and executorship of his father's will each rate a mention in the *Sydney Morning Herald* (14 June 1924 [14] and 10 August 1949 [14]).

Meanwhile Lovecraft, as an English surname, appeared in six front-page advertisements in the Adelaide *Advertiser* in 1895–96 (6 and 27 April, 25 May, 14 December, 25 January, and 1 February), as part of a large listing of surnames of persons listed in "A Register, containing names of 70,000 persons advertised for, to claim property and money since 1703. Every man and woman in the world should buy this book, as instructions are given how to recover property from Chancery." Published by the London firm

---

sixth position appears inexplicable. However, once post-1954 papers from the rest of the country are digitized, a breakdown more in line with relative populations (NSW, Vic, Qld, WA, SA, Tas, ACT, NT) is expected.

of F. H. Dougal & Co. since 1844, the index of advertisements in worldwide newspapers for missing heirs to unclaimed estates, was a mere 2/6 and full details of the original advertisements was available upon application for a £1 fee. Dougal & Co. would then assist a claimant recover the monies for a commission. The 1888 and 1910 editions of the index[11] do indeed list a Chancery case of Baker v. Lovecraft, with at least £50 unclaimed (11). A similar advertisement, masquerading as the article "Lost owners of £1,250,000" and still including the name Lovecraft, appears in Dunedin's *Otago Daily Times* of 3 June 1914 (8).

Otherwise, Lovecraft disappears from the papers as a surname with local connections. It is initially replaced by an intriguing prophetic conjunction of stagecraft, Lovecraft, madness, and suicide in America. Two Tasmanian papers, Hobart's *Mercury* and Launceston's *Daily Telegraph*, on 12 and 13 April 1894 respectively, report news from the San Francisco mail:

> May Brooklyn, the young actress, who committed suicide in San Francisco lately, was a native of Cornwall, England, and was so deeply imbued with theosophy and spiritualism as to be insane at times. Melancholia on account of the death of her lover—an actor named Lovecraft—was the proximate cause of her self-destruction. (3 & 3)

A similar but more detailed item appears in the "Musical and Dramatic" column of the Christchurch *Star* for 2 June 1894 (6), noting that Lovecraft had taken carbolic acid and shot himself.

Then the *Yea Chronicle* (Vic.) of 2 December 1897 uses "love-craft" literally: "the happy couple left for some distant port to sail their love-craft on the blissful waves of honey-moon" (2). Likewise did the Christchurch *Press*, reviewing the Comic Opera Company's production of *Dorothy* (6 June 1922): "In the domain of the comedian, Mr Charles Workman proved irrepressible as usual [. . .]. It was a foregone conclusion that his courting of the much-widowed lady, [. . .] displayed all the art and science of up-to-date lovecraft" (11). Following up on other non-surname uses of the word, a weekly column by "Oriel," titled "The Passing Show," in

---

11. F. H. Dougal & Co., *Dougal's Index Register to Next of Kin, Heirs at Law and Cases of Unclaimed Money Advertisements*, London.

Melbourne's *Argus* for 25 August 1928 comments on "the discovery in the County Court a few days ago of a young man who did not know how to kiss or make love, who did not know what a glory-box was, and did not even seem to be aware that an engagement ring is worn neither through the nose nor on the right thumb" (7)—a description that could apply to HPL. Oriel continues: "Education in courtship is a matter most vital to the future of the race; yet, in a presumably civilised community, there are allowed to run the streets young men who, if a knowledge of lovecraft entitled them to matriculation, could not obtain their sixth grade qualifying certificates" (7). Likewise in a piece of short fiction, "The Feminine Touch" by "Laicus," in Ipswich's *Queensland Times* for 4 September 1937: "It was man's first venture into the art of love-craft" (14).

An eldritch unspeakableness associated with the name "lovecraft" lurks unexpectedly in Margaret Drabble's essay "Children—A Brief History of My Addiction" in the *Australian Women's Weekly* for Wednesday 10 October 1973:

> I have heard from American friends that the anti-baby movement is so well in hand over there that they are surprised to see how openly and proudly baby shops and maternity shops still display their wares over here: perhaps they will end up discreetly in back alleys, where lovecraft used to conceal its offerings. (55)

Indeed, Lovecraft was the name of a chain of, er, lovecraft shops in Adelaide, which managed to get an advertisement inserted in the December 1979 issues of the South Australian Police Association's *Police Journal*, to the delight of mainstream media (*CT*, 12 December 1979 [3]). Oddly, the one Lovecraft shop still operating in Adelaide is not listed in the online White or Yellow Pages.

Finally, Paul Theroux comments on the confounding of surname and noun in an extract from his *Sunrise with Seamonsters* ("The adventure now standing on platform 1. . .," *CT*, 30 June 1985): "I [. . .] bought a biography of the writer of weird tales, H. P. Lovecraft, and boarded the train for New York [. . .] and en route my book proved an invaluable conversation piece, since most of my fellow passengers took the title, Lovecraft, to be that of a sex manual" (54).

Apart from eight nationwide references between 1913 to 1919, and a ninth in 1926, to a racehorse, sister to Lovelorn, named Lovecraft (one paper mistakenly spells it Lovegraft), the remaining fifty-three instances of the word "Lovecraft" include forty-seven direct references to HPL himself and six derived from, if not trading on, his name. The first appear over a three-month period in 1906–07, when six separate non-metropolitan papers reproduce HPL's letter of 16 July 1906 to the *Scientific American*, published in that magazine on 25 August 1906. These six references are all syndicated copy, reproducing verbatim a column titled "Science and Invention," with seven items, of which HPL's letter is the sixth.[12]

The papers are:

> Fri 23 Nov. 1906, *Burrowa News* (Burrowa, NSW), Supplement, p. 3.
> Sat 24 Nov. 1906, *Liverpool Herald* (Liverpool, NSW), p. 9.
> Sat 24 Nov. 1906, *Dubbo Liberal and Macquarie Advocate* (Dubbo, NSW), p. 7.
> Fri 7 Dec. 1906, *Gosford Times* (Gosford, NSW), p. 4.
> Fri 7 Dec. 1906, *Narandera Argus and Riverina Advertiser* (Narrandera, NSW), p. 7.
> Sat 23 Feb. 1907, *Eastern Districts Chronicle* (York,[13] WA), Supplement p. 1.

---

12. The seven items in order of appearance are: A Bright Black Varnish for Leather [a recipe from "a German inventor"]; A New Bridge [over the St. Lawrence near Montreal "will be built in the immediate future"]; The Use of Salt ["discussed by a Dutch scientist" concluding that excessive use is harmful]; Another Flat Earth Man ["John Edward Quinlan, commissioned land surveyor of St. Lucia and St. Vincent, British West Indies," issues a pamphlet, *The Earth a Plane*]; Paraffin Oil in a Well [a water well at the Graziers' Arms, Husbands Bosworth, England yielding paraffin oil]; Trans-Neptunian Planets; Metallised Paper [a new electric process for giving paper a metallic surface, published in *Paper and Pulp*].

13. Of the towns, Liverpool is now part of Sydney's western sprawl; Dubbo is a large rural service centre in central NSW; Gosford is part of the central coast between Sydney and Newcastle; Burrowa and Narrandera are small towns in southern NSW, while York in WA is inland east of Perth. The first national census, in 1910, did not compile data for individual towns, but none of the six would have exceeded 5000, and most would likely have been only 1000 or so. By 1930, Dubbo had 5000 people, York 4000 and Liverpool 3000. The other three were much smaller.

In five of the six papers, the entire broadsheet page in which this column appears is reproduced identically, including its short fiction, housekeeping tips, and jokes. The *Liverpool Herald*, however, with a smaller page size (four columns instead of seven), reproduces this content only in part, but including the entire "Science and Invention" column, over two pages.

The Australian papers all make the following changes to the letter's text as published in *Scientific American:*

Trans-Neptunian Planets.

[To the Editor of the SCIENTIFIC AMERICAN:]
In these days of large telescopes and modern astronomical methods, it seems strange[, says Mr H. P. Lovecraft,] that no vigorous efforts are being made to discover planets beyond the orbit of Neptune, which is now considered the outer-most limit of the [sS]olar [sS]ystem. It has been noticed that seven comets have their aphelia at a point that would correspond to the orbit of a planet revolving around the sun at a distance of about 100 astronomical units [(]9,300,000,000 miles).[¶] Now several have suggested that such a planet exists, and has captured the comets by attraction. This is probable, as Jupiter and others also mark the aphelia of many celestial wanderers. The writer has noticed that a great many comets cluster around a point 50 units out, where a large body might revolve. If the great mathematicians of the day should try to compute orbits from these aphelia, it is doubtful if they could succeed; but if all the observatories that possess celestial cameras should band together and minutely photograph the ecliptic, as is done in asteroid hunting, the bodies might be revealed on their plates. Even if no discoveries were made, the accurate star photographs would almost be worth the time and trouble.
[H. P. LOVECRAFT.
Providence, R. I., July 16, 1906.]

None of the papers give any indication that the piece is a letter, let alone its date or place of initial publication, and while HPL is named, exactly who he is or where he is from is left unstated. While the "Science and Invention" column includes short pieces from around the world, because HPL's affiliation and address are not provided, the reader would be forgiven for thinking him a leading global astronomical expert, if not an Australian.

These appear to be the only instances of HPL's own work appearing in the Australian press. HPL then disappears from the Australian press record for almost four decades, until on 26 August 1944 the *Sydney Morning Herald*, the leading metropolitan daily in the country, finally makes reference to HPL's horror stories. R. G. Howarth's book review column titled "Ghosts and Goose-flesh" reviews the recently released Random House title *Great Tales of Terror and the Supernatural.* While citing several stories and authors in this anthology by name, the review discusses the genre of ghost stories more generally, as well as those collected in this title, Howarth commenting that few ghost stories occur in the age of electric light and enlightenment:

> Rather, their themes come out of the past. Black magic is the commonest of these, and it seems extraordinary to find one H. P. Lovecraft writing of conjurations and pacts with the Devil in contemporary New England—machinations which were to repeople the earth with an ancient evil race of monsters that first possessed it. But Lovecraft is here following Arthur Machen, whose "Great God Pan" develops the same idea. Machen, curiously enough, uses modern medical science as the means of working a spell. (6)

The next HPL reference is the *Argus* (Melbourne, Vic.) for 19 February 1949. A book review column ends with the brief note:

> THE LURKER AT THE THRESHOLD, by H. P. LOVECRAFT and A. DERLETH. Museum Press.
> THE LURKER ON [sic] THE THRESHOLD is written in the Dracula tradition, with horror piled on horror, so that midnight becomes a terror session and the moon rises on monsters hitherto fortunately not on the visiting lists of most of us. In short, a pleasurable fright-maker. – G.A.H. (11)

By now HPL was also a household name in France. On 28 August that same year, the Francophone Sydney weekly *Le Courier Australien* (pp. 1 & 5), reprinting an article by Jerome Cardan from the Paris hebdomadal *La Tribune des Nations*, linked HPL with Kafka as stereotypical of an inescapable nightmare scenario.

Describing the situation of American Edward U. Condon (1902–1974), Director of the National Bureau of Standards—who in 1948 learnt only through the press of his accusation, by J. Edgar Hoover and the House Committee on Un-American Activities, of alleged and unsubstantiated communist sympathies—Cardan reviewed a February 1949 article "Trial by Newspaper" in *Scientific American* (180(2):11–16), in which Klapper and Glock of Columbia University's Bureau of Applied Social Research applied content analysis to New York newspaper coverage of the Condon affair:

La dernière née des sciences modernes, c'est la calomnie

[. . .]
Cette étude porte sur la campagne de presse et non sur l'affaire elle-même. Elle ne touche donc ni au problème de la "culpabilité" du professeur Condon, ni au drame humain lui-même: ce drame d'un accusé à qui on refuse tout moyen de se justifier et qui ne voit l'acte d'accusation qu'à travers des articles de journaux. Cette tragédie, qui n'est possible qu'à notre époque, tentera certainement un Kafka ou un Lovecraft de l'avenir et donnera naissance à quelque nouvelle ou pièce de théâtre hallucinante.[14] (5)

That HPL's surname alone was needed, without any initials, proves how synonymous that surname had become with a single man and a single concept of unnamable terror, even outside the Anglophone world.

Finally, in 1951, HPL's works, issued by the British publisher Victor Gollancz, reached antipodean shores:

Tales of Terror

"THE Haunter of the Dark" (H. P. Lovecraft) has been edited and an introduction written by August Derleth. This volume contains

---

14. **The latest creation of modern science: slander. [. . .]** This study focuses on the press campaign, not the case itself. Therefore, it does not touch the issue of Professor Condon's "guilt", nor the human drama itself: the drama of an accused who is denied any means to justify himself and only sees the indictment through newspaper reports. This tragedy, which is only possible in our time, definitely will tempt a Kafka or a Lovecraft of the future and will give birth to some mind-blowing short story or play.

not only the title story, but nine others of the "terror" writings of Howard Phillips Lovecraft, who at 47 years [*sic*] died in 1937. Only a few of his macabre creations were published during his lifetime. (Victor Gollancz Ltd., London.) ["Books in Brief," *West Australian* (Perth, WA), 7 April 1951 (15)]

Other reviews occur in the "Latest Fiction" column of Adelaide's *Advertiser*, 12 May 1951:

> "The Haunter of the Dark," by H. P. Lovecraft.
> (Gollancz, London, 13/6).

H. P. LOVECRAFT, who died in 1937, was an American writer who achieved distinction in the genre of the fantastic.

He specialised in themes of cosmic terror and spiritual horror. Many of his stories were based on what he called Cthulhu mythology—based on "the fundamental lore or legend that this world was inhabited at one time by another race who, in practising black magic, lost their foothold and were expelled, yet live on outside ever ready to take possession of this earth again."

"The Haunter of the Dark" and the other tales that make up the first selection of Lovecraft's stories to be published outside America is representative of his best work—memorable stories that occupy a place in the classic niche reserved for minor masterpieces of the macabre. (6)

and in Brisbane's *Courier Mail*, 29 September 1951:

A browse through the bookshelves
By Warwick Lawrence

[. . .]

An American writer, H. P. Lovecraft, brings you in THE HAUNTER OF THE DARK (Gollancz), a fantastic and macabre collection of stories told in the tradition of Edgar Allan Poe.

[. . .]

H. P. Lovecraft (who died in 1937) first wrote his stories for the "penny dreadfuls," but in time his writing drew the serious attention of both critic and connoisseur.

He turned to themes of cosmic terror and spiritual horror, basing his stories on the fundamental lore or legend that the world was once inhabited by another race, who, in practising black magic, lost their foothold and were expelled, yet still live on the out and outer, every ready to take possession of the earth again.

This eerie belief forms the basis of many of his most hair-raising tales, among them "The Rats in the Wall[s]," which is by far one of his best.

This story, which concerns an American grown rich, who goes to England to restore an ancestor's ruined castle, has such a sense of mounting horror that it is impossible to put it aside until you come to the end.

The same strain of suspense runs through all his stories, especially "The Outsider," "The Colour Out of Space" (strangely suggestive of events in our own atomic age), "The Dunwich Horror," "The Thing on the Door-step," and "The Haunter of the Dark," from which the book takes its title. (2)

The "Books Received" column of several papers listed HPL titles without further comment in 1951–52:

"The Haunter of the Dark and Other Tales of Terror," by H. P. Lovecraft (Victor Gollancz Ltd., London). [*West Australian*, 14 April 1951 (19); "Book News," *Sydney Morning Herald*, 3 May 1952 (8); and "Wagga City Library Book List," the *Daily Advertiser* (Wagga Wagga, NSW), 10 September 1952 (5)].

"The Case of Charles Dexter Ward," by H. P. Lovecraft (Victor Gollancz Ltd., London). [*West Australian*, 29 March 1952 (28)]

The latter title received a brief review in the *West Australian* of 13 September 1952:

Books In Brief
Review

Scare Technique. "The Case of Charles Dexter Ward" (H. P. Lovecraft), described by the publishers as "a novel of terror" runs on the lines of his earlier success "The Haunter of the Dark." The author has made a name for himself as a "fantasy writer," with a gift for giving "overwhelming conviction to the wildly abnormal" and he does it again. (Victor Gollancz Ltd., London.) (16)

HPL gets no further mention in the Australian press before the beginning of the current copyright period (1955 at time of writing in late 2014). After that, our sample is restricted to the *Australian Women's Weekly* (to 1982), the *CT* (to 1995), and *Woroni* (to 2007). This is the period in which HPL becomes an Australian household name, mentioned not as a new writer, but as a stylistic descriptor, to which others are compared. Thus the *CT* on 7 March 1964, described an exhibition at the Art Club of Canberra:

New Exhibition
EIGHT ARTISTS

The other striking pictures in the show are those of Elwyn Lynn. He has used cloth and glue to give depth and texture to his painting, to convey sinuous movement in his material. The chief impact of his work is sensual, but it has emotional over tones like a Lovecraft mythology: the primeval matter which determines its own shape. (2)

Occasional reviews still do surface:

Fiction
Life in a tank
By Chris Bryant

DAGON. By H. P. Lovecraft. Gollancz. 413 pp. Price $3.85.
'Dagon and Other Macabre Tales' really needs no comment from me. All those who are addicted to supernatural fiction will know the work of H. P. Lovecraft. Some of his stories are comparable with those of Edgar Allan Poe, and he succeeds consistently where the writers in the previous volume fail—although, to be fair, his own contribution to it was not notable. However, 'Dagon' is an excellent accumulation of Lovecraft's short stories, and as a companion to his other books also published by Gollancz, is great value for money. [*CT*, 23 December 1967 (12)]

But with most of HPL's work now available to the Australian public via the Gollancz editions, Lovecraft is from now on mainly mentioned only in passing as one of the authors included in an anthology (e.g. *CT*, 28 March 1975 [6]), as a descriptor of the style of writing used by others (e.g. *CT*, 11 July 1993 [26]), or as a standard

of horror writing to which other writers are measured (and usually found wanting).

Besides books, reviews and advertisements appear for films and
TV movies based on Lovecraft's work, such as *The Dunwich Horror* (in the *CT* for a week or so from 4 February 1971 [19]); *Re-
Animator* (*CT*, 26 September 1988 [38]); *Bride of Re-Animator*
(*CT*, 1 December 1990 [24]); or reruns of *Die, Monster, Die!* (*CT*,
27 November 1989 [38]; 10 June 1991 [28]). The Lovecraftian film
Cthulhu, filmed in Canberra in the mid-1990s and released in
2000, is also mentioned. Robert Macklin's "A Capital Life" column
in the *CT* of 24 June 1995 ends with: "A feature film of the thriller
genre is about to be shot in Canberra—*Cthulhu*, based on the
writings of H. P. Lovecraft. According to producer Damian Heffernan it is the first movie to be shot entirely in Canberra for 22
years. However, all other details are secret at this time" (C8). A
fortnight later, on 7 July, much more detail emerged in the Geor-
gina Curry's *CT* article "Directing All the Action":

> Based on a selection of H. P. Lovecraft short stories, the psycho-
> logical thriller *Cthulhu* will employ 26 locals as cast and crew and
> 50 as extras. Canberra rock bands such as P. Harness and Three
> will contribute to the soundtrack.
>
> Onara Productions is the creation of 26-year-old Damien Hef-
> fernan. [. . .] "H. P. Lovecraft has got a big following—he wrote
> *The Call of Cthulhu* about cult worship and five other pieces
> which are all the Cthulhu [mythology]," he said. "We've based it
> on three of those five stories and added role playing to it like in a
> dungeons-and dragons game." [. . .] The 100-minute film culmi-
> nates in a violent massacre scene to be shot near Hume. [. . .] Like
> other short-stories written by Lovecraft, *Cthulhu*'s setting will use
> older style buildings and homesteads. Hall Village has been cho-
> sen to double for the fictitious town of Dunwich and to achieve a
> New England feel. Batemans Bay's southern beaches will also be
> used to portray an eerie shore-line near the imaginary town of
> Innsmouth and the old Royal Canberra Hospital will serve as the
> interior of the Arkham Asylum in which Ed finds himself impris-
> oned. (11)

And two years later in *Woroni* (21 February 1997):

Culture
Tell me a story

[. . .]

Damien Heffernan, 27, has been described by an anonymous colleague as the only serious film maker in Canberra, yet he too is about to pack up his bag and hit the road for Sydney. Damien seems very disillusioned and frustrated with the dearth of opportunity for his craft here. He told me of the difficulty of making his latest film, a feature (76 mins) called Cthulhu, a horror/psychological thriller based on a series of stories by 1930s writer H. G. [sic] Lovecraft. Damien made Cthulhu with no financial support on an ultra low budget. It became prohibitive to finish it on film, so shooting was completed on video. The actors were paid a daily stipend to cover expenses and were all made associate producers with a share in any profits. (34)

By the 1970s, Lovecraft had also become a cliché. The TV schedule in the CT (5 June 1972 [17]) for Channel 7 on the following Friday, includes an episode of *Night Gallery*, with four stories including "Miss Lovecraft Sent Me." The film *Cast a Deadly Spell*, reviewed in the CT's "TV Guide" for 1 June 1992 (36), has as lead character a Detective Harry Lovecraft. And a (Miss) Linda Lovecraft, conjoining the reputations of porn actress Linda Lovelace and HPL, in the persona of the presumably pseudonymous anthologist of a (second) book of horror and heavy-breathing has her work reviewed ("Books in Brief," CT, 20 August 1978):

MORE DEVIL'S KISSES. Edited by Linda Lovecraft. Corgi. 188pp. $2.00.
This is a book to be read in bed with the companion of one's choice by the light of a flickering candle. Miss Lovecraft has collected 13 stories, each of which combines terror and titration, and so, should the reader enter into the spirit of the volume, he or she will have two good reasons to clutch the beloved. All of the stories are clever. Two of them are genuinely funny. One of them, a tale of bestiality and paedophilia, is comparably vile. Beautiful women couple with huge bats and are ravaged by Things. A libidinous Swede makes the two-backed beast with an ice woman at the North Pole. A predatory male chauvinist wart hog receives his come uppance when he is literally eaten by a vengeful spirit dis-

guised as just another promiscuous strumpet. All good filthy fun. L.W. (13)

HPL also manages to worm his way into officialdom and bureaucracy, with a public notice of intention to apply for incorporation, dated 16 March 1989, inserted by David Gregg Tansey, on behalf of the Esoteric Order of Dagon, the objects of which society were given as "(i) To promote discussion and appreciation of horror, science fiction and fantasy literature and other media, with special reference to the works of H. P. Lovecraft & his contemporaries; (ii) To develop the talents of amateur writers, poets and artists within the above field" (CT, 26 May 1989 [29]).

By the 1990s, Lovecraft's influence has devolved to even the youngest ages, with a (very) short story by Ashley Homann, age eleven, published in the "Mailbag" section of the CT children's supplement *Junior Times*, on 19 April 1992 (2). The story, "The Beast," features a reanimation following a lightning strike on the grave of one Edward T. Lovecraft. The name cannot be a coincidence.

Sydney hard-rock band Lovecraft was promoted, along with fellow Sydneysiders Hell Yes, in a puff piece and advertisement for their Friday the 13th concert in the CT, 12 November (17 & 19). And even Woody Allen referenced Lovecraft in his own love life (*Woroni*, 1 March 1993 [34], reviewing Allen's *Complete Prose*).

The final digitized Lovecraft reference in the online Australian press is the most enthusiastic ("H. P. Lovecraft," *Woroni*, 8 September 2003 [37]), a "Lovecraft 101" if you will, with the appropriate byline of "Brown Jenkins," which opens by asking: "Sick and tired of the same old serial killers? Want at least 10% more tentacles, and up to 20% more fungi from other planets? Feel like some horror that's a bit more on the cosmic side? Then perhaps a taste of the somewhat different literary delights of H. P Lovecraft is just the thing you need."

III. *Conclusion*

Despite its obvious Englishness, and simple etymology, Lovecraft is a rare and unusual surname, with only six persons of that name being listed on current electoral rolls in Australia, and none in New Zealand, giving an antipodean frequency of less than 1 in 2

million persons. Of 358 references to "Lovecraft" in digitized Australasian newspapers since 1803, there are a handful of literal references to lovecraft as the art of wooing, and which by the late
1900s become euphemistic references to sex shops. Otherwise,
apart from a racehorse named Lovecraft and a half-dozen advertisements referring to an unclaimed chancery estate owing to a
Lovecraft, about three-quarters are references to nineteenth-
century Sydney draper Joshua Lovecraft, mainly in advertisements
and shipping freight news. A handful of other Lovecrafts, several
being Joshua's relatives, also appear. References specifically to HPL
make up a mere 20% of the total, beginning with six separate reproductions of his 1906 letter to *Scientific American*, but HPL citations dominate after 1944, when the first reference to his published
fiction appears in a book review. From then on, the word Lovecraft
becomes almost entirely synonymous with HPL, with direct references to the man being joined by references to his genre of horror
writing, to the quality benchmark he set, and lastly as a cultural
icon and even cliché, referenced in advertisements or reviews of
(often loose) film adaptions of his work, and the names of fictional characters or authorial pseudonyms of the works of others.

Briefly Noted

The recent and unexpected discovery of a cache of Lovecraft's letters to Zealia Brown Reed Bishop has generated considerable excitement in the world of Lovecraft criticism, and their imminent
publication by the H. P. Lovecraft Historical Society will be eagerly awaited. These letters shed tremendous light not only on Lovecraft's relations with Bishop, a persistent revision client from 1927
onward, but also on Lovecraft's general practices in his chosen occupation as literary revisionist and ghostwriter. Curiously, there is
no overlap between these newly discovered letters and those letters that Arkham House transcribed decades ago for publication in
the *Selected Letters*. In all, the letters come to nearly 85,000 words.

The Search for
Joseph Curwen's Town Home

Donovan K. Loucks

My House opp. Mr. Epenetus Olney's Tavern off ye Towne Street, Ist on ye N. side of Olney's Court. Distance from Boston Stone abt. XLIV Miles. *(The Case of Charles Dexter Ward* [CF 2.270])

The *approximate* location of Joseph Curwen's house has never been a mystery. The "Towne Street" was the colonial-era name for Providence's Main Street, and "Olney's Court" has long been thought to be a short extension of Olney Street on the *west* side of Main Street. Since the house is described as being on the *north* side of Olney's Court, it would be logical to assume that it was at the *northwest* corner of North Main Street and Olney Street.

But did Lovecraft have an actual house in mind? And, if he did, what became of it? More importantly, why did he choose it? And does any evidence remain of it? More than four years ago, I set out to answer these questions.

Examining old plat maps of Providence, one can see that a house once stood at this location with an address of 6 Olney Street. Though the house number does not appear on the following scan from a 1918 plat map (see p. 100), it is designated by an "X" just to the left of the center.

The intersection of North Main Street (extending north and south through the middle of the image below) and Olney Street (entering from the east/right of the image) is at the center. The entire row of houses on the west side of North Main Street is no longer extant, nor are there any along Stampers Street. For that matter, Stampers Street itself no longer exists.

Originally, Olney Street began at Stampers Street and contin-

ued east. Likewise, the numbering of Olney Street began at
Stampers Street, with the houses on the north side being numbered 2, 6, 10, 14, 16, and 20—these last three numbers can be
seen on the image below.

So what became of the house at 6 Olney Street? By May 1931
the house was owned by the city of Providence and in 1932 it was
listed as being vacant. Around the same time, Lovecraft mentions
the area in a letter:

> Right now the ancient colonial houses on Stamper's or Constitu-
> tion Hill at the foot of Olney St.—a niggerville—are about to suc-
> cumb in the course of a widening of North Main's notorious
> bottleneck. (Lovecraft to Wilfred Blanch Talman, 24 March 1931)

Looking over later maps of the area, one finds that this portion
of North Main Street was widened in 1931 and renamed Captain
J. Carleton Davis Memorial Boulevard. If one overlays a modern
map of the area on the 1918 plat map, one finds that what was
formerly North Main Street is now the northbound (eastern) lanes
of the new boulevard. Again, everything along the west side of the

street has been demolished all the way to Stampers Street. In fact, part of what was once Stampers Street now serves as the southbound (western) lanes of the new boulevard. The house at 6 Olney Street would have been in the very center of today's intersection, right in the middle of North Main Street's southbound left-turn lane just before it meets the northbound lanes.

But why did Lovecraft choose this address? A search through Providence city directories around the time Lovecraft wrote *The Case of Charles Dexter Ward* turns up a "Delilah Townsend" living at that location. A search through Lovecraft's letters finds a black housekeeper named Delilah who worked for Lovecraft and his aunts from at least April 1923 to May 1930. Lovecraft nowhere explicitly gives her last name, but a letter to his aunt Lillian makes everything clear: "On this occasion I met for the first time the Michigan amateur Clyde G. Townsend (no relative of Delilah's, but a fine Nordic specimen with yellow hair and blue eyes!)" (Lovecraft to Lillian D. Clark, 1 August 1924; ms., John Hay Library).

Delilah *Robinson* Townsend (December 1872–21 November 1944) lived at 6 Olney Street from 1918 to 1928. City directories variously give her name as "Delia," "Deliah," "Delila," "Dilah," "Dillia," or even "Lila." Delilah was born in Virginia but on 11 February 1895 married William J[oseph] Townsend (May 1872–?) in Lincoln, Rhode Island. William was from New Bedford, Massachusetts, but was living in Central Falls, Rhode Island, at the time. They had a son, William Joseph Townsend, who was born in March 1896 in Rhode Island.

In the 1900 census, the family was living at 46 Thayer Street in Providence (no longer extant). By the 1905 Rhode Island census, Delilah was listed as divorced and the head of the family. However, a dozen city directories after this point list her as widowed. (It is possible that Delilah found it easier to claim she was widowed rather than to admit to her divorce.) Delilah's son died of "angina pectoris" on 21 July 1915 at the age of just nineteen. Delilah, her son, her mother Amanda Robinson (1849?–5 March 1941), and her sister Mary Robinson (?–14 January 1934) are all buried in the cemetery of Providence's Grace Episcopal Church.

At this point, I had concluded that the house was real, found why it was no longer extant, and determined why Lovecraft had chosen it. But was there a chance I could find an actual *photograph* of it? Given that many historic areas in New England have been thoroughly documented before demolition, I decided I'd try to locate such documentation for the Olney Street house. But given that I lived in Minnesota at the time, most of this research could only be done while on my (frequent) vacations to Rhode Island.

In July 2011 I began with the Providence Department of Public Works which was able to show me some old construction maps, but could not offer any documentation on what existed before that construction. I got in touch with Paul Campbell, Providence City Archivist, who showed me documentation of several other construction projects, but we found nothing for the North Main and Olney Streets area.

At the Rhode Island State Archives, Reference Archivist Ken Carlson showed me some maps and photos, but we turned up nothing. I contacted Paul Wackrow, Director of Preservation Services, at the Providence Preservation Society, who sent me an image from a 1919 Sanborn fire insurance map. This map confirmed the house's address, but that was all. I also met with Rick Greenwood, Deputy Director at the Rhode Island Historic Preservation and Heritage Commission, which is housed in Rhode Island's Old State House (1762). He took the time to examine several maps and documents with me. Unfortunately, we still discovered nothing new.

Ken Carlson had suggested that I contact Michael A. Hebert, Supervising Historic Preservation Specialist/Archaeologist for the Rhode Island Department of Transportation. After some brief research, Mr. Hebert concluded that the widening of North Main Street probably was a city project, rather than a state project. Nevertheless, he took me back to the Rhode Island State Archives, where we examined some maps and photographs from the Howard W. Preston collection, but to no avail.

Mr. Hebert then suggested to me a collection of photographs that had been compiled by the National Society of Colonial Dames in Rhode Island. Their collection is housed in the basement of the Governor Stephen Hopkins House (1707, 1742), which is open to the public as a museum. Among many other distinctions, Hopkins was one of the signers of the Declaration of Independence. Hopkins and his home even figure in *The Case of Charles Dexter Ward:* "Late in December 1770 a group of eminent townsmen met at the home of Stephen Hopkins and debated tentative measures" (*CF* 2.249).

Mr. Hebert put me in touch with Kim Clark, Chair of the Stephen Hopkins House Board, who invited me to the house to see the photo collection in October 2012. The significance of my circumstance was not lost on me—I was going to the home of a signatory of the Declaration of Independence who was mentioned in *The Case of Charles Dexter Ward*, in the hopes of locating information regarding the home of the story's villain. In the basement of the house Ms. Clark showed me the collection: dozens of binders full of photographs of locations all over Rhode Island taken in the 1920s and 1930s by members of the Colonial Dames. The binders were grouped by township, and sometimes into individual neighborhoods, so I began searching through the one for this particular portion of Providence.

And there it was—after four separate trips to Providence over a fifteen-month period—just as Lovecraft had described it:

> The place, now crumbling with age, had never been a mansion; but was a modest two-and-a-half story wooden town house of the familiar Providence colonial type, with plain peaked roof, large central chimney, and artistically carved doorway with rayed fanlight, triangular pediment, and trim Doric pilasters. (*The Case of Charles Dexter Ward* [*CF* 2.271])

There was also a close-up photograph of the front door labeled as "10 Olney St.," but it was clear by comparing the doorways in the two photos that it was actually of 6 Olney Street. In addition, several photos of 10 Olney Street—a very large gambrel-roofer at the northeast corner of North Main and Olney Streets—made it clear it wasn't the same house. For that matter, the "6" on the door was a dead giveaway!

Questions still remain. Was the house actually razed or could it have been moved? It is possible that it could still exist somewhere, since many New England houses were moved, Lovecraft's final home being an example. However, this seems unlikely given that this area was a near slum and historic preservation wasn't very widespread in the 1930s. Also, determining this would probably require extensive searching through City Hall archives. And when was the house actually built? Lovecraft uses a date of 1761, but perhaps this simply best fit the narrative of the story. That answer may also be buried in archives somewhere.

The Case of Charles Dexter Ward is probably Lovecraft's most detailed work, with countless elements of Providence's history finely woven into its fabric. It should come as no surprise that nearly ninety years after its writing it is still yielding up fascinating secrets.

Special Thanks

Thanks to Paul Campbell, Ken Carlson, Rick Greenwood, Michael A. Hebert, and Paul Wackrow for their assistance in tracking down this information. Thanks especially to Kim Clark and the Colonial Dames of Rhode Island for permission to publish the photos of the house at 6 Olney Street. For further reading on this subject, see "The Site of Joseph Curwen's Home in H. P. Lovecraft's *The Case of Charles Dexter Ward*" (Moshassuck Monograph Series No. 15) by Kenneth W. Faig Jr. and Jason C. Eckhardt. The monograph covers some of the same ground but further discusses the Stampers Hill area around the North Main and Olney Streets intersection.

Works Cited or Consulted

Plat Book of the City of Providence, Rhode Island from Official Records, Private Plans and Actual Surveys. Philadelphia: G. M. Hopkins Co., 1918.

Charles Baxter on Lovecraft

S. T. Joshi

[The 18 December 2014 issue of the *New York Review of Books* contained a lengthy review-article of Leslie S. Klinger's *The New Annotated H. P. Lovecraft* (Liveright, 2014). The article seemed to me so filled with errors—and written with such an evident hostility to Lovecraft the man and writer—that a detailed rebuttal seemed in order. I sent such a rebuttal (printed below) to the editor of the *New York Review*, but the editor stated that only a relatively short, 400-word rebuttal would be accepted. Although I prepared such a rebuttal (published in the 19 February 2015 issue), I feel it is worth printing my full rebuttal here.—S.T.J.]

To the Editor:

I was taken aback at the vehemence of Charles Baxter's screed on the American supernaturalist H. P. Lovecraft ("The Hideous Unknown of H. P. Lovecraft," Dec. 4), nominally a review of Leslie S. Klinger's *The New Annotated H. P. Lovecraft*. It seems as if Mr. Baxter has some kind of personal animus against Lovecraft. Whatever the case, I think some words on the other side might be useful.

I was initially puzzled as to why Mr. Baxter was assigned to write the review in the first place. So far as I know (and I have prepared two versions of a comprehensive bibliography of Lovecraft that lists every article written about him from the 1910s to the present day), Mr. Baxter has done no original research on Lovecraft or published anything about him. There is little evidence that Baxter has read the leading scholarship on Lovecraft (he claims to have read my biography, but does not appear to have done so comprehensively or sympathetically) or is aware that the scholarly work of the past half-century has revolutionised our understanding of this author—work by such critics as Dirk W. Mosig, Donald R. Burleson, David E. Schultz, Steven J. Mariconda, Robert M. Price, Robert H. Waugh, and countless others. This work has definitively removed Lovecraft from the realm of pulp fiction and enshrined him as a canonical figure in American literature—a status endorsed by the Library of America, which published a volume of his *Tales* in 2005.

There is also little indication of Mr. Baxter's familiarity with the tradition of "weird fiction" (Lovecraft's felicitous term) in which Lovecraft was working—a tradition that stretches back to the Gothic novelists and Poe and progresses through Ambrose Bierce, Arthur Machen, Lord Dunsany, Algernon Blackwood, M. R. James, Walter de la Mare, L. P. Hartley, Ray Bradbury, Richard Matheson, Shirley Jackson, William Peter Blatty, Stephen King, Ramsey Campbell, Peter Straub, Clive Barker, Anne Rice, Thomas Ligotti, Caitlín R. Kiernan, Laird Barron, and many others. Lovecraft is at the focal point of this genre, drawing upon the best that preceded him and fueling much of the work that followed in his wake. If Mr. Baxter is indeed familiar with this entire tradition, then he has been singularly adept at hiding his light under a bushel.

Charles Baxter appears determined to pigeonhole Lovecraft— and, indeed, the entire genre of weird fiction—as of interest only to "adolescents." He cites certain works of weird fiction written by youthful writers (e.g., Mary Shelley, who wrote *Frankenstein* when she was about twenty); but I don't think Mr. Baxter quite realises the hot water he has gotten himself into. First, it cannot exactly be said that Bram Stoker (b. 1847) was a young man when he wrote *Dracula* (1897), or Henry James (b. 1843) when he wrote *The Turn of the Screw* (1898); many other examples of oldsters writing canonical weird fiction could be cited. Second, I assume Mr. Baxter knows of a certain spouse of Mary Shelley who wrote most of his poetry when he was fairly young; and many other instances of youthful poetic genius could be cited. On Mr. Baxter's own reasoning, it would therefore seem that all poetry is written by adolescents for adolescents, even though Tennyson (b. 1809) wasn't exactly spry when he wrote *Idylls of the King* (1859– 85), or Thomas Hardy (b. 1840) when he wrote *The Dynasts* (1904–08).

As for Lovecraft, while it is true that a substantial number of devotees initially read him as adolescents, a fair number of these fans grow up to be reasonably mature writers in their own right who continue to draw upon Lovecraft's writings for aesthetic inspiration. I would hope that Mr. Baxter would admit that such writers as Jorge Luis Borges (whose story "There Are More Things" [1975] is dedicated "to the memory of H. P. Lovecraft"), Joyce Carol Oates (who has written several Lovecraft pastiches), and Peter Straub (whose novel *Mr. X* [1999] is a riff on "The Dunwich Horror") are sufficiently mature for his tastes. In my recent anthology, *A Mountain Walked: Great Tales of the Cthulhu Mythos*, I have included work by such undeniably mature writers as Neil Gaiman, Caitlín R. Kiernan, Patrick McGrath, and T. Coraghesson Boyle. Dozens of other fans, critics, scholars, writers, and filmmakers who are well beyond their babbling infancy also admit to an admiration of Lovecraft.

Baxter goes on to assume—based on a stray comment made early in his career ("Adulthood is hell")—that Lovecraft himself remained an arrested adolescent. In fact, he was largely successful in overcoming the severe psychological damage resulting from his early upbringing (he was raised by two parents who were borderline psychotics) and became a surprisingly well-adjusted and outgoing individual, and one who exhibited a keen interest in the world around him. In the four million words of his surviving correspondence, Lovecraft spoke perspicaciously on the political, intellectual, and cultural events of his time—from T. S. Eliot to Einstein to Max Planck to the depression to Brancusi to technocracy. I imagine readers of this paper in particular would conclude that Lovecraft's radical transformation from political conservatism to moderate socialism is a sign of advancing maturity (conservatives may think otherwise).

In his superficial and misleading portrayal of Lovecraft, Baxter has carefully chosen quotations from Lovecraft's letters and other work that appear to verify his presuppositions rather than allowing the totality of the evidence to guide his analysis. He notes, for example, that Lovecraft was a "stranger to joy" and that he had "the timid shut-in's phobia of difference, variety, and diversity." In fact, Lovecraft found a great many things to enjoy in life (aesthetic expression, astronomy, chemistry, anthropology, travel, cats, colonial architecture); his wide correspondence put him in touch with an extraordinarily diverse band of friends and colleagues, ranging from the rugged frontiersman Robert E. Howard (creator of Conan the barbarian) to the highbrow poet Hart Crane; and his travels during the last decade of his life took him far from his native Providence, R.I.—to such places as Quebec, Richmond, Charleston, Key West, New Orleans, and Natchez. A remarkably active "shut-in"!

Baxter's prejudice is no more evident than in his treatment of Lovecraft's undeniable racism. His simple-minded caricature of this phase of Lovecraft's thought (which he has clearly absorbed only at second hand) depicts him as a "pathological racist." If Baxter had read some actual treatises of the period—such things as William Benjamin Smith's *The Color Line: A Brief in Behalf of the Unborn* (1905), Madison Grant's *The Passing of the Great Race* (1916), or Lothrop Stoddard's *The Rising Tide of Color against White World-Supremacy* (1920)—he would see that Lovecraft's opinions on the subject are relatively mild in the context of his times.

Baxter allows himself to be snookered by citing a passage about a black man in a story, "Herbert West—Reanimator": "He was a loathsome, gorilla-like thing, with abnormally long arms which I could not help calling fore legs, and a face that conjured up thoughts of unspeakable Congo secrets and tom-tom poundings under an eerie moon" (*CF* 1.306). Sounds pretty bad, no? But there are two things one can say about this:

1) One can find passages of a similar sort in stories by other writers of the period. Consider this from Raymond Chandler: "The Negro was enormous in stature, gorillalike, and wore a baggy checked suit that made him even more enormous" ("Pickup on Noon Street" 448). (Chandler's story also contains repeated references to a "little Jap.")

2) The over-the-top language of the passage makes it evident that it was meant as a parody (to say nothing of the fact that it was spoken by a first-person narrator). The element of parody is underscored when we understand the progression of the story, which deals with a physician's invention of a drug that will reani-

mate the dead. When Herbert West injects the dead boxer with his formula (a formula that he explicitly stated was created with white people in mind), nothing seems to happen, thereby apparently confirming the racist subtext of the story. But the boxer is in fact reanimated and goes on a murderous rampage (as a white patient had done in a previous episode), thereby validating the physiological and psychological similarity of blacks and whites.

Baxter is also apparently unaware of the extent to which Lovecraft moderated his racist outlook over the decades. By the 1930s he had come to adopt a belief in cultural integrity, whereby a given nation's culture should be preserved for its own sake: "a real friend of civilisation wishes merely to make the Germans *more German*, the French *more French*, the Spaniards *more Spanish*, & so on" (*SL* 4.253). And while retaining his belief in the biological inferiority of blacks (a view endorsed by any number of American and European anthropologists of the time), he could make so relatively humane an utterance as this: "It is possible that the economic dictatorship of the future can work out a diplomatic plan of separate allocation whereby the blacks may follow a self-contained life of their own, avoiding the keenest hardships of inferiority through a reduced number of points of contact with the whites... No one wishes them any intrinsic harm, & all would rejoice if a way were found to ameliorate such difficulties as they have without imperilling the structure of the dominant fabric" (*Letters to James F. Morton* 254).

There is also the question of exactly how much racism enters into Lovecraft's fiction. Baxter maintains that it is central. Another reviewer of the Klinger book—John Gray, writing in the *New Republic*—offers a different opinion: "Fortunately, the core of his work has nothing to do with his social and racial resentments." I am inclined to agree with Gray. Such things as atheism (for which see my philosophical study *H. P. Lovecraft: The Decline of the West*), devotion to science, and love of the past are all far more central to both his philosophy and to his fiction than racism. Among his sixty short stories, novelettes, and short novels, I have counted only five that have racism as their thematic foundation, and only one of these— "The Shadow over Innsmouth" (1931), where the unwholesome mating of fishlike creatures from the sea with humans is generally interpreted as a metaphor for Lovecraft's disdain for "miscegenation" (intermarriage between members of different races)—is a major tale. And yet, this remains one of Lovecraft's great narratives, an imperishable account of regional decay worthy of Faulkner.

Baxter now makes a new accusation against Lovecraft—that he was a misogynist. This would come as a considerable surprise to those many women—his mother, his two aunts, his wife, and such friends and correspondents as Helen V. Sully, Elizabeth Toldridge, and the science fiction writer C. L. Moore—whom Lovecraft treated with unfailing courtesy and with several of whom he established close bonds of affection. Baxter's chief evidence for his charge is another story, "The Thing on the Doorstep" (1933), where it is said of Asenath Waite: "She wanted to be a man" (*CF* 3.339). (Oddly enough, Baxter does not quote an earlier passage that would seem even more damning to Lovecraft: "Her crowning rage, however, was that she was not a man; since she believed a male brain had certain unique and far-reaching cosmic powers. Given a man's brain, she declared, she could not only equal but surpass her father in mastery of unknown forces" [*CF* 3.330]).

But Baxter has again been snookered. First, this passage is placed in the mouth of a first-person narrator, Daniel Upton, and moreover he is merely reporting the opinion of Asenath Waite. Surely Mr. Baxter cannot wish to commit (again) the cardinal sin of criticism and assume that the views of a character are identical to the views of an author? Moreover, it has apparently passed his notice that Asenath herself is nothing more than the soul of her father, the wizard Ephraim Waite, who occupied his daughter's body upon the death of his own. I suppose it is too much to expect Mr. Baxter to know that, a little more than a year after writing this story, Lovecraft made the following utterance: "I do not regard the rise of woman as a bad sign. Rather do I fancy that her traditional subordination was itself an artificial and undesirable condition based on Oriental influences. . . . The feminine mind does not cover the same territory as the masculine, but is probably little if any inferior in total quality" (*SL* 5.64).[1] This would pass as fairly enlightened in his day—and, indeed, in our own.

---

1. This passage was cited in both versions of my biography.

The lengths to which Baxter will go in denigrating Lovecraft is indicated by his making unflattering (and unwarranted) assumptions about Lovecraft's character based on his appearance. I am saddened to see a respected academic resorting to such desperate expedients. It will no doubt be amazing to Baxter that Lovecraft was an almost universally beloved figure in his time, as evidenced by the dozens of memoirs written by his friends, colleagues, and relatives. A comment by Ernest A. Edkins is representative: "I think that the most lasting impression Lovecraft left me was one of essential nobility, of dauntless integrity... He remains enshrined in my memory as a great gentleman, in the truest sense of that much abused term" (cited in Cannon, *Lovecraft Remembered* 96).

Baxter has a low opinion of Lovecraft's prose. It is easy to quote Edmund Wilson's strictures from 1945, but there are several good reasons for not regarding Wilson as the voice of God on this issue. First, Wilson revealed a severe prejudice toward all genre writing, as witness his condemnations of detective fiction ("Why Do People Read Detective Stories?") and of J. R. R. Tolkien's *The Lord of the Rings* ("Oo, Those Awful Orcs"). Wilson was simply unable to acknowledge that non-mimetic literature can convey anything significant about humankind. (It will be news to Mr. Baxter that Wilson substantially revised—and revised upward—his view of Lovecraft about twenty years later, when he read the first volume of Lovecraft's *Selected Letters* [1965]; he even wrote a play, *The Little Blue Light*, with some Lovecraftian touches. See de Camp.)

Second, Wilson's review appeared when he and many others assumed that the barebones austerity of Hemingway was the only "correct" style that could be utilised in literary fiction (Lovecraft himself derided Hemingway's prose as "machine-gun fire" [*SL* 4.32]), but I thought we had learned something since then. Steven J. Mariconda, who has done more to analyze Lovecraft's prose style than any other scholar, has concluded that he was a "consummate prose stylist" and adds:

> The bulk of his stories are *atmospherically effective*... He wrote as he did for carefully considered reasons, leveraging a naturally erudite style into an effective instrument to create weird atmosphere... He plumbed the depths of fear, dream, time, and space as few others have, and nothing other than the unique style we

now know as "Lovecraftian" could have better conveyed the intense philosophical and psychological conceptions that were his concerns. (45)

If Mr. Baxter wishes the opinions of someone more eminent than Mariconda (and, indeed, than himself), I can cite Joyce Carol Oates, who has stated:

> Most of Lovecraft's tales . . . develop by way of incremental detail, beginning with quite plausible situations . . . One is drawn into Lovecraft by the very air of plausibility and characteristic understatement of the prose, the question being *When will the weirdness strike?* There is a melancholy, operatic grandeur in Lovecraft's most passionate work, like 'The Outsider' and 'At the Mountains of Madness'; a curious elegiac poetry of unspeakable loss, of adolescent despair and an existential loneliness so pervasive that it lingers in the reader's memory, like a dream, long after the rudiments of Lovecraftian plot have faded. (xiii, xv)

These sentences come from Oates's introduction to *Tales of H. P. Lovecraft* (Ecco Press, 1997), one of the best short analyses of Lovecraft ever written. It was originally written as a review-article of my *H. P. Lovecraft: A Life* in the *New York Review of Books* (October 31, 1996).

Baxter also underestimates the tonal and stylistic variety of Lovecraft's prose. He has made no attempt to seek out an entire group of imaginary-world fantasies (modeled largely after the work of Lord Dunsany), ranging from such exquisite early specimens as "The White Ship" (1919) and "Celephaïs" (1920) and culminating in the expansive short novel *The Dream-Quest of Unknown Kadath* (1926–27), that are very different from his dense tales of supernatural horror. These tales were deliberately excluded from Klinger's volume. Baxter also ignores such things as the melding of weirdness and pathos in "The Outsider" (1921; also not included in Klinger), the self-parodic humor in "Herbert West— Reanimator" (1921–22) and "The Lurking Fear" (1922), and the transmogrification of the horrific "other" to the horrific self in such existential fictions as "The Shadow over Innsmouth" (1931) and "The Shadow out of Time" (1934–35).

Moreover, Baxter seems strangely tone-deaf to the radical change from Lovecraft's early "first-person hysterical" style, as seen in such tales as "The Tomb" (1917) and "Dagon" (1917), to the far more sober, scientifically based fictions of his last decade. I for one would find it difficult to find a passage of more effective rhythmic modulation than in the first paragraph of "The Call of Cthulhu" (1926):

> The most merciful thing in the world, I think, is the inability of the human mind to correlate all its contents. We live on a placid island of ignorance in the midst of black seas of infinity, and it was not meant that we should voyage far. The sciences, each straining in its own direction, have hitherto harmed us little; but some day the piecing together of dissociated knowledge will open up such terrifying vistas of reality, and of our frightful position therein, that we shall either go mad from the revelation or flee from the deadly light into the peace and safety of a new dark age. (CF 2.21)

The first sentence is now cited in *Bartlett's Familiar Quotations*. I trust Mr. Baxter is prepared to admit that the editors of *Bartlett's* know a bon mot when they encounter one.

Even when Lovecraft seems to be at his flamboyant worst, he reveals a sensuous love of language that can be intoxicating, as in this celebrated example from "The Outsider": "It was the ghoulish shade of decay, antiquity, and desolation; the putrid, dripping eidolon of unwholesome revelation; the awful baring of that which the merciful earth should always hide" (CF 1.271). At least one dictionary has quoted a part of this sentence as an example of the metaphorical use of the word "eidolon."

Lovecraft made every word count. He adhered as rigidly to Poe's theory of the "unity of effect" as Poe himself did. He recognised that a richly textured prose style was perhaps the best means to convey the *realism* that the supernatural tale required if it were to be convincing to a skeptical audience. He outlines his principles in the seminal essay "Notes on Writing Weird Fiction" (1933):

> In writing a weird story I always try very carefully to achieve the right mood and atmosphere, and place the emphasis where it belongs. One cannot, except in immature pulp charlatan-fiction, present an account of impossible, improbable, or inconceivable

phenomena as a commonplace narrative of objective acts and conventional emotions. Inconceivable events and conditions have a special handicap to overcome, and this can be accomplished only through the maintenance of a careful realism in every phase of the story *except* that touching on the one given marvel. This marvel must be treated very impressively and deliberately—with a careful emotional "build-up"—else it will seem flat and unconvincing. Being the principal thing in the story, its mere existence should overshadow the characters and events. . . Atmosphere, not action, is the great desideratum of weird fiction. Indeed, all that a wonder story can ever be is *a vivid picture of a certain type of human mood.* (CE 2.177)

The upshot of all this is that Lovecraft developed, in the course of a relatively short career spanning less than twenty years, a highly coherent aesthetic of the weird and developed a prose style that he believed was appropriate to its expression. Whatever one may think of Lovecraft's prose, I would suggest to Mr. Baxter that he be a little less intolerant when assessing work that doesn't accord with his own presuppositions.

I would not have thought that, at this late juncture, there would be any need to defend the aesthetic value of weird fiction as a whole (or of fantasy fiction, science fiction, or crime fiction); but, in the opinion of dinosaurs like Mr. Baxter, evidently there is. The matter is too involved for discussion here, but I would recommend that he consult the works of such historians and theoreticians as Tzvetan Todorov (*The Fantastic: A Structural Approach to a Literary Genre*, 1973), Terry Heller (*The Delights of Terror: An Aesthetics of the Tale of Terror*, 1987), Noël Carroll (*The Philosophy of Horror*, 1990), and myself (*The Weird Tale*, 1990; *Unutterable Horror: A History of Supernatural Fiction*, 2012).

Indeed, I begin to wonder whether the hostility that Mr. Baxter shows toward Lovecraft—and, by extension, the entire realm of weird fiction—is based on a dim (and, to him, unwelcome) realisation that, for at least the past century or so, many of the most dynamic aesthetic developments in Anglophone literature have come from what used to be derided as "genre fiction"—especially the vital interrelation between literature and media—and that the mainstream fiction in which Mr. Baxter himself has worked for his entire career now occupies a lesser place, with a dwindling readership and decreased relevance in today's culture. Such writers as Raymond Chandler, Ray Bradbury, Richard Matheson, Stephen King, Philip K. Dick, James Ellroy, Neil Gaiman, George R. R. Martin, and the like are what even highly educated people want to read—not because the work of these writers constitutes some kind of escape from "reality," but precisely because it offers provocative insights into human life and its relations to the universe that cannot be found in mainstream literature. Geoffrey O'Brien, editor of the Library of America, has recognised that fact in publishing editions of several of these authors. Lovecraft is again the lynchpin of this development, as testified by the H. P. Lovecraft Film Festival, which draws thousands of enthusiasts to Portland, Oregon, every year.

I hear on almost a daily basis from figures in film, television, video games, and comic books about adapting Lovecraft's tales. I also hear regularly from editors and publishers from around the world who are interested in disseminating his entire work—stories, essays, poems, even letters—to a worldwide audience. Collected editions of his fiction have appeared in France, Italy, Germany, Greece, Japan, and elsewhere, and the imminent publication of a large omnibus of his work in Brazil this spring will be a major publishing event. Lovecraft has even inspired a new philosophical movement, weird realism, led by the philosopher Graham Harman. It is difficult to find, in the entire range of world literature, a writer who so unites critical acclaim and immense popular interest as H. P. Lovecraft. Charles Baxter has tried his hardest to knock Lovecraft from his pedestal, but his effort comes up considerably short of the mark.

[As mentioned earlier, a 400-word version of the above letter was published in the 19 February 2015 issue of the *New York Review of Books*. There followed a response to my letter by Baxter himself and a letter of comment by another writer. I felt that there were errors and misconceptions in these writings as well, so I wrote the following response (published only on my website).—S.T.J.]

I was a bit surprised to see that a highly truncated version of my response to Charles Baxter's article in the *New York Review of Books* has been published in the new issue of that paper (dated 19 February 2015). I had sent my response to the editors of *NYRB* and was told that only a 400-word letter could be published. (My full response was ten times that length.) I hastily prepared such a letter, but then never heard from the editors as to whether it would be published.

Adding to the bizarrerie, Mr. Baxter has appended a reply that addresses, not the letter as published in *NYRB*, but my full response! I am not particularly impressed by Mr. Baxter's reply, which I will hereby subject to a sentence-by-sentence analysis:

- "One would think, reading S. T. Joshi's response to my book review, that I had attacked the object of a cult." [If correcting the errors of a critic's analysis of a given writer constitutes defending a cult writer, then Poe, Melville, Whitman, Bierce, Hemingway, Mencken, and dozens of other writers are all cult writers. All these writers have faced, during and after their lifetimes, malicious and error-riddled attacks exactly along the lines of Baxter's screed on Lovecraft.]

- "His lengthy letter never acknowledges that my review of Lovecraft's stories was divided into two parts: the first containing my misgivings about the fiction, the second containing guarded praise." [This is a deliberate mischaracterisation of Baxter's article. In fact, the first part of it was a grotesque slander against Lovecraft the person (as one who was "a stranger to joy" and who was a "shut-in," etc. etc.). And while I could have addressed some errors and distortions in the "guarded praise" in the second part of the article, that didn't seem to me sufficiently important to discuss.]

- "I am not surprised that Joshi, who has spent much of his life studying Lovecraft, was affronted by my review, but he doesn't seem to understand the distinction between matters of fact and matters of judgment. Readers of Lovecraft can judge for themselves whether Lovecraft's prose contains infelicities of style, along with misogyny and racism." [Mr. Baxter stubbornly refused to acknowledge the numerous errors of "fact" that he made in his review; and many of his "judgments" on Lovecraft are based directly on those errors of fact.]

- "Joshi's argument against the stories' misogyny is of the some-of-his-best-friends-were-women variety, a confusion of the work and the life." [To call someone a "misogynist," as Baxter did in his article, is to make a fairly clear personal comment—or attack—on a writer's character, and it is false and disingenuous to claim that the assertion merely reflects an interpretation of the author's literary work. In any event, I have clearly established that Baxter has misinterpreted key elements of the stories in finding a misogynist undercurrent where there is none.]

- "As for Lovecraft's racism, Joshi's defense of Lovecraft's views in his letter is astonishing in this day and age; he quotes, with apparent approval, Lovecraft's suggestion of apartheid as a benevolent remedy." [My whole argument, in discussing HPL's racism, is that it is unfair and unwise to judge him based on the standards of "this day and age"—very few (including such known racists and anti-Semites as Jack London, T. S. Eliot, and Roald Dahl) would come away unscathed from such scrutiny. In any event, the "apartheid" that HPL recommended was one that a number of black leaders of his day (e.g., Marcus Garvey) had themselves advocated.]

- "Joshi seems unable to grasp my argument that the racism is at the core of the stories' horror of aliens." [I can't grasp this argument because it is nonsensical and belied by the plain facts of the case. It is a highly tortuous and prejudicial reading of Lovecraft's stories to maintain that any of his extraterrestrial "gods" and monsters—with the exception of the Deep Ones in "The Shadow over Innsmouth"—are somehow meant as stand-ins for ethnic minorities. See more on this below.]

- "I never denied that the stories have a disturbing power. What readers should certainly note, however, is that Joshi is territorial; while I grant him the right to his opinions, he does not grant me a right to mine." [Now Baxter has descended to whining. It is the last, desperate ploy of persons losing a debate to plead that their opponents are trying to "silence" them. Baxter is free to express his views on Lovecraft; but surely I am free to rebut his arguments and point out their errors and fallacies. No one is trying to abridge Baxter's freedom of speech; but "freedom of speech" does not imply freedom from criticism. Baxter seems to think he can say anything he wants on Lovecraft and not face critical scrutiny—but that would be a denial of *my* freedom of speech, and of the speech of any others who don't agree with him.]

Things get curiouser and curiouser. Another letter published in the *NYRB* issue is by one Mark Halpern. It addresses nothing in Baxter's own article but attacks *me* for some perceived failings in my biography of Lovecraft—or, rather, one failing in particular, to wit: "Joshi must have been suffering from one of his rare moments of fatigue when it came to linking his subject's attitude toward Jews and other sorts of non-Nordic immigrants to New York's Lower East Side to the emotional source of Cthulhu and his like, because he writes not one word about the topic in his otherwise painfully detailed biography." Well, lordy me! I confess to be guilty as charged—because there *is* little or no connection between Lovecraft's racism and his creation of the "gods and monsters" in his fiction.

It is most curious how many recent critics (Charles Baxter, Laura Miller, and now Mr. Halpern) have put forth this view without providing the slightest evidence for it. Let us examine the physical properties of Lovecraft's iconic creation, Cthulhu. When the narrator of "The Call of Cthulhu" first sees Wilcox's bas-relief of the creature, he describes it as follows: "If I say that my somewhat extravagant imagination yielded simultaneous pictures of an octopus, a dragon, and a human caricature, I shall not be unfaithful to the spirit of the thing. A pulpy, tentacled head surmounted a grotesque and scaly body with rudimentary wings; but it was the *general outline* of the whole which made it most shockingly frightful" (*CF* 2.24). Lovecraft's description of the actual sight of Cthulhu by Johansen is deliberately vague, but we do have this: "The Thing of the idols, the green, sticky spawn of the stars, had awaked to claim his own" (*CF* 2.53). Uh-oh—Cthulhu is *green!* Maybe this means that he is a stand-in for "people of colour"! If you believe that, there's a bridge nearby that I'd like to sell you.

It is true that the Cthulhu cultists in Louisiana do symbolise Lovecraft's disdain of certain types of foreigners: they were "men of a very low, mixed-blooded, and mentally aberrant type. Most were seamen, and a sprinkling of negroes and mulattoes, largely West Indians or Brava Portuguese from the Cape Verde Islands, gave a colouring of voodooism to the heterogeneous cult" (*CF* 2.37). Well and good; but this whole passage (the second section of the story) is largely an elaborate "info dump" whereby we learn the basic properties of Cthulhu and his "spawn," as recounted by "old Castro." I don't see that there is anything specifically anti-Semitic in the passage above. Mr. Halpern (who predictably refers to Lovecraft's "pathological anti-Semitism") will be surprised to learn that Lovecraft repeatedly declared his belief that Jews in both America and Europe were in several ways culturally superior to Anglo-Saxons—something that could certainly not be said of the Cthulhu cultists in Louisiana.

How about Lovecraft's other "gods and monsters"? Azathoth? He is described in one story as follows: "that shocking final peril which gibbers unmentionably outside the ordered universe, where no dreams reach; that last amorphous blight of nethermost confusion which blasphemes and bubbles at the centre of all infinity—the boundless daemon-sultan Azathoth, whose name no lips dare speak aloud, and who gnaws hungrily in inconceivable, unlighted chambers beyond time" (*CF* 2.100). Any racist implications there, people?

Yog-Sothoth, maybe? We hear of him as "a congeries of iridescent globes" (*CF* 4.438). There *must* be a racist implication there somewhere, but—Gawdelpme—I just don't have the critical acumen to detect it.

Shub-Niggurath? Well, she is usually mentioned in the same breath as "The Black Goat of the Woods with a Thousand Young" (*CF* 2.487). Omigod!—*black* goat! All right, that's it: she must be a stand-in for HPL's disdain for black women who breed a lot! What else is possible? Well, wait a minute . . . HPL does describe her elsewhere as "a kind of sophisticated Astarte" (*CF* 4.270), so I guess we can presume that HPL was prejudiced against the ancient Mesopotamians.

Nyarlathotep also seems very promising. He is first described as having the bearing of a Pharaoh. OK, no question about it—this must reflect HPL's prejudice against Arabs! But it seems that Nyarlathotep emerged "from the blackness of twenty-seven centuries" (CF 1.203)—meaning that he emerged about thirteen centuries before the birth of Mohammad. But didn't HPL describe him as the "Black Man" in "The Dreams in the Witch House"? Oh, wait—that was the standard designation for the leader of a witch coven. And HPL states specifically that the Black Man in that story was devoid of negroid features.

How about the fungi from Yuggoth in "The Whisperer in Darkness"? Well, they're described as "half-fungous, half-crustacean creatures from a planet identifiable as the remote and recently discovered Pluto" (CF 3.104); so unless we assume that HPL had a prejudice against mushrooms or crabs, I don't see any racist undercurrent here.

The Old Ones of *At the Mountains of Madness*? They are barrel-shaped creatures with starfish-heads and tentacles. Again I struggle to connect them with HPL's racism. Anyway, aren't they substantially superior to humans in intellect and many other qualities? What about those loathsome shoggoths? I suppose something could be made of the fact that they are immense, amorphous masses of *black* protoplasm . . .

The Great Race of "The Shadow out of Time"? They are huge, rugose, cone-shaped creatures who are also vastly superior to human beings, since they are virtually omniscient and have conquered time. Not much racism there, I fear.

I have repeatedly maintained that the only major story by Lovecraft based on racist presuppositions is "The Shadow over Innsmouth." And (*pace* Mr. Halpern) I do in fact discuss this matter at length in my biography. Here is some of what I wrote there: "'The Shadow over Innsmouth' is . . . clearly a cautionary tale on the ill effects of *miscegenation*, or the sexual union of different races . . . It is, accordingly, difficult to deny a suggestion of racism running all through the story" (*I Am Providence* 793). There is much more to this effect, but I trust that will do.

Our valiant critics have also failed to notice the several stories in which various unsavoury characters are unmistakably Caucasian. This applies particularly to the aristocratic Dutch-American family in "The Lurking Fear," the wealthy Anglo-American family in "The Rats in the Walls," and even the "decadent" inhabitants of Dunwich in "The Dunwich Horror." The Dunwich denizens are clearly a racially homogeneous (white) clan of backwoods New England farmers; there seem to be no ethnic minorities there. If one didn't know who wrote these stories, one could easily conclude that their author was prejudiced against white people!

The plain fact is that most of Lovecraft's "gods and monsters" are meant to symbolise the immensity—both spatial and temporal—of a universe where human beings occupy a derisively insignificant place. Their titanic power and anomalous physical properties are metaphors for the inscrutability of a universe where things may be very different from the way they are here.

Those hostile critics seeking to maintain some intimate connection between Lovecraft's racism and the creation of these alien entities will have to put forth more than mere assertions to make their case. In my mind, the evidence is overwhelmingly against them.

Works Cited

Cannon, Peter, ed. *Lovecraft Remembered*. Sauk City, WI: Arkham House, 1998.

Chandler, Raymond. "Pickup on Noon Street" (*Detective Fiction Weekly*, May 30, 1936). In *Collected Stories*. New York: Knopf/Everyman's Library, 2002. 425–72.

de Camp, L. Sprague. "H. P. Lovecraft and Edmund Wilson." *Fantasy Mongers* 1 (March 1979): 5.

Gray, John. "H. P. Lovecraft Invented a Horrific World to Escape a Nihilistic Universe." *New Republic* (14 October 2014).

Harman, Graham. *Weird Realism: Lovecraft and Philosophy*. Winchester, UK: Zero Books, 2012.

Joshi, S. T. *H. P. Lovecraft: A Comprehensive Bibliography*. Tampa, FL: University of Tampa Press, 2009.

———. *H. P. Lovecraft: A Life*. West Warwick, RI: Necronomicon Press, 1996.

———. *H. P. Lovecraft: The Decline of the West*. Mercer Island, WA: Starmont House, 1990.

———. *H. P. Lovecraft and Lovecraft Criticism: An Annotated Bibliography*. Kent, OH: Kent State University Press, 1981.

————. *I Am Providence: The Life and Times of H. P. Lovecraft.* New York: Hippocampus Press, 2010.

Joshi, S. T., ed. *A Mountain Walked: Great Tales of the Cthulhu Mythos.* Lakewood, CO: Centipede Press, 2014.

Lovecraft, H. P. *Letters to James F. Morton.* Ed. David E. Schultz and S. T. Joshi. New York: Hippocampus Press, 2011.

Mariconda, Steven J. "H. P. Lovecraft: Consummate Prose Stylist." In *H. P. Lovecraft: Art, Artifact, and Reality.* New York: Hippocampus Press, 2013). 13–45.

Oates, Joyce Carol. "Introduction." In *Tales of H. P. Lovecraft.* Ed. Joyce Carol Oates. Hopewell, NJ: Ecco Press, 1997. vii–xvi.

Briefly Noted

The spate of neo-Lovecraftian fiction continues unabated. Among recent items that may be noted are a sheaf of volumes by Hippocampus Press: Lois H. Gresh's *Cult of the Dead and Other Weird and Lovecraftian Tales;* W. H. Pugmire's *Monstrous Aftermath: Stories in the Lovecraftian Tradition;* and Ann K. Schwader's *Dark Equinox and Other Tales of Lovecraftian Horror.* Other Hippocampus volumes, such as Jonathan Thomas's *Dreams of Ys and Other Invisible Worlds* and Robert H. Waugh's *The Bloody Tugboat and Other Witcheries,* contain their share of Lovecraftian material. Pugmire and David Barker have written an intriguing collaborative volume, *In the Gulfs of Dream and Other Lovecraftian Tales* (Dark Renaissance Books, 2015), which feature imaginative ruminations on both Lovecraft's and Clark Ashton Smith's stories. Among anthologies, we may note S. T. Joshi's *Black Wings IV* (PS Publishing, 2015) and the forthcoming *Madness of Cthulhu, Volume 2* (Titan Books). A new edition of Joshi's *Rise and Fall of the Cthulhu Mythos* (2008)—now retitled *The Rise, Fall, and Rise of the Cthulhu Mythos* (Hippocampus Press)—is also imminent.

Six Degrees of Lovecraft: Henry Miller

Bobby Derie

"Not since H. P. Lovecraft has there been such a lover of language."
—Gore Vidal, "The *Sexus* of Henry Miller" (115)

From 1924 to 1926, Brooklyn played host to two of the great un-hatched writers of the twentieth century. Brooklyn native Henry Miller was on his second marriage and had quit his job to focus on being a writer; H. P. Lovecraft was a newcomer to New York City, on his first (and only) adventure in marriage, and desperate to find work. If the two men ever met, over some Brooklyn bookstall or at the New York Public Library, no record has survived, despite the many volumes of their letters that have been published.

Nor are the men known to have read each other's work. On the surface, this looks understandable: Miller's first book, *Tropic of Cancer*, was published in Paris in 1934 and, deemed obscene, was banned from sale in the United States; Lovecraft's only book published and distributed during his lifetime was *The Shadow over Innsmouth* in 1936, when Miller was still in Paris. On closer inspection, however, here again they nearly encountered each other in the pages of the pulp magazine the *Black Cat* (1895–1922).

Lovecraft had first noticed the *Black Cat* around 1904, as a result of its inclusion of weird stories, and bought it regularly for a period, although he was apparently surprised to learn that it had run until 1922 (*O Fortunate Floridian* 29; *Letters to James F. Morton* 372). In 1921, following the urging of his friend James F. Morton, Lovecraft attempted to sell his story "The Tomb" in the magazine, but was answered with a rejection slip. (*Letters to James F. Morton* 40; cf. *Letters to Alfred Galpin* 84). In so doing, Lovecraft missed by a couple of years Henry Miller's first published work—a series of reviews of stories previously published in the *Black Cat*, running from May 1919 to October 1919. Miller had published his work under the auspices of "The Black Cat Club," which for a subscription to the magazine solicited short critical reviews, with the offer that the best of them might be published for one cent per word. The policy ended with the October 1919 when the magazine was sold. (Miller, *Letters to* The Black Cat 10–16).

Yet even if they never encountered each other physically or on a literary level, there are some fine threads that connect the two—particularly the shared love for the works of the Welsh mystic Arthur Machen. The two men's mutual appreciation of Machen was both immediate and effusive, finding expression in their letters and their fiction—but for different reasons.

Lovecraft discovered Machen in 1923, through the Knopf reprint of *The House of Souls*, which contained some of the Machen's best weird novellas, including "The Great God Pan" and "The White People," and in that same year devoured Machen's novel *The Hill of Dreams* in a single sitting (*Letters to James F. Morton* 40, 47). By 1924, Lovecraft had purchased or read practically the entire corpus of Machen's weird fiction, as well as the three volumes of Machen's autobiography and *Hieroglyphics*, and would continue to do so in later years. (*SL* 1.358).

Lovecraft hailed Machen as a master of the weird tale and devoted a significant portion of his seminal essay "Supernatural Horror in Literature" to the Welsh mystic; but while he lauded Machen's "exquisitely lyrical and expressive prose style" and "refreshing essays," Lovecraft's appreciation for Machen was always primarily—almost exclusively—as an author of weird fiction, especially in regard to Machen's oblique hints of a dark, hidden mythology expressed in some of his best fiction (*Annotated Supernatural Horror in Literature* 80–87). The peak of Lovecraft's Machenmania was "The Dunwich Horror" (1928), which is both inspired by and pays homage to "The Great God Pan" and "The White People," both through subtle references to Machen's pseudomythology and more directly in one passage: "'Inbreeding?' Armitage muttered half-aloud to himself. 'Great God, what simpletons! Shew them Arthur Machen's Great God Pan and they'll think it a common Dunwich scandal!'" (*CF* 2.436).

Henry Miller did not discover *The Hill of Dreams* until 1925, but if anything his response to Machen's fabulous story of a penniless, struggling writer in a strange city was even greater. As he wrote to Emil Schnellock:

> Stolen this day—3/18/25—from my good friend, Emil Schnellock, never to leave my possession until death and dissolution. No more wonderful epic of the artist's soul have I seen till now. This I write solemnly in the flyleaf of your book, so generously loaned me and so wantonly filched. But this is a gift from the high places. This is an involuntary gift which can never be requited fully. (*Letters to Emil* 11)

Miller apparently quoted from Machen's book for five pages in that letter, adding in a postscript that he would buy Schnellock another copy.

But their appreciation was not identical. For Lovecraft, it was the subtle and sublime horror of Machen's short fiction that most affected him, themes that he would use and expand on in his own stories. For Miller, it was Machen's capture of ecstasy and sin, the Welshman's ability to defend the profanity of Rabelais as well as capture the plight of the struggling novice. Yet both men loved Machen for his language, his rich vocabulary and meter, and would carry their influence on in their very different works. Where Lovecraft glossed over some of Machen's more "picaresque" works—bowdlerized translations of the memoirs of Casanova, the *Heptameron* of Margaret of Navarre, references to Rabelais and obscenity in *Hieroglyphics*—in favor of the weird, Miller appears to have been the exact opposite. There is scant mention of Machen's weird fiction in any of Miller's letters or writing, yet Miller cites several passages from Machen's *Hieroglyphics* in his essay "Obscenity in Literature" (196).

Miller too would go on to pay further homage to Machen in his own works, particularly *The Hill of Dreams*, which would appear in his novels *Nexus* and *Sexus*:

> "Oh," I said, "you called me a dreamer a moment ago. Let me read you a passage—it's short—from *The Hill of Dreams*. You should read the book some time; it's a dream of a book." (*Nexus* 215–16)

> He threw the book aside. It was *The Hill of Dreams*. (*Sexus* 193)

Both men likewise shared their discovery with others. Lovecraft found fellow-admirers in such colleagues as Donald Wandrei and August Derleth, who would go on to found Arkham House after Lovecraft's death. In her diary Anaïs Nin recollects how Miller would read to her from the book (as first noted by Don Herron in "Analects from the Mainstream #2: Of Machen and Henry Miller: Or, Anais, Meet Arthur"): "Henry was telling me about a book I had not read. It was Arthur Machen's Hill of Dreams" (Nin 80).

If Miller and Lovecraft shared a literary ancestor of sorts in Arthur Machen, they also shared a kind of mutual descendent in the form of British horror writer Ramsey Campbell. In the early 1960s, the teenaged Campbell contacted August Derleth at Arkham House about publishing a series of pastiches of Lovecraft; Derleth countered by asking Campbell to rewrite them using settings in England. During the writing and editing process they continued the correspondence, and in 1962 Campbell prevailed upon Derleth to send him copies of Miller's novels *Tropic of Cancer* and *Tropic of Capricorn*, which were still banned for sale in Britain as obscene, and Derleth complied (Campbell-Derleth 88–90). The two discussed Miller on occasion in their letters, as Derleth was editing stories for Campbell's *The Inhabitant of the Lake and Less Welcome Tenants*. Campbell would later write:

> This led me to assume he wouldn't mind if I introduced a different kind of shock into my Lovecraft imitations, but he took the shit out of a line of dialogue. I still think it's what the character would have said, but I see that that may not be relevant to such a stylised form as Lovecraft pastiche. (*Ramsey Campbell, Probably* 233)

Campbell would reply that "I'm afraid that the Henry Miller–Burroughs influence has been telling on me" (Campbell-Derleth 125), to which Derleth replied: "I think you may be mixing your liking for Miller (whose TROPIC OF CAPRICORN I sent off to you the other day) and Burroughs with your penchant for the weird, an insoluble combination, unfortunately" (127–28); and in greater detail:

> "Shit" etc. may be in place in TROPIC OF CANCER, but it is out of place in a weird tale. The reader is not concentrating upon any-

thing but the horror of your tale, and the intrusion of such language is unwarranted and distracting. It is certainly not a matter of
prurience on my part, but only of the fitness of things. Whenever
you use these offensive words (offensive in your context only,
that is) any other word will do as well; they are not vital to your
story, as they are vital to Miller's, by contrast. In a Miller story
"cunt" for women is inevitable, and "woman" would be as out of
place in his context as "shit" or "shitty" etc. are in yours. (129)

Despite Derleth's small editorial adjustments with regard to vulgarity, and his pronouncement that mixing Miller and Lovecraft
would produce an "insoluble combination," Campbell's first Lovecraftian pastiches such as "The Moon-Lens," and later "Cold Print"
and "The Faces at Pine Dunes," contained a heretofore unseen
flair, a touch of vulgarity and sexual taboo which had been heretofore missing in many Mythos tales.

The shadows of Miller and Lovecraft fall across the literary
landscape of the twentieth century, and it is impossible to say
how many more writers were influenced by both. At least one
wondered what it would look like had the two men not just met,
but collaborated together on a work of fiction. The result is Peter
Cannon's "Asceticism and Lust: The Greatest Lovecraft Revision."
Taking the form of a trail of fragmentary letters and obscure references familiar to many Lovecraft scholars, the parody supposedly traces the generation of the lost shared work "Tropic of
Cthulhu," done with all the skill of a good hoax and the love of
someone well-versed in not just the letters and fiction of the two
great authors, but of their respective mythology as well. Here is
juxtaposed Lovecraft's prudery against Miller's vulgarity, the Bo-
hemian Brooklynite paired against the Cosmic Yankee. As a "what
if?" it is a fitting tribute to both, who though they never quite met
in life, yet continue to cross paths today.

Works Cited

Campbell, Ramsey. *Ramsey Campbell, Probably.* Ed. S. T. Joshi.
    Harrowgate, UK: PS Publishing, 2002.
Campbell, Ramsey, and August Derleth. *Letters to Arkham: The
    Letters of Ramsey Campbell and August Derleth, 1961–1971.* Ed.
    S. T. Joshi. Hornsea, UK: PS Publishing, 2014.

Cannon, Peter H. "Asceticism and Lust: The Greatest Lovecraft Revision." *Crypt of Cthulhu* No. 61 (Yuletide 1988): 29–31.

Herron, Don. "Analects from the Mainstream #2: Of Machen and Henry Miller: Or, Anais, Meet Arthur." *Crypt of Cthulhu* No. 65 (St. John's Eve 1989): 33.

Lovecraft, H. P. *The Annotated Supernatural Horror in Literature.* Ed. S. T. Joshi. New York: Hippocampus Press, rev. ed. 2012.

———. *Letters to Alfred Galpin.* Ed. S. T. Joshi and David E. Schultz. New York: Hippocampus Press, 2003.

———. *Letters to James F. Morton.* Ed. David E. Schultz and S. T. Joshi. New York: Hippocampus Press, 2011.

———. *O Fortunate Floridian: H. P. Lovecraft's Letters to R. H. Barlow.* Ed. S. T. Joshi and David E. Schultz. Tampa, FL: University of Tampa Press, 2007.

Miller, Henry. *Letters to* The Black Cat. Ann Arbor, MI: Roger Jackson, 1996.

———. *Nexus.* New York: Grove Press, 1965.

———. "Obscenity in Literature." In *Henry Miller on Writing.* New York: New Directions, 1964.

———. *Sexus: The Rosy Crucifixion I.* New York: Grove Press, 1965.

Miller, Henry, and Schnellock, Emil. *Letters to Emil.* Ed. George Wickes. New York: New Directions, 1989.

Nin, Anaïs. *The Diary of Anais Nin, Volume I (1931–1934).* New York: Harcourt, 1996.

Vidal, Gore. "The *Sexus* of Henry Miller." In *Reflections upon a Sinking Ship.* New York: Little, Brown, 1965.

Cassie Symmes: Inadvertent Lovecraftian

David Goudsward

The Long family obelisk in the Prospect section of Woodlawn Cemetery in the Bronx is well known to horror and science fiction devotees as the final resting place of the cremains of Frank Belknap Long (1901–1994), whose name is listed below those of his grandparents. The family plot contains Long's paternal family members, but Long's maternal Doty kin are scattered across the cemetery in family plots, including a small mausoleum. It stands out not only by its size but also by its design, an Egyptian Revival crypt in a field of headstones. The façade is triangular to evoke a pyramid, with Art Deco–style lotus blossoms engraved on each side of the door. The Egyptian Revival flourished from 1820 to 1850 but made a comeback during the 1920s with an Art Deco flair in the aftermath of the discovery of King Tut's tomb. This particular example is the final resting place of William Bittle Symmes (1851–1928) and his wife, Cassie Mansfield Doty Symmes (1872–1935).

Cassie Mansfield Doty was born on 31 July 1872 in Bayonne, New Jersey, the second of the three children of Charles Edmund Doty and Emma Augusta Mansfield. The Mansfield and Dotys had been successful produce wholesalers and brokers in upstate New York, and Charles's move to Manhattan was a calculated risk to expand the business. It proved a wise choice. The family was successful, and the Dotys became active in the arts and society affairs.

Cassie was maid of honor when her sister May Mansfield Doty married Frank Belknap Long Sr. in 1891 (although the society pages neatly overlooked the fact that Dr. Long was a mere DDS, not an MD). Frank Belknap Long Jr. was born in 1901, much to the delight of doting Aunt Cassie. Cassie's brother Mansfield Mudge Doty married in 1902. Cassie lingered at the fringes of New York's society crowd, but no potential suitors seemed to strike her fancy.

When her mother Emma died in 1907, Cassie, as the unmarried daughter, was expected to serve as head of the household. Both her father's age and his distraction over his wife's death caused the produce business to suffer. Cassie made a decision and moved with her father from their house into a smaller apartment. In 1908, Mansfield's wife died after a long illness, an invalid since the death of her month-old second son four years earlier. Suddenly Cassie was caring for Mansfield's five-year-old son as her brother mourned and attempting to rebuild the family fortunes.

In 1910, Mansfield remarried and formed a new produce brokering business with his father. With the family business again thriving, and her father and brother resuming their lives, Cassie took a break. Her cousin Roxy Smith (first cousin once removed) invited her to join her and her son William at the Hotel Griswold in New London, Connecticut, a glamorous summer playground for the wealthy.

In short order, a summer romance blossomed into a betrothal between William Smith and his second cousin, Cassie. She was given an engagement ring soon after he learned his divorce from his wife was final. A wedding was planned for 1916, and Smith basically told Cassie to handle the details as the date neared. The five-year engagement was deliberate for propriety's sake. It would be a minor scandal for Smith to remarry so soon after his divorce. Things started to go bad almost immediately. The Smiths had barely returned to New York when Roxy's husband, William Van Rensselaer Smith, died. When the estate will was released, New York society was astounded. It was known Smith had made his fortune as a founding partner in the Arbuckle Brothers coffee empire. What wasn't known was that Smith was worth over $5 million ($120 million in 2015 dollars). Suddenly, the only thing between William and a fortune was his seventy-eight-year-old mother, who knew of her son's irresponsible lifestyle. William began backing away from discussing his commitment with Cassie. As 1916 rolled around, Cassie was beginning to suspect Smith had lost interest, and in February he called off the wedding, citing a variety of reasons but mostly the purported fact that his mother did not want him to marry. Cassie knew that was nonsense, and with few other options, she stunned the society pages by suing William Smith for breach of promise. This was, by itself, not unusual, but what set New York society atwitter was the amount Cassie demanded—$1 million. The *New York Times* had a field day. Under oath, Smith admitted to proposing, but claimed it was invalid because Cassie knew he was married. The case was settled out of court for an undisclosed amount. It would not be Smith's only romance-inspired lawsuit by the time Smith's mother died in 1921: two of his ex-wives would also sue him, as well as his niece, who claimed he had reneged on an agreement to give her a larger portion of the estate if she did not tell Roxy that William had again married. Under William's litigious lifestyle, the family sued and countersued one another into penury by the late 1930s. Cassie may not have thought so at the time, but subsequent events among the Smiths undoubtedly gave her some satisfaction at how things turned out.

Whatever the amount for which Cassie settled out of court, it was substantial, because she began to appear in the society columns at a much more rarefied level. At the same time, she met William B. Symmes, a widowed associate of her father, another successful produce wholesaler who had branched out into brokering manufacturing.

In April 1917, three days before the U.S. entered World War I, forty-five-year-old Cassie Mansfield Doty married sixty-six-year-old William B. Symmes Sr. at the home of her sister, May Long. It was a quiet affair, just close friends and family. Cassie was still skittish from the Smith affair, and Symmes was trying to be low-key about a second marriage to a younger woman.

The newlyweds settled into a new home at the Hotel Theresa on Manhattan's Seventh Avenue, and as William began to plan his retirement, Cassie immersed herself in the society arts scene. William's official retirement allowed them to spend autumns in Europe and winters in Florida. Based in Miami, they began to explore the area. In 1923, they learned that a new community was being planned south of Fort Lauderdale called "Hollywood by the Sea." William was interested in the new city as a real estate investment. Cassie was interested because the community was planned as a motion picture colony. The next year, they commissioned the most sought-after architect in south Florida, Martin L.

Hampton, to design a building for them on the Broadwalk at Harrison Street. The "Symmes Shops" would be a two-story building in the popular American Southwest style with apartments above and an arcade below with space for nine small, exclusive shops.

Construction on the shops began in 1925. Cassie had become a patroness of the arts, offering to underwrite the publication of a book of verse by her nephew Frank Belknap Long. By November 1925, the book's contents had been compiled. The book contained a preface by Samuel Loveman, and Long dithered as to whether Loveman's own publications should be listed on the title page under his name as credentials. (In the end, he simply listed Loveman as author of the preface.) His friend and advisor H. P. Lovecraft similarly was unsure, and Lovecraft's friend James F. Morton was drawn in to the debate (see *SL* 2.30). W. Paul Cook was commissioned to produce the 31-page book. Cook completed presswork on *A Man from Genoa and Other Poems* in 1926, the latest work from the Recluse Press. It was a handsome volume and Cassie was impressed when given a copy. She and William were on their way to Europe, and her nephew's book gave her the idea of keeping a travel journal with an eye toward her own little book.

Any literary aspirations were cut short in September when the Symmeses received a cable while still in Europe. The telegram was from Florida. On 18 September, a hurricane roared ashore in Hollywood, destroying the town. The recently completed Symmes Shops were among the casualties. Photos show a twisted pile of wood and masonry, the wreckage unrecognizable as having once been a building. Under today's Saffir-Simpson Hurricane Scale, the storm would be classified as Category 4 with sustained 150 mph winds. The building was a total loss, and the local economy took years to recover. The Symmeses simply sold the land at a loss and walked away, not the first and certainly not the last to lose money in the Florida real estate market.

The Symmeses made their annual trip to Europe, then Miami, in 1927. Cassie had again jotted down travel notes. Now she would produce her travel book. She contacted her nephew Frank and had him make arrangements with Cook. Unbeknown to her, it would be the last trip with her husband. William B. Symmes Sr. died in Manhattan on 30 May 1928, two months after their return from Florida. Cassie made a final change to her book, dedicating it to the memory of her husband.

W. Paul Cook published *Old World Footprints* by Mrs. William B. Symmes in June 1928 under the imprint of the Recluse Press; 300 copies of the slim 32-page book were produced, with a foreword credited to Frank Belknap Long Jr. H. P. Lovecraft confided to several correspondents that he had actually written the foreword because Long was too overwhelmed with work to meet such a short deadline for Cook. Lovecraft was being polite. In an unpublished letter to Clark Ashton Smith of 1929, Lovecraft admits that Long was so bored by Cassie's "tame travel-book" that he was unable to come up with anything (see *CE* 5.287n), so Lovecraft stepped in and penned some "amiable ambiguities" for him.

Reading the text, Lovecraft's "ambiguities" are indeed subtle, and knowing how Long and Lovecraft felt about the text, the foreword proceeds with tongue firmly planted in cheek, containing such backhanded compliments as "The scenes are familiar, and the style is artless and without pomp or pretense; but the account is delightful because of these very things."

In 1929, Cassie resumed the scheduled trips to Europe and Florida, but traveling alone did not sit well with the widow. She tried a trip to Cuba in 1930, with similar disinterest. Instead, she focused on the arts and limited her travels to winters in Florida. Soon after William's death, she acquired a winter home at the Cavanaugh Apartments in Hollywood, one-third of mile north of where the Symmes Shops had briefly stood. Hollywood was convenient; it was less than 20 miles to the art scene in Miami, and less expensive. William Symmes's estate was a tad sparse after the Symmes Shops débâcle, and Cassie was becoming more reliant on her own resources.

Thanks to *Old World Footprints*, she was now a card-carrying member of the National League of American Pen Women, whose membership was limited to professional women of the arts. She was an active member and was even a featured speaker at the November 1934 American Pen Women meeting in Miami, speaking on the Damascus Blade. She attended meetings regularly in Miami. But trips to Miami proved to be her undoing. Cassie Symmes was killed in a motor accident in Miami Shores en route to Miami on 20 October 1935. Lovecraft mentions his authorship of

Long's foreword to R. H. Barlow in a letter of September 1936, noted only in passing, suggesting it was commonly known among his circle, now that Cassie was deceased (*O Fortunate Floridian* 362).

Cassie Symmes's ties to Lovecraft and his circle are unquestionable, although it is doubtful she was aware of Lovecraft as anything but a friend of her nephew, Frank Belknap Long Jr. This is not to imply that Lovecraft was any more familiar with Mrs. Symmes. He casually mentions her death in a letter to Alfred Galpin, identifying her only as the underwriter of Long's *A Man from Genoa* and that the timing of her death was a "tragick irony" because Barlow had been binding a complimentary copy of Long's second book of poetry, *The Goblin Tower*, as a gift for her (*Letters to Alfred Galpin* 220). Lovecraft helped set type for the book, published by R. H. Barlow.

Lovecraft also corrected some of Long's meter while setting type on *Goblin*, and this brings up an interesting point. In *Dreamer on the Nightside*, Long admits he really didn't know W. Paul Cook, having only met Cook twice (neither time with Lovecraft present) and corresponding with him only in "a few brief letters" (xiii). One would assume that arranging for the publication of two books by Cook would involve more than a few brief letters. If Long was not coordinating texts, layout, editing, and Cassie's payments for the work, Lovecraft would be a logical intermediary between his two friends. And there are certain suspiciously archaic spellings and terms in *Old World Footprints* that seem more like the phrasing of the Old Gent from Providence than a novice travel diarist. It seems quite possible that Lovecraft also tweaked the text.

Frank's Aunt Cassie may owe Lovecraft a bigger debt than we have previously suspected.

Works Cited

Long, Frank Belknap. *Howard Phillips Lovecraft: Dreamer on the Nightside*. Sauk City, WI: Arkham House, 1975.

Lovecraft, H. P. *Letters to Alfred Galpin*. Ed. S. T. Joshi and David E. Schultz. New York: Hippocampus Press, 2003.

———. *O Fortunate Floridian: H. P. Lovecraft's Letters to R. H. Barlow*. Ed. S. T. Joshi and David E. Schultz. Tampa, FL: University of Tampa Press, 2007.

Clergymen among Lovecraft's Paternal Ancestors

Kenneth W. Faig, Jr.

In Memory of My Friends Chris J. Docherty and A. Langley Searles

Rotten with Reverends?

Lovecraft wrote to his friend Frank Belknap Long in November 1927: "The Lovecraft line is fairly rotten with Reverends. It trickles Theology and radiates rural rectors. God help it" (*SL* 2.182). He expounded further in his letter to Maurice W. Moe dated 5 April 1931:

> The overwhelming majority—virtually totality—of my ancestry on both sides is of the staid and stolid country-gentry class, with an abnormally high percentage of *clergymen* droning their amiably well-meaning matins and liturgies across the well-clipt hedges of a subdu'd and commonplace rural mead. I can scare up a full-fledged cleric—the Rev. Francis Fulford, Vicar of Dunsford—in four generations, that is, he is my great-great grandfather—and by two generations behind him they come thick and fast. (*SL* 3.359)

Undoubtedly, Lovecraft harbored mistaken notions regarding the social class and occupations of his paternal ancestors. In *Devonshire Ancestry of Howard Phillips Lovecraft* (2003), my co-authors Chris J. Docherty, A. Langley Searles, and I found these occupations for Lovecraft's ancestors in his direct paternal (Lovecraft) line in England: great-grandfather Joseph Lovecraft (1774–1850), carpenter and worsted-spinner (declared bankrupt in 1831, after his emigration to America); 2×-great-grandfather John Lovecraft (1742–1780), mariner; 3×-great-grandfather Joseph Lovecraft (1703–1781), farmer; 4×-great-grandfather Will Lovecraft (c. 1675–1736+), weaver (DSF 18–24, 42). In fact, both Will Lovecraft and his bride George1 Merifeild, who married in Broadhempston parish, Devonshire, on 27 December 1699, were weavers. Will's and George's son Joseph and their grandson John both resided in adjoining Woodland parish, while their great-grandson the emigrant Joseph Lovecraft lived in Pulsford (Woodland parish) (1813- to 1820+) and Bickington parish (1828 to 1831) before his emigration to America in 1831 (DSF 13–17). S. T. Joshi mentioned our research on Lovecraft's paternal ancestry in the latest edition of his biography of Lovecraft (*I Am Providence* 3). We acknowledge that Lovecraft's beliefs concerning his ancestry remain important even when they have been proven erroneous (*QAT* 27).[2]

Rev. Francis Fulford (1734–1772),[3] Vicar of Dunsford, cannot have been Lovecraft's ancestor, since he had in fact been dead for

---

1. George was an uncommon, but not unknown, given name for females; some given names were borne both by males and by females. Today the female version of this name would usually be Georges, Georgene, or Georgette.

2. In my essay on HPL's ancestry (2008), I wrote: "My colleagues and I have certainly caught the Lovecraft family genealogist—be it great-aunt Sarah Allgood or some other person—in a number of apparently deliberate falsehoods, but we realize at the same time that what HPL believed is important, whether it is true or not. Nevertheless, we take much greater pride in Will Lovecraft and George Merifeild, weavers, married in Broadhempston Parish (Devon) in December 1699, than we do in highly questionable noble or royal descents" (QAT 27).

3. Most of the royal descents published for HPL have depended upon his claimed descent from Rev. Francis Fulford; e.g., the descent published by Gary Boyd Roberts in *The Royal Descents of 500 Immigrants to the American Colonies or the United States* (Baltimore: Genealogical Publishing Co., 1993), 136–38 (removed in later editions of the book). HPL has bona fide royal descents in his maternal Place-Hutchinson-Marbury line through his 6x-great-grandmother Anne (Marbury) Hutchinson (1591–1643) (see pp. 233–35 of Roberts's book) [QAT 22]. Through his maternal Place-Hutchinson-Marbury and Whipple-Millard-Shores lines, respectively, HPL could also have claimed the poet John Dryden (1631–1700) [QAT 27, 39, 47n60] and the author Nathaniel Hawthorne (1804–1864) [QAT 28] as remote cousins. (Cousins share a common ancestor but do not appear in each other's ancestor table; the more remote their common ancestor, the higher their degree of cousinship. Thus, first cousins share a common grandparent; second cousins, a common great-grandparent; and so forth. Individuals sharing a common parent are of course siblings or half-siblings, not cousins.) To the best of my knowledge, HPL never claimed either Dryden or Hawthorne as his relative; had he become aware that these eminent literary figures were his relatives, he

nearly a decade by the time Lovecraft's great-grandmother was born during the summer of 1782.[4] In fact, Lovecraft's great-grandfather, the emigrant Joseph Lovecraft, married Mary Full (1782–1864), the daughter of Richard and Elizabeth (Brusey) Full of Denbury parish, in Woodland parish church on 26 September 1805 (DSF 12).[5] The maiden name of Joseph Lovecraft's 1805 bride Mary was Full, not Fulford.[6] Her parents, Richard Full and Elizabeth Brusey of Torbryan parish, had been married in Torbryan parish church on 15 August 1782, with James Brusey and William Hooper as witnesses. Mary's father Richard Full had been baptized at Woodland parish church on 18 June 1758, the son of Richard[7] and Mary (Tapper) Full. Mary's mother, Elizabeth Brusey, had been baptized at Denbury parish church on 24 May 1763, the daughter of John and Joan (Knapman) Brusey. Mary Full herself was baptized privately at Denbury parish church on 10 September 1782, less than a month after her parents' marriage, and was publicly received into the church two weeks later on 24 September 1782 (DSF 12–13). There is not a

---

would probably have broadcast the discovery to his correspondents. He was desperate to find intellectuals, other than clergy, among his ancestors and rejoiced when in 1936 he was informed, probably incorrectly, that the sixteenth-century English astronomer John Field (c. 1525–1587) was his ancestor through his maternal Whipple-Mathewson-Field line (*RFS* 77; QAT 29, 45n42).

4. Francis Fulford's Prerogative Court of Canterbury will [vol. 983 (1772), folio 441, LDS film 92955] was made 16 1772 and admitted to probate on 24 December 1772. Fulford was described as "Clerk [in holy orders] and Batchelor" in the probate record (IFW 1–3, DSF 11–12). The author is grateful to Henry L. P. Beckwith, Jr. for pointing him to this record.

5. This was probably the single most important parish record found by DRO for Docherty, Searles, and me. (This record is also included in the DFHS Devon marriage index.) I published a broadside, *A Bicentenary Celebration*, in an edition of 50 copies from my Moshassuck Press to celebrate the bicentenary of this marriage on 26 September 2005.

6. The fact that Joseph and Mary Lovecraft named their first child, baptized in Woodland parish on 7 September 1806, John *Full* Lovecraft provides a substantial clue regarding Mary's maiden name (DSF 13).

7. Richard Full, the husband of Mary Tapper, can probably be identified as the son of Richard and Joanna (Earle) Full, both of Painton, married in Denbury in 1733 (DSF 13). So we can describe Mary (Full) Lovecraft, the wife of emigrant Joseph Lovecraft, as Mary(1) Full [Richard (A-C)].

clergyman in sight among Lovecraft's Full family ancestors for three generations in back of Joseph Lovecraft's 1805 bride Mary Full.

Reaching for Ancestors among the Landed Gentry (With Family Seats and Coats of Arms)

Lovecraft was at best an amateur family historian. The paternal family charts that he borrowed from his great-aunt Sarah Allgood[8] for copying in 1905 (SL 2.179) themselves contained substantial inaccuracies. On the basis of these charts, Lovecraft claimed that his 2x-great-grandfather Thomas Lovecraft (1745–1826) had been forced to sell his property, Minster Hall near Newton Abbot, in 1823 (SL 2.182, SL 3.361), evidently in order to liquidate debts in-curred for "wine, horses, and the fair"[9] (SL 3.360). According to a note in the Allgood chart, one Thomas Lovecroft bore as arms "a chevron[10] or [i.e., gold] between three towers or on a field vert [i.e., green]" as early as 1500 (SL 2.182).[11] According to the same source, Lovecraft's ancestor John Lovecroft of Minster Hall bore as arms in 1560 "a chevron, engrailed,[12] or, between three foxes' heads,

---

8. Sarah Allgood (1830–1908) was a younger sister of Helen Allgood (1820–1881). Helen married HPL's grandfather George Lovecraft (1815–1895) in 1839.

9. By "the fair" HPL means women. It is interesting to note that Thomas Love-craft (1745–1826) apparently preferred horses to the "song" of the proverbial triad "wine, women and song." We do not know whether it was ownership of horses, betting on horse races, or both that hastened the financial downfall of Thomas Lovecraft, as recorded by his great-great-grandson HPL. Even today the ownership of horses, especially race horses, is a rich man's hobby; horses are large animals and housing, feeding, and caring for them (including veterinary care) is expensive. To-day, some of the most valuable horses are owned by financial consortiums and covered by expensive insurance policies. Betting on horse races remains accessi-ble to both rich and poor and like lotteries makes some of the poor even poorer.

10. In heraldry, a chevron is an upside-down V-shaped band.

11. Regarding the older version of the arms, Henry L. P. Beckwith, Jr. opines: "It appears that another branch of the family cadenced the coat by the substitution of towers for the heads, and it may be that the towers in this coat, and in H.P.L.'s crest, derive from the arms of a family with which the Lovecrafts were intermar-ried, the cadet line deriving from this match" (94).

12. An engrailed pattern in heraldry has boundaries or borders consisting of a se-ries of circular arcs with outward points. It is the chevron (i.e., the upside-down

erased,[13] or, on a field vert" (*SL* 3.360).[14] In fact, the arms "vert a chevron between three towers or" occur only with different tinctures as quarterings in the arms of the Elliott and Boscawen families[15] in the 1620 Visitation of Cornwall (DSF 3). R. P. Graham-Vivian, M.V.C., Norroy & Ulster King of Arms, wrote to Henry L. P. Beckwith, Jr. concerning these arms on June 19, 1969: "The fact that it appears only as an ancient Quartering by the time of the Visitations means that whatever it was, and it was unnamed, was extinct in the male line, and even the name lost sight of" (DSF 3).

In fact, no Devonshire manor or estate bearing the name "Minster Hall" has been identified.[16] Docherty, Searles, and I were not

---

V-shaped band) that is engrailed in the Lovecraft arms.

13. The foxes' (or rather wolves') heads are erased in the Lovecraft arms, which means that only the heads are depicted, with jagged edges as if severed from their bodies at their necks.

14. The later Lovecraft family coat of arms and crest were blasoned by Henry L. P. Beckwith, Jr. and were reproduced first in Beckwith's book (95) and then (hand-colored by Beckwith) as the frontispiece for DSF. Beckwith believes that HPL was in error when he stated that the later version of the arms depicted foxes' rather than wolves' heads (94). He believes that the later Lovecraft family arms represent a "punning" coat, based on the French *louve* (meaning wolf bitch) and *croft* meaning place, farm, field, lair, cave, den (DSF 3). See also Beckwith's article "The Lovecraft Family Arms," which appeared in my own *Moshassuck Review* [Esoteric Order of Dagon Amateur Press Association] for February 1998 (2–3). Beckwith blasons the later arms as "Vert [green], a chevron engrailed and three wolves' heads gold," and the crest "A tower gold" (94).

15. For more on the Boscawen and Elliott families of Cornwall, see DSF 3–7.

16. A more extended treatment of Minster Hall may be found in DSF 8–11. The term minster (Old English *mynster*) was originally used for a monastic church or a religious house but later was applied to any large church, such as a collegiate or cathedral church, but especially to churches with secular canons (e.g., York, Beverley, Ripon, Southwell, Lincoln, Lichfield, and Wimborne). Both Cardiff, Wales, and Lichfield, Staffordshire, had twentieth-century public buildings called Minster Hall. There is a Minster parish on the north coast of Cornwall. The parish church St. Merteriana (restored in 1871) occupies the site of Talkarne Priory, a foreign monastic house confiscated by Parliament in 1407. It is also possible that Minster Hall recalls the Church House Inn, operated in the former Broadhempston parish house by Joshua Lovecraft (1739–1811) from 1774 to 1810. William Hooper (1762–1841), who married Joshua's daughter Ann Lovecraft (1771–1846) in Broadhempston in 1806, continued to operate the Church House Inn from his father-in-law's retirement in 1810 until 1832 (DSF 10–11). The Broadhempston

able to identify any Thomas Lovecraft[17] in Lovecraft's direct paternal line (DSF 26–27). Lovecraft probably used family resources, including his 1905 copy of the Allgood chart, and the Providence Public Library for most of the genealogical research he conducted prior to his 1924–26 residency in New York City. By 1927 his friend Wilfred B. Talman, a much more dedicated genealogist, had taught Lovecraft to use the richer genealogical resources of the Rhode Island Historical Society, then housed in its cabinet on Waterman Street in Providence[18] (QAT 15–16). Lovecraft's introduction to these resources, which included Burke's *Peerage* and Burke's *Landed Gentry*, proved to be a mixed blessing. Like many amateur family historians of his day, Lovecraft could not resist linking the surnames he found in the Allgood chart to the principal lines included in these references.[19] Lovecraft probably de-

---

innkeeper Joshua Lovecraft was the son of Joshua Lovecraft (b. 1706) and his wife Elizabeth (Willinge) Lovecraft. Joshua Lovecraft (b. 1706) was a younger brother of HPL's ancestor Joseph Lovecraft (1703–1781) (DSF 43). Minster Hall has fascinated readers and students of HPL's work over the decades. It is the setting for a major part of S. T. Joshi's novel *The Assaults of Chaos*. David Haden features an illustration reflecting his own conception of Minster Hall in the 7 November 2013 post on his Lovecraft blog (tentaclii.word.press.com/2013/11/page/3/), viewed 15 May 2014. I fantasized about a daguerreotype of Minster Hall owned by a remote cousin of HPL in the first of my "Tales of the Lovecraft Collectors" (*LP* 32). In my story the barely literate carpenter John Luckcraft, a son of Thomas Luckcraft, the last proprietor of Minster Hall, had the daguerreotype of Minster Hall taken just before the former family seat was demolished in 1848, after having been out of the family for a quarter century. HPL's cousin, a grandson of John Luckcraft, had a copy of the daguerreotype made for his Providence correspondent and kinsman in 1915. Needless to say, all these alleged details concerning Minster Hall were my own invention.

17. A son Thomas Lovecraft of Jonah and Elizabeth (Ludgar) Lovecraft was baptized in Woodland parish on 22 November 1736. Thomas Lovecraft and Martha Hollock (or Hollett) of Torbryan were married in Torbryan parish church on 4 August 1772; it is not certain that the 1772 Torbryan groom Thomas Lovecraft was the son Thomas Lovecraft of Jonah and Elizabeth (Ludgar) Lovecraft baptized in Woodland parish in 1736 (DSF 26–27). Jonah Lovecraft (1705–1780) was a younger brother of HPL's ancestor Joseph Lovecraft (1703–1781) (DSF 43).

18. The Rhode Island Historical Society Library is now located on Hope Street; its former cabinet on Waterman Street is now the copying center for Brown University.

19. HPL was not immune to "reaching" for illustrious ancestors even before his

introduction to new resources by his friend Talman in 1927. For example, as early as his letter to Edwin Baird dated 3 February 1924 (*SL* 1.296), he claimed that his maternal ancestor Michael Phillips (c. 1630–1676 or earlier), 1668 freeman of Newport, Rhode Island, was the youngest son of Rev. George Phillips (1593–1644) of Watertown, Massachusetts (QAT 17). (Just as his ancestor Anne (Marbury) Hutchinson had three lines of descent from King Edward I of England, HPL had three lines of descent from his ancestor Michael Phillips, through Michael's sons Joseph [his direct Phillips line], James and Richard [QAT 26, 44n32, 34]. It is possible that HPL also descends from a fourth son of Michael Phillips, William, through his Rathbone-Casey-Babcock line (QAT 43n26).) HPL probably asserted this claim regarding his ancestor Michael Phillips's paternity based upon his familiarity with Albert M. Phillips's *Phillips Genealogies* (1885), which devotes most of its space to descendants of Rev. George Phillips (but shows no youngest son Michael for him) (QAT 18). It is possible that other Rhode Island Phillips family members and researchers shared HPL's belief concerning the paternity of his ancestor Michael Phillips. Family researcher Henry Byron Phillips (1850–1924), of Berkeley, California, whose collection of card files and other records is owned by the California Genealogical Society, stated his opinion that Michael Phillips was one of two brothers who emigrated from Wales, perhaps originally as members of Sir Fernando Gorges's colony, in a 1900 letter to James N. Arnold (1844–1927), the publisher of the *Narragansett Historical Register* and the *Vital Record of Rhode Island* and the friend of HPL's uncle Franklin C. Clark (1847–1915) (QAT 25–26). I cited the recurrence of the given name Asaph in HPL's family as further evidence pointing to Michael Phillips's possible origin in Wales in my essay on Lovecraft's ancestry (QAT 44n30). The name Asaph was famously borne by the Welsh St. Asaph (d. c. 600). However, Charles Reuben Phillips of Youngstown, Ohio wrote to Henry Byron Phillips: "the three [Phillips] brothers owned their ship and sailed from Ireland; one was Michael born in 1629" (QAT 44n30). In recent years, the Canadian researcher Richard Ripley has posted new theories regarding the origin of Michael Phillips on the Internet. Based on circumstantial evidence, Ripley identified Michael Phillips as a cousin, rather than a son, of Rev. George Phillips. He further identified Michael as the son of John Phillips and Mary Street, born in 1623 in Duncton, Sussex, England, and traced Michael's claimed ancestry seven generations back to Sir Thomas Phillips (d. 1520) of Picton Castle, Castleblythe, Haverfordwest, Pembrokeshire, Wales. From Sir Thomas Phillips, Ripley traced Michael Phillips's claimed ancestry through the Welsh nobility deep into the Middle Ages. In 2008, some of Ripley's research could be found on the Phillips-Weber-Kirk-Staggs family space on rootsweb (QAT 41n11, 44n30). Ripley has also proposed new theories regarding the identification of Michael Phillips's wife Barbara, who married Edward Inman as her second husband in 1689- after the death of her first husband Michael in 1676-. Based on circumstantial evidence, Ripley identified Michael's wife as Bar-

scended from "cadet" branches of families like the Allgoods and the Morrises rather than the principal lines that he claimed for his ancestors in his letters to Long and Moe[20] (QAT 21). Alan Taylor, the leading authority on the Edgecombe family, was unable to identify either of the Edgecombe brides (sisters Letitia and Ellen) whom Lovecraft claimed for Thomas Lovecraft and Rev. Francis Fulford, respectively (DSF 26).[21] In summary, many of the "great"

---

bara Pierce, born c. 1624 in Tewkesbury, Gloucestershire (QAT 47n56).

20. I question the credibility of HPL's account of his Allgood and Morris lines beyond his great-grandparents William Allgood and Rachel Morris, who married in Trevethin, Monmouth, on 8 June 1817. I doubt whether Rachel Morris (b. 1790? Pontypool, Monmouth) was the daughter of Thomas Morris (1777–1817), M.A. (Oxon.) and the granddaughter of Sir John Morris, Baronet, of Clasemont, Glamorganshire, Wales, as HPL asserted in his letter to Frank Belknap Long in November 1927 (SL 2.180). HPL probably lifted these claimed Morris ancestors directly from the Morris entry in Burke's *Landed Gentry*. Similarly, HPL probably lifted the father Lancelot Allgood and the grandfather Sir Lancelot Allgood, whom he claimed for his great-grandfather William Allgood (b. 1786, Trevethin, Monmouth), directly from the Allgood entry in Burke's *Landed Gentry*. I did include a "cadet" line of Allgood ancestors in my article on HPL's ancestry (QAT 21). My Allgood "cadet" line differs from HPL's account of his Allgood ancestry, although both lines originated in Northumberland.

21. In his 1927 letter to Long, HPL wrote: "In 1766 Thomas Lovecraft . . . espoused Letitia Edgecombe of the Cornwall line" (SL 2.183). In the same letter, he wrote: "Thomas Lovecraft's son Joseph followed the favourite family pastime of cousin-marrying and espoused Mary Fulford, daughter of his mother's sister Ellen Edgecombe and of her husband the Reverend (again—the woods are full of 'em!) Francis Fulford, Vicar of Dunsford" (SL 2.183). In the same letter, HPL stated that Rev. Francis Fulford's "death date [was] missing" in the Allgood chart (SL 2.183). Fulford's actual death year (1772) would have been fatal for HPL's claim of descent from him. The Allgood chart gave 1735 as Rev. Francis Fulford's birth year (SL 2.183), only about a year off. One intriguing Devon parish record concerns the baptism of one "Mary Anne Edgecombe Full" (an illegitimate child born 1 February 1811) in Ugborough parish on 21 February 1811 (DSF 21n88, IFW 1–3). The name of this child combines the actual given name (Mary) and surname (Full) of HPL's great-grandmother Mary (Full) Lovecraft (1782–1864), and includes the Edgecombe surname that HPL claimed for the wives (Letitia and Ellen) of his alleged 2x-great grandfathers Thomas Lovecraft (1745–1826) and Rev. Francis Fulford (1734-1772). The Ugborough parish records for this period have many entries for the Full and Luscombe surnames. I do not know how the illegitimate child Mary Anne Edgecombe Full might figure, if at all, in HPL's an-

lines claimed by Lovecraft on the authority of the Allgood chart probably do not actually occur among his ancestors: e.g., Fulford, Edgecombe, Chichester, Carew, Musgrave, and Reed (QAT 21).[22]

---

cestry. It is difficult to believe that HPL's great-grandmother Mary (whose maiden name was Full) could have borne a child out of wedlock on 1 February 1811, not quite five and a half years after her marriage to Joseph Lovecraft in September 1805. For one thing, Mary and Joseph Lovecraft's third son Joseph, Jr. had been baptized in Woodland parish as recently as 22 November 1810 (DSF 13), so that Joseph, Jr. would have had to have been some seven months old (and his mother in her seventh month of pregnancy) at the time of his baptism in order for his mother to have been able to give birth to a subsequent child on 1 February 1811. Yet the existence of a Thomas Maye Luscombe at Broadhempston Hall in 1850, the abundance of Fulls and Luscombes in the Ugborough parish register, and the claim of two lines of Edgecombe ancestry in the Allgood chart lead one to ask whether there might be some connection between this mother and her illegitimate child and the Lovecraft family. Perhaps a close Full relative of Mary (Full) Lovecraft did become pregnant with a child out of wedlock through intercourse with a male member of the prominent Edgecombe or Luscombe families. The Edgecombes or the Luscombes may have made financial provision for the support of the mother and her illegitimate child. Is it possible that Joseph and Mary (Full) Lovecraft may have taken this child (or even the child and her mother) into their household in respect of the financial provisions made by the Edgecombes or the Luscombes? Might the father of the child have borne the name Thomas, resulting in the interjection of this given name in the Allgood account of the Lovecraft ancestry? After spinning such a web of theories, I must of course ask: what became of the mother (surname Full?) and her illegitimate daughter Mary Anne Edgecombe Full, born in Ugborough on 1 February 1811? I must leave this question for resolution by a future researcher.

22. Other surnames mentioned by HPL in his descriptions of the Allgood chart include Collins, Martin of Lindridge (Devon), Harvey (SL 2.182), and Washington (SL 3.360). In his published letters, HPL did not specify the exact linkages of these lines with his direct paternal line, which was the principal subject of the Allgood chart. After his death, HPL's genealogical papers became the property of his aunt Annie E. (Phillips) Gamwell (1866–1941), and after her death they passed to Annie's cousin Ethel M. (Phillips) Morrish (1888–1987). I hope that the Phillips family, which still owns HPL's genealogical papers, will at some time in the future make a copy of HPL's 1905 transcription of the Allgood chart(s) available to researchers at the John Hay Library. HPL's full transcription of the Allgood chart(s) might enable researchers to settle a number of still unresolved questions concerning the author's paternal ancestry. HPL wrote of the chart(s) in his letter to Frank Belknap Long dated November 1927: "There was a chart—one of those partitioned compartment affairs with broad spaces for one's parents and little narrow

We must probably reject Lovecraft's claim that his paternal ancestry was dominated by landed gentry and clergymen. In my essay "Quae Amamus Tuemur: Ancestors in Lovecraft's Life and Fiction" (2008), I wrote:

> Where he sought for intellectuals, he generally found sturdy yeomen and their wives, earning a hard living from the soil. His spurious English ancestry may have been ridden with clergymen, but his real English ancestry included carpenters, mariners, farmers, weavers. Lovecraft's ancestors prove that ordinary seed may produce from time to time an extraordinary flowering. (QAT 29)

I think I can write with confidence that my late co-authors Chris J. Docherty, A. Langley Searles, and I regarded the weavers, farmers, mariners, carpenters, and spinners whom we discovered among Lovecraft's paternal ancestors with as much pride as we would have felt had we discovered landed gentry[23] or clergy. In

---

spaces for one's remote forbears. I had copied it from my late great-aunt Sarah Allgood's chart (plus a chart of the Lovecraft side) in 1905, and it had nearly fallen to pieces" (SL 2.179). HPL seems to indicate that his own 1905 copy was fragile by the time he wrote to Long in 1927, not that his great-aunt Allgood's chart was fragile when he borrowed it for copying in 1905. Perhaps HPL made a new, sturdier copy, hopefully still surviving today, of his own fragile 1905 copy of the Allgood chart(s) after his friend Wilfred B. Talman reawakened his interest in family history in 1927.

23. As early as his letter to Maurice W. Moe on 1 January 1915, HPL asserted that "The Lovecrafts were a family of small country gentry in Devonshire" (SL 1.5). In his history of Woodland parish, Rev. H[enry] R[ichard] Evans recorded that the major landowning families of the parish were the Cullings, Dyers, Neyles, Pinsents, and Abrahams (EVW 195–96). Dochery, Searles, and I examined the Woodland Parish Property Tax Assessments (LDS film 1526151) for the period 1780–1830 and found no Lovecra(o)ft property owners. William Lovecraft was the tenant of landowner Robert Abraham on one of the "Lake" farms of Woodland parish from 1780 to 1801 (DSF 38). Local historian Rev. Henry Richard Evans (1885–1960), rector of Broadhempston parish in 1919–38 and rector of the combined Broadhempston-Woodland parish in 1938–58, published parish histories of Broadhempston (EVB) and Woodland (EVW) in the *Transactions of the Devonshire Association*, for 1958 and 1960, respectively. Moira Mellor's book *Looking Backward: People and Places in Broadhempston* contains a well-illustrated chapter on Rev. Evans and his wife (Mellor 48–49). The former Dorothy Maneer

many ways, the ancestors whom we discovered for Lovecraft reflect more closely the mainstream of social and economic life in
Devonshire, particularly Broadhempston and Woodland parishes,
than would more illustrious putative predecessors.[24] We concluded our study *Devonshire Ancestry of Howard Phillips Lovecraft*
with these remarks: "That the Devon Lovecrafts and Lovecrofts
were ancient but hardly illustrious families seems apparent. This
fact, however, does not reduce the interest of the family's Devon
origins for the many thousands of readers who admire the work of
Howard Phillips Lovecraft" (DSF 40–41).

The History of the Lovecraft and Lovecroft Surnames

Lovecraft's account of the Lovecroft and Lovecraft name variants
is especially interesting. Richard D. Squires's *Stern Fathers 'neath
the Mould: The Lovecraft Family in America* (1995) contains an
excellent chart that carefully reflects Lovecraft's account of his
paternal line in England (*Squires* 49). Therein George Lovecraft,
great-grandson of the 1560 armiger John Lovecroft of Minster
Hall, married Hester Lovecroft in 1649. In his November 1927 letter to Long, Lovecraft describes Hester Lovecroft as "one of the
old line with uncorrupted name and the original arms with the
three towers instead of foxes' heads" (*SL* 2.182).[25] In Lovecraft's account, the surname of the proprietors of Minster Hall changed

---

of Ogwell parish married Rev. Evans in 1925. Mellor includes a photograph of
their wedding (49) and other photographs of Rev. Evans (52). In 1958 Rev. Evans
and his wife retired to Harpford, near Sidmouth, in East Devon; his widow Dorothy was still living there when she was interviewed by Mellor in 1978 (48).

24. According to Rev. H. R. Evans, Devonshire was a major exporter of wool by the
fifteenth century. Evans wrote further that Woodland parish in particular lent
itself to sheep pasture and that local water sources served admirably for the washing of wool (EVW 168–69, 196; DSF 38). So, it is not surprising that Will Lovecraft
and his 1699 Broadhempston bride George Merifeild were both weavers. It is possible that the weaver John Lovecraft, who was buried in Broadhempston in
1705/06, was Will Lovecraft's father or grandfather, so that multiple generations
of the Lovecraft family may have worked as weavers, a very common occupation
in Broadhempston and Woodland parishes and all of Devonshire from the fifteenth century onward.

25. HPL noted that Hester's father was one Richard Lovecroft (d. 1642), but stated that the Allgood chart did not trace her ancestry beyond her father (*SL* 2.182).

from Lovecroft to Lovecraft during the interval between John Lovecroft in 1560 and his great-grandson George Lovecraft in 1649. Henry L. P. Beckwith, Jr. joins Lovecraft in believing that Lovecroft was the older form of the surname (DSF 3).

In *A Dictionary of Surnames* (1988), Patrick Hanks and Flavia Hodges assert that the Old English *croft* refers to an arable enclosure, normally adjoining a house. Thus, they believe that the "croft" suffix surnames are habitation names deriving from the dwelling places of the bearers of the name. According to the same source, the Old English *croeft* refers to a craft, skill, machine, engine or mill. Regarding the prefix "Love," Hanks and Hodges state: "English and Scots: nickname from ANF *louve* female wolf (a fem. Form of *lou* cf. Low 3). This nickname was fairly commonly used for men, in an approving sense. It may have been bestowed on a staunch soldier, with reference to the ferocity with which the she-wolf defends her young."

Beckwith, who notes that there were wolves in the Exmoor area as late as 1200,[26] believes that the later surname Lovecraft may have been borne by families whose living (i.e., craft) included wolf-hunting, hence the three wolves' heads, not foxes' heads as Lovecraft incorrectly states, in the later version of the coat of arms (DSF 3). Whether they were soldiers or wolf-hunters or both, the early male bearers of the Lovecraft surname were doubtless brave men and skilled fighters. Perhaps the prowess of the Lovecraft men caused the family arms to be added as quarterings in the Boscawen and Elliott family arms when women of the Lovecraft family married into these families centuries before the final flourishing of the Lovecraft family name in Broadhempston and Woodland parishes in the seventeenth and eighteenth centuries—perhaps as early as the twelfth or thirteenth centuries, long before the Lovecroft name first appeared in the Teign Valley in the middle of the fifteenth century according to the Allgood chart (SL 2.182). Beckwith opines that the Lovecraft family arms are ancient: "Though it is impossible to establish the date of first usage of the coat by H.P.L.'s ancestors, internal design evidence suggests that it is of considerable antiquity. I refer here specifically to the use of

26. Letter from Beckwith to me dated 4 April 1997.

the tincture vert (green), and to the composition of the coat—a chevron between three items" (94)

The Lovecra(o)ft and the Luc(k)raft surnames probably have common origins in the remote past. Hanks and Hodges state that Lucraft is a habitation name deriving from Luckcroft in Ashwater, Devon, whose name derives from the Old English *loca* (enclosure) and the Old English *croft* (paddock). They state that the Luckraft variant is first found c. 1554 in Stoke Gabriel (335). Luc(k)raft family authority Ian Lucraft, in his presentation "Devon Origins in the South Hams," delivered before the Luc(k)raft Family Conference in Exeter in May 1999, identified one Richard de Loccroft, assessed for eighteen pence in Essewater (Ashwater) parish of Black Torrington, north of Okehampton, in the 1332 lay subsidy. In the 1524 lay subsidy, Lucraft found five occurrences of the Lovecroft and Lovecrofte surnames (four in Loddiswell parish and one in Harberton parish), one occurrence of Lowcrofte in Harberton parish, one occurrence of Lomecrofte in Bridford parish, and one occurrence of Lowcroffthe in Exeter St. Sidwell parish.[27] The Devon muster role for 1569 includes three occurrences of these related surnames: pikeman Luke Luckrafte in Revelstock parish, Plympton hundred; archer William Lockroste in Littlehempston parish, Haytor hundred; and billman John Lovecroft, South Milton Parish, Stanborough hundred. [28]

The earliest Lovecraft surname parish records found by the Devon Record Office (DRO) for Docherty, Searles, and me, by type, relate to the baptism of Richard Lovecraft, son of Xpofer [Christopher], in Loddiswell on 20 November 1559; the burial of Agnise Lovecraft in Loddiswell on 30 August 1560; and the marriage of Steven Lovecraft and Joane Wakeham in Loddiswell on 3 June 1567 (DSF 29–30, DSF2 90). The earliest Lovecroft surname parish records, by type, were those for the marriage of Margaret Lovecroft and Vincent Cutmore in Stokeinteighhead on 2 July 1576; the burial of Walter Luckroft in Loddiswell on 30 May 1591;

27. Ian Lucraft published his findings in *The Luc(k)raft Newsletter* [Sheffield, UK] no. 7 (December 1999). Lucraft maintains a website for his Luc(k)raft One Name Study at www.lucraft.org.
28. See A. J. Howard and T. L. Stoate, *The Devon Muster Roll for 1569* (Bristol, UK: T. L. Stoate, 1977).

and the baptism of Jehan Loveroft, daughter of William, at Loddiswell in 1605 (DSF 29–30, DSF 2.91–92]. By the time of the Devon
protestation returns of 1641, there are only four occurrences of the
Lovecraft surname: one (Henry) in Cornwood parish, Ermington
hundred; and three (John, Samuel, and Thomas) in Broadhempston parish, Haytor hundred. By way of contrast, there are no occurrences of the Lovecroft surname and twenty-one occurrences
of the more common Lu(k)raft surnames and variants (DSF 29).[29]

The Lovecroft variant of the surname had become uncommon
by the seventeenth century.[30] In Loddiswell parish, even the more
common Lovecraft surname was beginning to wane in favor of
Luc(k)raft. The last Lovecraft baptism in Loddiswell was 17 December 1628; the last marriage, 1 November 1617; the last burial,
5 May 1624 (DSF 2.94).[31] The Lovecraft surname held out the
longest in any number in Broadhempston and Woodland parishes,
where the earliest baptisms for the surname were recorded in 1613
and 1692, respectively (DSF 37). Of eighteen seventeenth-century
Lovecraft and Lovecroft marriages in Devon found for us by
DRO, Docherty, Searles, and I identified six in Broadhempston,
five in Torbryan, five in Loddiswell, and one each in Ashburton

---

29. See A. J. Howard, *The Devon Protestation Returns 1641* (privately printed, 1973).

30. A few occurrences of the Lovecroft variant can still be found in the nine-
teenth century. Samuel James Augustus Leowcroft, the son of James and Ann
Jane, was baptized at St. Mary Magdalene, Woolwich, Kent, on 26 November
1843 (DSF 2.121). John Lovecroft, master of the schooner *Gleaner* of Torquay,
Devon, died while in the port of Tynemouth, Northumberland, and was buried
there on 29 July 1844 (DSF 33–34; DSF 2.122). Mary Jane Lowcroft, daughter of
Mary of Union House, was baptized in Tavistock, Devon, on 18 November 1846
(DSF 2.123). Elizabeth Anne Lovecroft, widow, the daughter of William Thorne,
deceased linen draper, married John Daniel Radick, son of Daniel Radick, deceased carriage builder, at St. James, Westminster, London, on 10 June 1878. The
bride resided at St. James, Clerkenwell, at the time of her marriage. The 1881 UK
census recorded Dawlish as her place of birth (DSF 34; DSF 2.127). It would be
interesting to discover the name of her deceased Lovecroft husband, the date and
place of his death, and the date and place of their marriage.

31. That some memory of the Lovecraft surname was retained in Loddiswell parish in the eighteenth century is indicated by the fact that the 8 December 1735
Loddiswell burial record of John Luccraft has his surname struck out and replaced by Lovecraft (DSF 31).

and Littlehempston (DSF 29). Of the forty-four eighteenth-century Lovecraft marriages contained in the index maintained by the Devon Family History Society (DFHS), more than seventy percent occurred in Broadhempston or Woodland parishes: Broadhempston, sixteen; Woodland, fifteen; Denbury, Torbryan, and Staverton, two each; Chagford, Ashburton, Cornworthy, Widdecombe in the Moor, St. Peter Exeter, Plymouth St. Charles, and Rockbeare, one each (DSF 29).

The last Lovecraft burial in Woodland parish was that of John Lovecraft, age seventy-one—perhaps an older brother of the emigrant Joseph Lovecraft (1774–1850)—on 4 December 1844 (DSF 32).[32] The last Lovecraft burial in Broadhempston parish was that

---

32. John Lovecraft, the eldest son of mariner John Lovecraft (1742–1780) and his wife Mary (Tapper) Lovecraft, and the older brother of the emigrant Joseph Lovecraft (1774–1850), was baptized in Woodland parish on 9 October 1768 (DSF 20), which would have made him seventy-six years old if he was the John Lovecraft buried in Woodland on 4 December 1844. However, in former centuries many common people, especially the illiterate, knew their ages only approximately. So it is not impossible that John Lovecraft's survivors misstated his age. Joseph, baptized in Woodland parish on 20 November 1774, also had a younger brother Joshua Lovecraft (1776–1850), baptized in the same parish church on 15 September 1776 (DSF 20). Although Joshua Lovecraft remained in England, his family had many connections with the family of his brother the emigrant Joseph Lovecraft. Joshua Lovecraft married Elinor Gaskin (1778–1872) in Torquay St. Marychurch parish on 12 June 1806. He and his wife had two daughters baptized in Stokeinteignhead parish, Mary on 11 November 1810 and Elizabeth on 20 February 1812. Elinor Gaskin (1806–1890), probably a close relative of Joshua's wife Elinor Gaskin, married Joseph's eldest son John Full Lovecraft (1806–1877) on 8 June 1833 at St. Luke's Episcopal Church in Rochester, New York (DSF 18–19; Squires 14, 51). Joshua's older daughter Mary Lovecraft married shoemaker Joseph Taylor in Combeinteignhead parish on 16 February 1836. Their son John Lovecraft Taylor (1836–1899) was baptized in the same parish on 29 December 1836. John Lovecraft Taylor emigrated to America, where he married Augusta Charlotte Allgood (1842?–1884), a younger sister of George Lovecraft's wife Helen Allgood (1820–1881) and the adoptive daughter of George himself, on 24 December 1862 (Squires 31, 55; Everts 16). Their son George Lovecraft Taylor (1877–1900) is buried in George Lovecraft's lot in Woodlawn Cemetery (DSF 19). Joshua's younger daughter Elizabeth Lovecraft (1812–1896) married her cousin Joseph Lovecraft, Jr. (1810–1879) on 10 October 1839 at St. Paul's (Episcopal) Church in Rochester, New York. White's 1850 Devon directory listed Joshua Lovecraft as a farmer in Combeinteignhead parish, but he died in September 1850 (as recorded the Newton

of William Lovecraft (1776–1855) on 20 February 1855. William, the son of innkeeper Joshua Lovecraft (1739–1811) and his wife Sarah (Ashweek) Lovecraft (1740–1808), was baptized in Broadhempston on 6 February 1776 and married Elizabeth Bennett there on 3 December 1799. He and his wife raised a family of twelve children baptized in Broadhempston between 1800 and 1823. William moved to London to conduct his tailoring business after the death of his wife, Elizabeth (Bennett) Lovecraft, in 1835, but retired to Broadhempston in 1850 and built the handsome home "Greenhill" (known today as "Sneydhurst") (DSF 33).[33]

By the later nineteenth century, the Lovecraft name was dying out in England. There were only six Lovecrafts enumerated in the 1881 UK census, two of them being London residents William Lovecraft (1803–1883) and Sarah Lovecraft (1800–1889), both children of the Broadhempston tailor William Lovecraft and his wife, Elizabeth (Bennett) Lovecraft (DSF 34).[34] The last English

---

Abbot civil registration district) and was buried in Stokeinteignhead parish on 8 September 1850 (DSF 18–19). After the death of her husband, Joshua Lovecraft's widow Elinor (Gaskin) Lovecraft joined her daughter Elizabeth and her son-in-law Joseph Lovecraft, Jr. in Rochester, New York. She died in Rochester on 17 April 1872, at age ninety-four, and was buried in Mt. Hope Cemetery in the same lot as her daughter and son-in-law (Squires 29; DSF 19n67).

33. Moira Mellor's book *Looking Backward: People and Places in Broadhempston* contains a chapter on Sneydhurst (formerly Greenhill), including a photograph of the house (53). I acknowledge the assistance of Steve Sneyd, who was the first, in 1999, to identify Broadhempston parish in print as a center for the Lovecraft family (Sneyd 2–3). Bob Nield, Richard McWilliams, and Rev. Nicholas Pearkes, rector of Broadhempston-Woodland, also helped Docherty, Searles, and me with the Broadhempston and Woodland parish Lovecrafts.

34. William Lovecraft (1803–1883) and his sister Sarah Lovecraft (1800–1889) were living in comfortable circumstances in London when the 1881 UK census was enumerated. William Lovecraft lived with his second wife Elizabeth Whithear (Knowles) Lovecraft (1809–1893) and their three servants at 69 South Hill Park in Hampstead, London. Sarah Lovecraft lived with her widowed brother-in-law Bernard John Muller, his two daughters, and their four servants at 158 Highbury NP, Islington, London. Sarah's younger sisters Elizabeth Lovecraft (b. 1819) and Jane Lovecraft (b. 1823) had married George Kerby, Jr. and Bernard John Muller, respectively, in a double wedding at Old Church, St. Pancras, London, on 31 March 1844 (DSF 34; DSF 2.30, 122, 129). In his letter to Maurice W. Moe dated 5 April 1931 (*SL* 3.361–62), HPL wrote that he had seen an advertise-

Lovecraft, excluding non-bloodline Lovecrafts who later assumed the surname in honor of H. P. Lovecraft, was apparently John Lovecraft, who died at St. Thomas, Devonshire, at the stated age of seventy-one during the first quarter of 1911 (DSF 2.66).[35] It seems likely that H. P. Lovecraft was the last surviving male bloodline Lovecraft when he died in 1937, unless he was survived by his elusive second cousin George Elliott Lovecraft (1866/67–1933/34+) (a.k.a. George A. Lovecraft and Eliot George Lovecraft), last noted in the 1933–34 New York City directory.[36]

---

ment of a Lovecraft estate in chancery court in London "about twenty years ago" (i.e., c. 1911) but did not elect to answer the advertisement. ("I let chancery take care of its own"). If the c. 1911 chancery case related to the estates of William Lovecraft and his second wife Elizabeth Whithear (Knowles) Lovecraft, it seems unlikely that HPL would have had any claim that could have prevailed in chancery court. HPL's grandfather George Lovecraft (1815–1895) and William Lovecraft were third cousins, through common descent from Will Lovecraft (c. 1675–1736+) and his wife George (Merifeild) Lovecraft, married in Broadhempston on 27 December 1699. HPL was thus a third cousin twice removed of William Lovecraft (DSF 36). In 1911, the tailor William Lovecraft (1776–1855), father of William Lovecraft (1803–1883), had living descendants in the female line in both England and Australia. These descendants would have had a stronger claim to the estate of William Lovecraft than HPL, who was probably wise to decline to involve himself with the chancery court case. The English chancery courts had a reputation for moving very slowly and for consuming most of the estates assigned to their jurisdiction through legal and administrative expenses before turning any remaining assets over to the residual beneficiaries. Many estates in chancery were exhausted before any assets could be turned over to the residual beneficiaries. In some cases, no qualifying residual beneficiaries were ever identified.

35. The 1891 UK census recorded John Lovecraft, a fifty-year-old pauper and former agricultural laborer, born in Princetown (Lydford), Devon, as a patient in the Exminster Lunatic Asylum in Woolborough, Devon. The 1901 UK census recorded John Lovecraft, a sixty-one-year-old imbecile and former agricultural laborer, in the same institution. Despite the age discrepancy, it seems probable that the John Lovecrafts in the 1891 and 1901 UK censuses were the same person as the forty-four-year-old unmarried farm servant John Lovecraft (born in Lydford, Devon) recorded in the household of John Hannaford in Widdecombe, Devon, in the 1881 UK census (DSF 35; DSF 2.66). This John Lovecraft was the seventh child of John Lovecraft (1794–1861+) and Elizabeth (Soper) Lovecraft (c. 1789–1861+) of Princetown (Lydford), baptized there on 13 March 1831 (DSF 2.35). Note that the 1881, 1891, and 1901 UK censuses all understated John Lovecraft's age, by six, ten and nine years, respectively.

36. For George Elliott Lovecraft, see my work *George Elliott Lovecraft: Lost Scion*

Willimus Lovecroft(e)

Although Docherty, Searles, and I questioned Lovecraft's assertion that landed gentry and clergymen predominated among his paternal ancestors, the Clergy of the Church of England database does tell us of one Lovecroft (note the use of the early spelling) who attained major orders. Record ID 66335 of the database[37] indicates that one Willimus Lovecroft,[38] residing in the diocese of Exeter,

---

of the House of Lovecraft [LSHL]. HPL was the son of Winfield Scott Lovecraft (1853–1898) [WSL], the grandson of George Lovecraft (1815–1895), and the great-grandson of the emigrant Joseph Lovecraft (1774–1850). George Elliott Lovecraft (1866/67–1933/34+) was the son of Joshua Elliott Lovecraft (1844–1898) [JEL], the grandson of Joseph Lovecraft, Jr. (1810–1879), and the great-grandson of the emigrant Joseph Lovecraft (1774–1850). First cousins WSL and JEL were both declared incompetent to manage their own affairs and hospitalized for the treatment of syphilis at the ends of their lives, in 1893–98 and 1896–98, respectively (Joshi, I Am Providence 21–28 for WSL; Squires 26–28 for JEL). They died within four months of each other, WSL on 19 July 1898 and JEL on 7 November 1898. Both men lived substantial parts of their lives in their Rochester, New York, birthplace; the question may be asked whether some common element in their lives led to their ultimate illnesses.

37. db.theclergydatabase.org.uk/jsp/DisplayOrdination.jsp?CDBOrdRedID=66335, viewed 11 May 2014. The source of this record is given as OCRO Oxf. Dioc. Papers d. 105 (Episcopal Register).

38. The English given name William would ordinarily be Latinized as Gulielmus; however, Willimus and Willielmus are found as unlearned (or naïve) Latinizations of the English given name William. (For example, see the listing of bailiffs and of members of Parliament in Thomas Gardner's An Historical Account of Dunwich [London: Printed for the author, 1754], 77–91, esp. 78, 87, 89. Today this rare book can be consulted on Google Books. For Latinizations of English given names, one may refer to homepages.rootsweb.ancestry.com/~oel/latingivennames.html.) I do not know what English given name other than William would be Latinized as Willimus; one might speculate that the short form Will (as was borne by HPL's 4×-great-grandfather Will Lovecraft) might be Latinized as Willimus. I assume that Wilfred or Wilfrid would be Latinized as Wilfredus or Wilfridus; Wilber(t) or Wilbur(t) as Wilbertus or Wilburtus. Other less likely male saints' names commencing in "Wil" listed in F. G. Holweck's A Biographical Dictionary of the Saints (St. Louis: B. Herder Book Co., 1924) include Willebald (French), Willebold (German), Willebrand (Italian), Willehad (Danish), Willehad (German), Willeic (German), Willeric (German), Willibald (German), Willibrand (Italian), Willibrord (Dutch), Willigis (German), Willow (English [Cornwall]), and Wilphin (French).

Devonshire, was ordained to the subdiaconate in the parish church of Hanborough, Oxfordshire, on 19 December 1556 by Bishop John Holyman of Bristol. Holyman had been born in Cuddington, Buckinghamshire, and became a fellow of Oxford as early as 1512, attaining a bachelor's degree in canon law in 1514 and a doctorate in canon law in 1526. He became rector of Hanborough in 1534 and retained this holding when he was consecrated as Bishop of Bristol in November 1554. He resigned his rectorship in February 1558, shortly before his death. Hanborough, where Lovecroft was ordained as subdeacon, belonged to the diocese of Oxford under Bishop Robert King. Holyman, the Bishop of Bristol, probably performed the ordination because of his close association with Hanborough, where he still served as rector. Originally a Cistercian monk, Robert King became Bishop of Thane and Oseney in 1541 and the first Bishop of Oxford in 1542. He returned to the Catholic faith under Queen Mary and was one of the judges of Archbishop Thomas Cranmer, burned at the stake on 21 March 1556. Bishop King died in 1558.[39]

The second record relates to Willimus Lovecrofte, doubtless the same man despite the slight difference in the spelling of his

---

The Cornish associations of the Lovecra(o)ft name remain—the quarterings of the ancient Lovecroft family arms in the Boscawen and Elliott coats of arms (DSF 3); the parish of Minster on the north coast of Cornwall with its ancient church of St. Merteriana (located close to a scenic 150-foot waterfall and home to England's only known maternity roost of horseshoe bats) (DSF 9n26), today part of the combined parish of Boscastle with Davidstow, which also embraces Forrabury and its church dedicated to St. Symphorian, whose lost bells (originally ordered by the lord of Bottreaux Castle to ward off the plague in the mid-fourteenth century) are supposedly still heard ringing from beneath the waters in Boscastle harbor (where they were lost by shipwreck) whenever a storm is brewing (DSF 9); the wolves that still roamed across Exmoor in search of prey until the close of the twelfth century and the linkage of the Lovecra(o)ft family name with brave wolf-hunters in the later form of the family coat of arms (which replaced towers with wolves' heads) (DSF 3n12). It is a pleasant fancy to wonder whether Willimus Lovecoft(e) may have been named in honor of the Cornish hermit and martyr St. Willow. www.ukattraction.com/west-country/church-of-st-willow/, viewed 17 May 2014, has photographs of the church. St. Willow should not be confused with St. Winnow, whose church is further up the river Fowey, south of Lostwithiel.

39. The information relating to Anglican Bishops Holyman and King derives from Wikipedia, viewed 11 May 2014.

surname. Record ID 64454 of the database[40] indicates that Willimus Lovecrofte was ordained to the diaconate in the Capella Sancti Gabrielis (chapel of St. Gabriel) in Cliste (probably Bishop's Clist) in the diocese of Exeter on 13 March 1557 by Bishop James Turberville of Exeter. Born in Beare, Dorsetshire, Turberville received his bachelor's degree from Oxford on 17 June 1516 and his master's degree from the same institution on 26 June 1520. He was consecrated as Bishop of Exeter on 8 September 1555. He refused the oath of supremacy instituted under Queen Elizabeth in 1559 and was deprived of his office in 1560. He retired to private life and died about the year 1570.[41]

There end the facts I have so far been able to discover about Willimus Lovecroft(e). He attained major orders (subdeacon, deacon) in the Church of England under Queen Mary and therefore probably recognized the supremacy of the Pope over the English church.[42] I have not been able to determine what became of him

---

40. db.theclergydatabse.org.uk/jsp/DisplayOrdination.jsp?CDBOrdRedID=64454, viewed 11 May 2014. The source of this record is given as Devon RO. Chanter 18 (Register).

41. The information relating to Anglican Bishop Turberville derives from Wikipedia, viewed 11 May 2014.

42. Bishop Robert King of Oxford, within whose diocese (at Hanborough) Willimus Lovecraft(e) was ordained as subdeacon in 1556, became a Roman Catholic under Queen Mary. Bishop James Turberville of Exeter, who ordained Lovecrof(e) as deacon in Clist in 1557, was also a Roman Catholic who refused the oath of supremacy under Queen Elizabeth in 1559 and was deprived of his office in 1560. I am not positive about the status of Bishop John Holyman (d. 1558) of Bristol, who ordained Lovecroft(e) as subdeacon in Hanborough in 1556. Note that Holyman served as rector of Hanborough even after his consecration as Bishop of Bristol in 1554. Holyman's connection with Hanborough was doubtless the reason why he (rather than Bishop King of Oxford) ordained Lovecroft(e) to the subdiaconate there in 1556. I am led to speculate that Willimus Lovecroft(e) followed Bishops King and Turberville into the Catholic Church, but I have no proof of this assertion. As of this writing, the only known facts concerning Willimus Lovecroft(e) are his subdiaconal (1556) and diaconal (1557) ordinations in the Church of England. Note that Lovecroft(e)'s subdiaconal ordination record specifies his place of residence as Exeter despite the fact that his subdiaconal ordination took place in Hanborough, Oxfordshire. Perhaps Willimus Lovecroft(e) was ordained to the subdiaconate in Hanborough because he was pursuing his

after he was ordained as deacon on 13 March 1557. Queen Mary died on 17 November 1558 and was succeeded by her half-sister Elizabeth, who severed ties with the papacy and restored the independence of the Church of England. Like his superior, Bishop Turberville of Exeter, deacon Lovecrof(e) may have refused the oath of supremacy required by Parliament in 1559 and, like Turberville, may have been deprived of his office. On 25 February 1570, with his bull *Regnans in Excelsis*, Pope Pius V excommunicated Elizabeth and released her subjects from obedience to her. In 1588 Catholic Spain sent the Armada against England and persecution of Catholics reached full tilt, to continue with somewhat diminishing severity into the following century under Elizabeth's successors, James I and Charles I. The Act Against Jesuits and Seminarists (27 Elizabeth, Cap. 2) adopted by Parliament in 1585[43] declared Catholic priests ordained abroad after 1559 who entered English territory guilty of treason, punishable by hanging, disemboweling, and quartering, and persons who aided them guilty of a felony, punishable by hanging only. Several hundred Catholic priests and laypersons were executed under this act; some of these have subsequently been beatified or canonized as martyrs by the Catholic Church.[44] Catholics did not attain full civil rights in England until 1829, and a Catholic diocesan structure was not instituted until 1850. The Act of Settlement of 1701[45] still prohibits Catholics

---

studies at Oxford University, where both Bishops Holyman and Turberville had been fellows earlier in their lives. It would appear that Lovecroft(e) was the subject of Bishop James Turberville of Exeter (consecrated in 1555) for his entire ecclesiastical career, or at least until Turberville was deprived of office in 1560 for refusing the oath of supremacy.

43. The text of this act may be viewed at history.hanover.edu/texts/ENGref/er85.html, viewed 15 May 2014.

44. Fifty-four martyrs were beatified by Leo XIII in 1886, followed by nine more in 1895. These were followed by 138 beatified by Pius XI in 1929, forty canonized by Paul VI in 1970, and eighty-seven beatified by John Paul II in 1987. That makes 288 (= 54 + 9 + 138 + 87) beatifications and forty canonizations.

45. The act was adopted because the former King James II (1633–1701), who succeeded his brother King Charles II in 1685 and reigned until he was ousted in favor of King William and Queen Mary in 1688, was a Roman Catholic, as were the succeeding Jacobite claimants: King James II's son James III (1688–1766) ("the Old Pretender"; claimant in 1701–66) and King James II's grandsons Charles III (1720–1788)

or individuals with Catholic spouses from being head of the Church of England, an office always held by the English monarch.[46]

If Willimus Lovecroft(e) did attain the priesthood, his priestly ordination is not recorded in the Church of England database. During this period subdeacon and deacon were usually temporary offices in preparation for the priesthood, both in the Church of England and the Catholic church. (Today the office of permanent deacon has been revived in the Catholic Church.) Did Willimus Lovecroft(e) complete his education at one of the continental seminaries established to educate Catholic priests for service in England? There were such institutions, sometimes called English colleges, in Rome, Douai, Valladolid, and Seville. Did he thereafter return clandestinely to England to serve as chaplain for one of the Catholic gentry, hiding in a "priest's hole" when necessary to avoid apprehension? Did he serve as a priest outside England? Did he abandon the clerical state once the oath of supremacy was required of Church of England clerics under Queen Elizabeth? It seems to me unlikely that he remained a deacon permanently, either in the Church of England or in the Catholic Church. It is possible that he died early, before he was able to complete the requirements for ordination to the priesthood.[47] I emphasize that I have at present no evidence that Lovecroft(e) ever held any clerical orders other than subdeacon and deacon in the Church of England.

Willimus Lovecroft(e)'s ordinations antedate any Devon parish record for the Lovecraft(e) or Lovecroft(e) surnames found by

---

("the Young Pretender," "Bonnie Prince Charlie"; claimant in 1766–88) and Henry IX (1727–1807) ("Cardinal York," who had been created a cardinal of the Catholic church in 1747; claimant in 1788–1807). There were subsequent Jacobite pretenders to the throne of England in Italian and German lines. Pretenders Charles III and Henry IX have a monument in the Vatican.

46. It has been proposed to amend the act to allow the head of the Church of England to marry a Catholic, but it has been objected that church requirements that Catholic parents raise their children as Catholics could pose a problem for the succession if the monarch is allowed to marry a Catholic.

47. I have no reason to think that deacon Willimus Lovecroft(e) should be identified with the William Lovecraft buried at Loddiswell on 12 December 1561, or with any of William Lovecrofte of Loddiswell, William Lowcrofte of Harberton, and William Lomecrafte of Bridford in the 1524 lay subsidy (DSF 2.85).

DRO for Dochtery, Searles, and me. Apart from the individuals identified in the 1524 lay subsidy, Willimus Lovecroft(e) is the earliest individual we know to have borne the Lovecraft(e) or Lovecroft(e) surnames, unless one accords that honor to Richard de Loccroft of the 1332 lay subsidy. How Willimus Lovecroft(e) links to H. P. Lovecraft's ancestral lines is unknown, although it seems likely that he is related to some degree, albeit remotely. (If Willimus became a celibate Catholic priest, he was probably not one of Lovecraft's direct ancestors, unless he broke his vows.) Willimus is to my knowledge so far the only Church of England clergyman who bore the Lovecroft(e) family name or any of its close variants (e.g., Lovecraft(e), Lowcroft(e), Lowcraft(e)).[48] If H. P. Lovecraft was troubled that his ancestry as revealed by the Allgood chart was "rotten" with Church of England clergymen, one wonders how he might have felt about Willimus Lovecroft(e), the Church of England subdeacon (1556) and deacon (1557) who may later have become a Catholic priest.

Did Will Lovecraft of Broadhempston Parish Have Father John Lovecraft and Grandfather John Lovecraft (Weaver)?

Docherty, Searles, and I speculated concerning the possible ancestors of Will Lovecraft (c. 1675–1736+) (DSF 24–25). A John Lovecraft, Jr. was buried in Broadhempston on 28 May 1696, while another John Lovecraft, a weaver, was buried there on 10 January

---

48. Jonah Lovecraft (1705–1780), a younger brother of HPL's ancestor Joseph Lovecraft (1703–1781), signed the Woodland bishop's transcripts as church warden c. 1745 (DSF 26n89). Church warden was a layman's, not a cleric's, office. The tailor William Lovecraft (1776–1855) was very active in Broadhempston parish affairs and served as a member of the "church band" (DSF 26n89, 33). As did his great-uncle Jonah Lovecraft, William Lovecraft participated in the Church of England as a layman. The fact that Docherty, Searles, and I, with the assistance of DRO, found their life events recorded in parish registers indicates that HPL's ancestors Will Lovecraft (c. 1675–1736+), Joseph Lovecraft (1703–1781), John Lovecraft (1742–1780), and the emigrant Joseph Lovecraft (1774–1850) were all members of the Church of England (albeit laymen rather than clerics). Joseph Lovecraft and his wife Mary (Full) Lovecraft maintained their affiliation with the Episcopal Church after their removal to Rochester, New York, in 1831 (Squires 12).

1705/06. It is possible that these two John Lovecrafts were father and grandfather of Will Lovecraft. Based upon the Allgood chart, Lovecraft gives his direct paternal line of descent as Howard(4) Winfield(3) George(2) Joseph(1) Thomas(A) John(B) Joseph(C) George(D) William(E) Richard(F) John(G) (*SL* 2.182). The emigrant Joseph Lovecraft (1774–1850) is Joseph(1) in this enumeration. Docherty, Searles, and I were in agreement with the Allgood chart for generations 1–4 in America, but we found that Lovecraft's paternal ancestors in England were John(A) Joseph(B) Will(C). Note how the succession of John(B) Joseph(C) in the Allgood chart matches John(A) Joseph(B) in the DSF account of Lovecraft's direct paternal (Lovecraft) descent. The Allgood chart interjects a generation George(D) between Joseph(C) and William(E), while the DSF account goes directly from Joseph(B) to Will(C). If we accept John Lovecraft, Jr. (d. 1696) and John Lovecraft (d. 1705/06) as father and grandfather for Will Lovecraft, the DSF account becomes John(A) Joseph(B) Will(C) John (D–E). Allowing twenty-five years for each generation, we might assign years of birth c. 1650 for John(D) (d. 1696) and c. 1625 for John(E) (d. 1705/06).

The abundance of seventeenth-century parish register entries for the Lovecraft surname in Broadhempston (DSF 2.92–101) makes it difficult to validate a father John and a grandfather John for Will Lovecraft (c. 1675–1736+). If the John Lovecraft, Jr. who was buried on 28 May 1696 is the same person as the John Lovecraft, son of John, baptized on 15 September 1687, then John, Jr. did not live long enough to form a link in Lovecraft's paternal ancestry. There were three marriages involving a John Lovecraft in Broadhempston parish in the 1680s: 9 November 1682, with Susanna Venning[49]; 5 August 1683, with Jane Predham; 26 February 1684/85, with Dorothy Furnace. The burial record does not disclose the age of John Lovecraft (weaver), buried in Broadhempston on 10 January 1705/06 (DSF 2.63). It is possible that he was young enough (say, born c. 1650) to have been one of the Broadhempston parish grooms of the 1680s; however, another John Lovecraft was buried in Broadhempston on 26 February 1724/25

---

49. This marriage was actually performed in the bride's home parish of Littlehempston, but the groom John Lovecraft was of Broadhempston parish (DSF 2.98).

(DSF 2.63). A John Lovecraft, son of Thomas Junier, was baptized in Broadhempston on 11 November 1638 (DSF 2.61), which is interesting because of the presence of the name Thomas in the Allgood chart. This John Lovecraft could also have been one of the Broadhempston grooms of the 1680s. John, Samuel, and Thomas Lovecraft were all residing in Broadhempston parish (Haytor hundred) in 1641 according to the 1641 protestation returns (DSF 2.95).

Does the Allgood Chart Invert George and William and Follow the Line of George's Wife Hester Lovecroft Rather Than George's Own Line?

DSF John(E) (born c. 1625) may possibly be identified with Allgood George(D), who Lovecraft states married Hester Lovecroft, son of Richard Lovecroft (d. 1642), in 1649 (SL 2.182). Allowing twenty-five years per generation in the Allgood chart, and starting with Thomas(A) (1745–1826), we derive as probable years of birth John(B) (c. 1720), Joseph(C) (c. 1695), George(D) (c. 1670), William(E) (c. 1645), Richard(F) (c. 1620), John(G) (c. 1595). Unless the generations were considerably longer than twenty-five years, it is difficult to identify Allgood George(D) with the 1649 husband of Hester Lovecroft and Allgood John(G) with the 1560 armiger John Lovecroft of Minster Hall. Is it possible that the Allgood chart inverted George(D) and William(E), thereby giving a corrected paternal descent Thomas(A) John(B) Joseph(C) William(D) George(E) Richard(F) John(G)? In the proposed correction of the Allgood chart, we have William(D) born c. 1670—in reasonable agreement with DSF Will(C) Lovecraft born c. 1675. In the proposed correction of the Allgood chart, George(E) would have been born c. 1645, still too late to have married Hester Lovecroft in 1649 unless the generations in back of Allgood Thomas(A) were longer than twenty-five years. Is it possible that the ancestors of George(E) in the corrected Allgood chart are actually those for his bride Hester Lovecroft? If this speculation is correct, then Richard(F) may be the individual Richard Lovecroft (d. 1642) identified by Lovecraft as the father of the 1649 bride Hester Lovecroft. However, even if we accept the corrected Allgood chart as Thomas(A) John(B) Joseph(C) William(D) Hester(E) Richard(F) John(G), it still takes generations longer than twenty-five years to be able to identify John(G) as the 1560 armiger John Lovecroft of Minster Hall. Note that apart from the inclusion of Thomas(A) in the Allgood chart, the corrected Allgood chart agrees with the DSF chart through DSF Will(C)—we have John followed by Joseph followed by Will in both accounts.

A Speculative Extension of Lovecraft's Paternal Line of Descent

I propose as a completely speculative extension[50] of the DSF chart the following (marking speculative generations with an asterisk): John(A) (1742–1780) Joseph(B) (1703–1781) Will(C) (c. 1675–1736+) John, Jr.*(D) (c. 1650–1696) John*(E) (c. 1625–1705/06) Richard*(F) (c. 1600–1642?) (possibly the father of the 1649 bride Hester Lovecroft) [no name]*(G) (born c. 1575) [no name]*(H) (born c. 1550) John*(I) (born c. 1525) (possibly the 1560 armiger of Minster Hall in the Allgood account) [no name]*(J) (born c. 1500) Thomas*(K) (born c. 1475) (possibly the Thomas Lovecroft who bore arms c. 1500 in the Allgood account) [no name]*(L) (born c. 1450) [no name]*(M) (born c. 1425) (possibly the unnamed Lovecroft observed in the Teign Valley in 1450 in the Allgood account, unless it was his father) [no name]*(N) (born c. 1400). The individuals identified only as [no name] in the DSF chart extension probably bore family names like George, John, Joseph, Richard, Thomas, and Will. (The name Samuel Lovecraft also appears in seventeenth-century entries in the Broadhempston parish register and in the 1641 protestation returns [DSF 2.79–80].) I was tempted to assume some recurring cycle of naming for the speculative generations, but I decided to restrain my imagination. It should be remembered that generations can run considerably longer (and sometimes somewhat shorter) than twenty-five years.[51]

---

50. Note that I bear sole responsibility for this speculative extension of HPL's paternal ancestry. My collaborators Chris J. Docherty and A. Langley Searles did not have any responsibility for my proposed extension and would surely have had their own, independent opinions of it. I have missed the wisdom and counsel of my collaborators in Lovecraft family research since their passing and I have dedicated this paper to their memory in appreciation of all that they contributed to our efforts.

51. It is not unknown for a husband as old as seventy or eighty years to father a child

The 1524 lay subsidy included William Lovecrofte and two John Lovecrofts in Loddiswell; William and Richard Lovecrofte in Harberton; William Lomecroft in Bridford; and John Lowcroffthe in Exeter St. Sidwell (DSF 30–31). The 1569 muster roll included Luke Luckrafte (pikeman) in Revelstock parish, Plympton hundred; William Lockroste (archer) in Littlehempston parish, Haytor hundred; and John Lovecroft (billman) in South Milton, Stanborough hundred (DSF 29–30). Whether any of the John Lovecrofts in the 1524 lay subsidy or the 1569 muster roll can be identified with the 1560 armiger John Lovecroft of Minster Hall in the Allgood chart is questionable. Docherty, Searles, and I did not find in Devon parish records any Thomas Lovecroft early enough to be identified with the c. 1500 armiger Thomas Lovecroft in the Allgood chart. Nor did we find any Richard Lovecraft buried in 1642, unless it might have been Rychard Lowecrafte, baptized on 11 May 1577 in Ipplepen (DSF 2.78). It is possible that this Rychard Lowecrafte could have fathered a daughter Hester marriageable in 1649 (born say 1625) if he married a woman younger than himself. However, the Allgood chart tells us that Richard and his daughter Hester bore the Lovecroft, rather than the Lovecraft, surname.[52] My extension of the DSF chart backward from the weaver Will(C) (c. 1675–1736+) derives primarily from my desire to make the DSF chart consistent with my proposed correction of the Allgood chart, to the extent possible, and is not supported di-

---

with a younger wife. The press reported in 2012 that a ninety-six-year-old Indian man named Ranajit Raghav had become a father, and fathers one hundred years old or more have been claimed. The reputed supercentenarian Thomas Parr (1483?–1635) ("Old Parr") famously performed public penance dressed in white sheets in Albery Church in 1588, at the claimed age of 105, for begetting a child by one Catherine Milton. Parr supposedly married for the first time at age eighty, and had two early-deceased children by his first wife. For Parr's alleged begetting of children as a very old man, see Rupert T. Gould, *Enigmas: Another Book of Unexplained Facts* (New Hyde Park, NY: University Books, 1965), 54. On the other hand, a young couple can bear children in their mid-teens. Kathleen Williamson, Lovecraft's 9x-great-grandmother in his maternal Place-Hutchinson-Marbury line, died in 1525 at the age of seventeen (perhaps in childbirth) (QAT 39, 48n61).

52. The only Hester Lovecra(o)ft found for Docherty, Searles, and me in Devon parish records by DRO was Hester Lovecraft, wife of Richd [Richard], buried in Broadhempston on 18 October 1793 (DSF 2.57).

rectly by any of the Lovecra(o)ft surname parish records found by DRO for Docherty, Searles, and me, the 1524 lay subsidy, the 1569 muster toll or the 1641 protestation returns.

The Allgood Chart's Thomas(A) Lovecraft and the Emigration of Joseph(1) Lovecraft

Docherty, Searles, and I (DSF 27–28) discussed the possibility that Thomas(A) of the Allgood chart may have been a family patron rather than an ancestor. For example, White's 1850 Devon directory recorded one Thomas Maye Luscombe as a gentleman residing at Broadhempston Hall (the former Rowe family dower house at Beaston). John Grant Luscombe, yeoman, was still in possession of Oakhill Farm at Beaston in Morris's 1870 Devon directory (DSF 27–28).[53] Is it possible that this Thomas Maye Luscombe assisted the Joseph(1) Lovecraft (1774–1850), financially or otherwise, in his emigration to America? The Allgood chart family historian may have chosen to interject an illustrious patron like Thomas Maye Luscombe into the family history.

Another possible reason for interjecting the name of Thomas Lovecraft (1745–1826) as the father of the emigrant Joseph Lovecraft might have been to deflect attention from Joseph himself. Writing to Moe in 1931, Lovecraft blamed the financial ruin of the family on Thomas Lovecraft:

> In 1745 we find born a restless egg who probably felt the blind stultification of all this oppressive respectability; for according to common report this Thomas Lovecraft struck out to live while he lived, aided by wine, horses, and the fair. I hope he had a good time, for his legacy to posterity was a general property scattering which shot everything to hell before he croaked—so that he had to sell even his family seat in1823 . . . historick date, on which the Lovecrafts ceased to be gentlemen according to the original and technical definition. Possibly the shock killed the old reprobate,

---

53. In his "Broadhempston" article in the *Transactions of the Devonshire Association*, Rev. H. R. Evans provides information concerning the Rowe family and its dower house at Beaston (EVB 107, 109, 117–18). His work (EVB 74, figure 7) also includes a photograph depicting the Georgian house erected by Austin Rowe at Beaston, connected to the older house by a later erection.

for he himself bumped off three years after that. Out of the wreckage climbed sundry of his numerous lawful progeny—I can't answer for the doubtless numerous rest—including his sixth child and their son[54] Joseph, already married and with six children of his own. (*SL* 3.360–61)

Writing to Rheinhart Kleiner in 1916, Lovecraft stated that his grandfather George Lovecraft (1815–1895) emigrated to America in 1847 "on account of a loss of fortune" (*SL* 1.31). Even once he acknowledged Joseph Lovecraft as the original emigrant in his 1927 letter to Long and his 1931 letter to Moe, Lovecraft minimized the role of Joseph by stating incorrectly that he died soon after his emigration to America (*SL* 3.361).

By 1828 Joseph(1) Lovecraft had left Pulsford, where he resided from 1813- to 1820+, to found his worsted spinning business in Bickington (DSF 14–15).[55] The sale of Minster Hall (1823) and the

---

54. By writing "their" son, HPL apparently intended to refer both to Thomas Lovecraft (1745–1826) and his alleged 1766 bride Letitia Edgecombe. According to HPL's account, Letitia and Ellen Edgecombe were sisters who married, respectively, Thomas Lovecraft and Rev. Francis Fulford (SL 2.183).

55. Sneyd (2–3) and Searles (DSF 19) record a tradition that Joseph Lovecraft (1774–1850) worked in a cotton mill in Coombe Cellars, a hamlet located on the south bank of the Teign estuary in Combeinteignhead parish. I would suggest the likeliest time would have been between his residence in Pulsford (1813- to 1820+) and his residence in Bickington (1828- to 1831-). The Ferry Boat Inn in Coombe Cellars, operated today under the name of the hamlet, was a famous place of resort and the hamlet served as the setting for Sabine Baring-Gould's novel *Kitty Alone* (Methuen, 1894) (DSF 19). Squires (10) states that family records show that one of Joseph's sons (unnamed) worked in Coombe Cellars. It should be noted that the emigrant Joseph's sons John Full Lovecraft (baptized 7 September 1806) and William (baptized 23 February 1808) were both of adult age before the family emigrated in 1831, and son Joseph Lovecraft, Jr. (baptized 22 November 1810), nearly so. Because there were no prohibitions against child labor at the time in England, it is possible that the emigrant Joseph's younger sons George Lovecraft (baptized 9 February 1815) and Aaron Lovecraft (baptized 6 November 1817) could also have been employed in a cotton mill before their emigration, particularly if their father Joseph was experiencing financial difficulties. The Cotton Factories Regulation Act of 1819 established the minimum age at nine (and the maximum workday at twelve hours) for child laborers, but even the youngest son Aaron Lovecraft would have been nine by 6 November 1826. The Regulation of Child Labor Act of 1833 instituted factory inspectors, and the

Ten Hours Act of 1847 established a maximum workday of ten hours for women and children. (On the Internet, eh.net/encyclopedia/child-labor-during-the-british-industrial-revolution/ and wathatcher.iweb.bsu.edu/childlabor/ [both viewed 17 May 2014] discuss child labor during the industrial revolution in England.) I have not been able to establish that Coombe Cellars or Combeinteignhead parish were ever the site of any cotton mills. That the emigrant Joseph and his wife Mary (Full) Lovecraft may have had other residences than Pulsford (in Woodland parish) and Bickington parish is suggested by the "disappearance" of their daughter Eliza Lovecraft (baptized in Woodland parish on 11 August 1820), who apparently did not accompany her parents to America (DSF 18). DRO did search Broadhempston, Woodland, Combeinteignhead, and Stokeinteignhead parishes (among others) for Lovecra(o)fts for Docherty, Searles, and me, but did not find a burial or a marriage for Eliza (or Elizabeth) Lovecraft compatible with the 1820 baptism of Joseph's and Mary's daughter. Civil records contain the death of an Elizabeth Lovecraft in London, Middlesex, in the first quarter (January–February–March) of 1840 (Public Record Office 2.114) and the marriage of an Elizabeth Lovecraft in Newton Abbot, Devon in the third quarter (July–August–September) of 1857 (Public Record Office 5b.235), but more details would be needed to associate either of these records with Joseph's and Mary's missing daughter Eliza (DSF 2.50). In his 1931 letter to Moe, HPL mentioned only sons John, William, Joseph, George, and Aaron and daughter Mary among the children who emigrated to America with Joseph and Mary Lovecraft (SL 3.361). (Joseph and Mary Lovecraft had had an earlier daughter Mary, who died at the age of two months in 1813 [DSF 13–14]. Their youngest child Mary, baptized in Bickington parish on 4 November 1828 [DSF 15], was named in remembrance of her early-deceased sister. Both sisters shared the given name Mary with their mother.) A third residence for Joseph and Mary Lovecraft, in addition to Pulsford (Woodland parish) and Bickington parish, would provide a location for their missing daughter Eliza to die or to marry. It is possible that Eliza Lovecraft remained in England with friends or relatives; the household of her uncle Joshua Lovecraft (1776–1850) in Combeinteignhead suggests itself as a possible place of residence for Eliza since the family of her uncle had many ties with the family of his elder brother the emigrant Joseph Lovecraft. If Eliza Lovecraft remained in England, the UK census is probably the next logical place to search for her, although the third quarter 1857 marriage of Elizabeth Lovecraft in Newton Abbot, Devon, may bear further investigation on the thesis that a left-behind daughter Eliza may have eventually married. Her uncle Joshua's home in Combeinteignhead was located in close proximity to Newton Abbot; a daughter of Joshua would have been more likely to marry in her own parish church in Combeinteignhead (as did his elder daughter Mary in 1836), but a niece who was boarding with her aunt and uncle might have been just as likely to marry in the nearby Newton Abbot metropolis. However, third quarter 1857 would be a late first

death of Thomas Lovecraft (1826) as narrated by Lovecraft initiate a period of major changes in Joseph(1) Lovecraft's life—i.e., his removal to Bickington (1828-) and his removal to America (1831-). In 1927 and 1931, Lovecraft dated Joseph's emigration to the year 1827 (*SL* 2.182, 3.361). In his 1931 letter to Maurice W. Moe, he stated that Joseph settled first in Ontario before arriving in New

---

marriage date for Eliza Lovecraft, baptized in 1820; moreover, Eliza's uncle Joshua Lovecraft had by that time already been dead for seven years and his widow Elinor (Gaskin) Lovecraft had already joined her daughter and her son-in-law in Rochester, New York. Thus, the likeliest family home for Eliza Lovecraft would likely have disappeared by the time of the third quarter 1857 Newton Abbot marriage. Of course, the disappearance of the family home in Combeinteignhead may have led Eliza Lovecraft to take up residence in Newton Abbot, where she may have found a husband. The first quarter 1840 London civil death record for Elizabeth Lovecraft should also be checked to determine if the decedent might have been Joseph's and Mary's daughter Eliza Lovecraft, who would have been nineteen years old at that time. Docherty, Searles, and I also discussed the possibility that Eliza Lovecraft did emigrate to America (DSF 18); she did not necessarily emigrate at the same time as her parents and her siblings. (It is possible that she accompanied her widowed aunt Elinor (Gaskin) Lovecraft to America after the death of her uncle Joshua Lovecraft in September 1850.) If Eliza Lovecraft did emigrate to America, the question must be asked why HPL failed to mention her among Joseph and Mary Lovecraft's children in his 1931 letter to Moe. It is possible that she was omitted from HPL's account because she died while still a child. If she survived so long, Eliza Lovecraft would have celebrated her eleventh birthday in 1831, the probable emigration year of her parents Joseph and Mary (Full) Lovecraft. On the other hand, if she accompanied Elinor (Gaskin) Lovecraft to America after the death of Joseph Lovecraft in September 1850, Eliza Lovecraft would have been at least thirty years old at the time of her emigration. At least one member of Joshua's family, his daughter Elizabeth Lovecraft (1812–1896), who married her cousin Joseph Lovecraft, Jr. in Rochester, New York, in 1839, did emigrate to America (c. 1836–37) while Joshua was still alive. (I do not know exactly when Joshua's grandson Joseph Lovecraft Taylor, the son of his daughter Mary and Joseph Taylor, emigrated to America. Perhaps he accompanied his grandmother Elinor (Gaskin) Lovecraft to America after Joshua Lovecraft's death in September 1850. Alternatively, Joseph Lovecraft Taylor may have accompanied his aunt Elizabeth Lovecraft to America when he was still an infant. I am not aware that Joseph Taylor and his wife Mary (Lovecraft) Taylor, the parents of Joseph Lovecraft Taylor, emigrated to America.) I hope this discussion provides a few clues concerning the missing Eliza Lovecraft, whose life story remains to be written by a future researcher.

York, "in whose northern reaches he settled down on an experimental farm and promptly died" (*SL* 3.361). In actuality, Joseph Lovecraft was listed in the first Rochester city directory in 1834 and continued to live there until his death at the age of seventy-five in March 1850 (Squires 11–12).

The Date(s) of Emigration of Various Members of the Lovecraft Family

Citing a family Bible record, Squires states that Joseph's son William (1808–1882) departed from England on 4 May 1831 (21). Squires states further that Joseph's son Joseph, Jr. (1810–1879) arrived in Rochester on 24 May 1831 (24).[56] If these dates are correct, Joseph, Jr. probably traveled in advance of William, because twenty days' passage from England to America would have been very fast for the times. Forty-seven days' passage from Torquay to Quebec (or longer if bad weather was encountered) was still typical in the 1850s (DSF 14n54). Exactly when Joseph (1774–1850) and Mary (Full) Lovecraft (1782–1864) emigrated is not known; Squires opines only that their emigration must have occurred between 1827 and 1831 (10). I do not believe they would have left England before the baptism of their youngest daughter Mary in Bickington on 4 November 1828 (DSF 15). Joseph Lovecraft probably departed before his bankruptcy proceedings in England transpired in September–October–November 1831 (DSF 15–16). It is possible that some of his children traveled separately—it seems natural to suppose that one or more of his sons, perhaps Joseph, Jr. who arrived in Rochester, New York, as early as 24 May 1831 went out first to reconnoiter before their parents, well beyond mid-life, sailed for America. (Joseph Lovecraft, baptized in Woodland on 20 November 1774, had celebrated his fifty-sixth birthday during the fall of 1830, while his wife Mary (Full) Lovecraft, baptized as Mary Full in Denbury on 10 September 1782, had celebrated her forty-eighth birthday during the summer of the same year.) One daughter, Eliza, baptized in Woodland parish on 11 August 1820, is not known to have accompanied her parents; it is

---

56. Squires kindly informed me that his source for the date of Joseph Lovecraft, Jr.'s arrival in Rochester was a newspaper obituary (DSF 14n54).

possible that she died in England before they emigrated or that she remained with friends or relatives in England or that she emigrated to America at another time than her parents (DSF 18). Overall, my considered opinion is that the likeliest time for the emigration of Joseph and Mary Lovecraft was the second quarter (April–May–June) of 1831. Finding them (or their children) in ship passenger lists would be the next step. The possibility that they may have arrived first in Canada (see Lovecraft's 1931 letter to Moe [SL 3.361]) and may possibly have traveled using assumed names should be borne in mind in conducting such an investigation.[57]

The Development of H. P. Lovecraft's Knowledge of His Paternal Ancestry

Lovecraft's knowledge of his paternal ancestry appeared to be considerably less in 1915–16 than it was in 1927–31. For example. on 1 January 1915 he wrote to Maurice W. Moe: "My paternal grandfather, George by name, (whom I never saw), emigrated to Rochester N.Y. in the first half of the nineteenth century" (SL 1.5). He refined this account somewhat when he wrote to Rheinhart Kleiner on 16 November 1916: "My father was the son of an Englishman who came from Devonshire to the state of New York in 1847 on account of a loss of fortune" (SL 1.31). In these two passages, Lovecraft appears to be referring to his grandfather George Lovecraft (1815–1895), who married Helen Allgood at Grace Episcopal Church in Rochester, New York, in 1839, as the original emigrant to America (Squires 30). Squires writes that George Lovecraft was about seventeen when he arrived in Rochester (30).[58] For that matter, George's eldest brother John Full Lovecraft (1806–1877) married Elinor Gaskin at St. Luke's Church in Rochester as early as 8 June 1833 (Squires 14, 51). The first Rochester directory (1834) included Joseph Lovecraft and his sons John

---

57. Docherty, Searles, and I speculated that the Lovecrafts probably traveled from Torquay in Devon to Quebec when they emigrated (DSF 15n57). We also speculated that the family may have traveled under an assumed name (or names) to escape their creditors because they were leaving England in advance of Joseph Lovecraft's bankruptcy proceedings in September–October–November 1831 (DSF 16).

58. Squires gives George Lovecraft's year of birth as 1814 (30). George Lovecraft was baptized in Woodland parish on 9 February 1815 (DSF 13).

Full Lovecraft, Joseph Lovecraft, Jr., and William Lovecraft
(Squires 11). (Joseph's two youngest sons George Lovecraft and
Aaron Lovecraft were still minors when this directory was published.) Perhaps Lovecraft did not bother to consult his 1905 copy
of the Allgood chart when he wrote to Moe and Kleiner a decade
later in 1915–16. It is also possible that he obtained additional information concerning his paternal ancestry during the decade
1917–27 from correspondence with other surviving Lovecraft
family members.

Was Lovecraft Suppressing Information about Joseph Lovecraft When He Wrote to Moe and Kleiner in 1915–16?

Another possibility is that Lovecraft did consult his 1905 copy of
the Allgood chart when he corresponded with Moe and Kleiner in
1915–16, but decided to describe his grandfather George Lovecraft
(1815–1895), rather than his great-grandfather Joseph Lovecraft
(1774–1850), as the original emigrant to America because he
wished to conceal the 1831 bankruptcy of Joseph Lovecraft. He
may have decided to describe his paternal ancestry more accurate-
ly when he corresponded with Long in 1927 and with Moe in
1931. To the best of my knowledge, Lovecraft never did disclose
that his great-grandfather Joseph Lovecraft had a bankruptcy—in
fact, he blamed his family's financial ruin on his putative 2x-great-
grandfather Thomas Lovecraft (SL 3.360–61), rather than upon his
great-grandfather Joseph Lovecraft.

Rather than hypothesizing an attempt by Lovecraft to conceal
his great-grandfather's 1831 bankruptcy, I believe it is preferable to
assume that Lovecraft's knowledge of his paternal ancestry gradually improved, with the assistance of one or more family inform-
ants, especially after his friend Wilfred B. Talman reawakened his
interest in his family history in 1927. This thesis of gradually improving knowledge seems likelier to me than any deliberate attempt by Lovecraft to (1) minimize the role of the emigrant
Joseph Lovecraft, (2) shift responsibility for the financial ruin of
the family to Joseph's putative father Thomas Lovecraft, and (3)
conceal Joseph's 1831 bankruptcy. In fact, Lovecraft may never
have been aware of his great-grandfather Joseph Lovecraft's bank-

ruptcy, rediscovered by Chris J. Docherty about 170 years after the original bankruptcy proceedings transpired in September–October–November 1831 (DSF 15–16).

Possible Family Informants in America

Lovecraft's younger aunt Mary Louisa (Lovecraft) Mellon (1855–1916) had died in Mount Vernon, New York, in 1916, leaving her nephew a legacy of two thousand dollars (de Camp 156). However, his elder aunt Emma Jane (Lovecraft) Hill (1849–1925), her husband Isaac Hill (1849–1932), their daughter Ida (Hill) Lyon (1874–1951), and their son-in-law David Lyon (1874–1945) all lived in Pelham, New York. About 1921, Lovecraft assigned his interest in his paternal grandfather George Lovecraft's lot in Woodlawn Cemetery in the Bronx to his aunt Emma Jane (Lovecraft) Hill. There is no indication that any financial consideration was involved; perhaps Lovecraft simply decided after the death of his mother in May 1921 that he wanted to be buried with his parents in Swan Point Cemetery in Providence and would not have any use for a burial place in the Lovecraft lot in Woodlawn Cemetery. Lovecraft is not known to have met his Hill and Lyon relatives when he lived in New York in 1924–26, but he did write to his aunt Lillian D. Clark of exploring the Mt. Vernon–Pelham area (located immediately north of New York City and readily accessible by public transportation) for ancestral homes c. 1925, so it is possible that he met the Hills or the Lyons. (He did look up a friend of his aunt Lillian.) In any case, he could have obtained additional information by correspondence with the Hills or the Lyons without ever meeting any of them in person.

There were also other American relatives, more distant than his aunts Emma Jane (Lovecraft) Hill and Mary Louisa (Lovecraft) Mellon, with whom Lovecraft could have corresponded after 1915–16, among them: Josephine (Lovecraft) Jordan (1842–1933) (Squires 20, 51), daughter of John Full Lovecraft (1806–1877); Bertha Avis (Andrews) Ratcliffe (1866–1928) and Harriet Eliza Andrews (1871–1957) (Squires 21–22, 52–53), granddaughters of William Lovecraft (1808–1882); George Elliott Lovecraft (1866/67–1933/34+)[59]

59. In his 1931 letter to Moe, HPL wrote of his second cousin George Elliott

Lovecraft: "Joseph [i.e., Joseph Lovecraft, Jr. (1810–1879]) had a grandson who went west in the 1880's and dropped from sight" (*SL* 3.361). George Elliott Lovecraft moved from Rochester, New York (his birthplace), to engage in business in Chicago in 1889–91 and married his first wife Celia Marchand (1871–1893) in Racine, Wisconsin, in 1890. He returned to New York City in 1892 to work for his cousin Frederick Aaron Lovecraft (1850–1893). George Elliott Lovecraft had lived in Chicago earlier, in 1870, when he was enumerated as a young boy in the ninth ward household shared by his grandfather Joseph Lovecraft, Jr., his grandmother Elizabeth (Lovecraft) Lovecraft (1812–1896), his father Joshua Elliott Lovecraft (1844–1898), and his mother Libbie M. (Vandervort) Lovecraft (1847–1873). In addition to young George, George's paternal great-grandmother Elinor (Gaskin) Lovecraft (1778–1872), the widow of Joshua Lovecraft (1776–1850), his maternal grandmother Louisa Vandervort (b. 1820 or 1821), and his maternal aunt Cora Vandervort (b. 1855 or 1856) were also part of this 1870 Chicago household. Joseph Lovecraft, Jr. His family did not remain in Chicago for long, but had moved back to Rochester, New York, by the time George's great-grandmother Elinor (Gaskin) Lovecraft died in 1872. George's mother Libbie M. (Vandervort) Lovecraft died in a boating accident on Lake Ontario in 1873; in 1875, his father Joshua Elliott Lovecraft took Alice Delia Ward (b. 1854) as his second wife. After the deaths of his first wife Celia (Marchand) Lovecraft and of his employer Frederick Aaron Lovecraft in New York City in 1893, George returned to Rochester to work for his father Joshua Elliott Lovecraft. George managed his father's heading mill in Olean, New York, from 1895 to 1898. Joshua Elliott Lovecraft was admitted to Rochester State Hospital in 1896, and George (who was initially appointed conservator) soon became embroiled in disputes over his father's estate. In 1898 George was arrested until he pledged assets to guarantee his performance; he was eventually replaced as conservator by John F. Brayer. Joshua Elliott Lovecraft died in November 1898, but the disputes over his estate continued. During the winter of 1898–99, George and his stepmother Alice D. (Ward) Lovecraft obtained a court ruling that George was not indebted to the estate of his deceased father, and the assets that George had pledged after his arrest were returned to him. Perhaps George and his stepmother made private financial arrangements between themselves at this time. George's stepmother Alice D. (Ward) Lovecraft married William Williams as her second husband in Rochester, New York, in September 1900. The disputes over the estate of Joshua Elliott Lovecraft were not finally settled until January 1901; most of the remaining estate of Joshua Elliott Lovecraft, inventoried at only $2,063.34 in March 1899, went to Brayer to cover his expenses. Squires states that Alice D. (Ward) Lovecraft Williams realized only $134.17 in cash from the settlement of the estate (28). George (using the assumed name Eliot George Lovecraft) was married at least one more time, to Norma Hanlon (1880–1910), in New York City in 1905. In 1922, George (as G. E. Lovecraft), together with D. E. Lovecraft

(Squires 28–29, 54; LSHL), grandson of Joseph Lovecraft, Jr. (1810–1879); Florence Veazie (Lovecraft) Salmons (1861–1950)[60] (Squires 44, 56), daughter of Aaron Lovecraft (1817–1870); George Francis Myers (1865–1937) (Squires 35–37, 56), grandson of Aaron Lovecraft; and Robert Bell Brown (1862–1934) (Squires 46, 57), son of Mary Lovecraft (1828–1907) and her husband James Brown (1806–1889). Of these, all were female line relatives except for George Elliott Lovecraft. It is difficult to speculate over which of these relatives, if any, might have imparted additional family data to Lovecraft. Robert Bell Brown and his wife Helen (Morgan) Brown honored the Lovecraft family name with the middle name that they chose for their son Gordon Lovecraft Brown (1901–1975). Gordon Lovecraft Brown and his wife Sarah S. (Bickford) Brown in turn named their own son Gordon Lovecraft Brown, Jr.

---

and S. W. Ferzon, incorporated the Lovecraft Safety Pocket Company in New York; it is possible that D. E. Lovecraft was a third wife of George. (No children are known to have been born to George's first two marriages.) As late as 1931, HPL was unaware of the survival or the whereabouts of his second cousin George Elliott Lovecraft, who surfaced for a (perhaps) final appearance (as George A. Lovecraft) in the 1933–34 New York City directory; he had earlier been identified as George A. Lovecraft when he testified in the matter of his former employer Frederick Aaron Lovecraft's contested will in 1894. We may speculate that his baptismal name was George Elliott while his confirmation name began with the letter "A" (perhaps "Aaron" in honor of his uncle Aaron Lovecraft) and that he from time to time chose to use the first letter of his confirmation name as his middle initial. (See LSHL and Squires 26–29 for extensive discussion of George Elliott Lovecraft.) Subject to his uncertainty regarding the survival of George Elliott Lovecraft, HPL believed himself to be the last survivor of the male Lovecraft line: "Of these lines, however, all but two [Joseph, Jr. and George] are definitely extinct [in the male line], and even one of these two [Joseph, Jr.] probably is" (SL 3.361).

60. Florence Veazie (Lovecraft) Salmons was the sister of the next most famous family member after HPL, Frederick Aaron Lovecraft (1850–1893), whose New York City suicide in 1893, followed by the suicide of his mistress May Brookyn and the contest of his will by his family in the following year, received national newspaper coverage. Squires (36–44) provides an extended treatment of Frederick Aaron Lovecraft. In 2013 journalist David Acord published an electronic book devoted to Frederick Aaron Lovecraft, *The Other Mr. Lovecraft: A True Story of Tragedy and the Supernatural from H. P. Lovecraft's Family Tree*. The cover of Acord's work reproduces contemporary portraits of Frederick Aaron Lovecraft and May Brookyn.

(1927–2003) (Squires 57). Perhaps the consciousness of the Lovecraft family name was highest among the descendants of Aaron Lovecraft (1817–1870), whose line also included the other famous Lovecraft, Aaron's son Frederick Aaron Lovecraft (1850–1893), whose 1893 suicide, combined with the suicide of his mistress May Brookyn and the contest of his will by his family in 1894, received national newspaper coverage (Squires 38–44; Acord].

Possible Family Informants in England

John Lovecraft (1831–1911), apparently the last male bloodline Lovecraft in England, died in the first quarter of 1911.[61] It is possible that the c. 1911 Lovecraft chancery court case in London mentioned by Lovecraft in his 1931 letter to Moe (*SL* 3.361–62) involved the estates of William Lovecraft (1803–1883), son of the Broadhempston tailor William Lovecraft (1776–1855), and his second wife Elizabeth Whithear (Knowles) Lovecraft (1809–1893).

---

61. The Lovecra(o)ft and Luc(k)raft family names in England continued to be somewhat malleable into the twentieth century. For example, the Public Record Office (PRO) records the death of Henrietta Lovecraft, age fifty-six, in Lincoln on 4 March 1923. However, the probate record gives the decedent's name as Henrietta Luckraft, spinster of Delhi Cottage, Mill Road, Lincoln. Administration was granted to her younger brother Frederick Luckraft (b. 1877?), who died aged fifty-four in Lincoln during the second quarter (April–May–June) of 1931. Henrietta's father William Lucraft had been a Sergeant Major in Her Majesty's 103rd Regiment (Royal Bombay Fusiliers) and both Henrietta (b. 1866?) and her older brother George (b. 1862?) were born in India, where their father was then serving in the military. By the time of the 1881 UK census, William Lucraft, a forty-eight-year-old pensioner (b. 1833?), his wife Jane Lucraft, and their children George, Henrietta, and Frederick were living in Chelsea, Lincoln. William Lucraft, who died in Lincoln on 13 March 1900, had been born in Loddiswell, one of the ancient "cradle" parishes of the Lovecraft family (with parish register entries for the Lovecraft surname as old as 1559) (DSF 2.55–56, 90]. By the end of the first quarter of the seventeenth century, the Loddiswell Lovecrafts had adopted the more common Luc(k)raft surname, although one 1735 burial record has the name Luccraft struck out and replaced by Lovecraft (DSF 2.105). The use of the Lovecraft surname for Henrietta Luckraft in the 1923 PRO record may reflect the continuing malleability of the related surnames, especially for the Loddiswell family, or it may simply reflect the pronunciation used by the informant for Henrietta's death record (probably her younger brother Frederick).

This chancery court case may have attracted some attention to the Lovecraft family name in England. A transcription of the 1901 UK census recorded two elderly Lovecroft sisters, Ellen, age seventy-one, and Henrietta, age sixty-six, in Lichfield, Staffordshire; but based upon earlier records relating to the sisters, Chris J. Docherty concluded that their surname was actually Laverock or Loverock and was transcribed incorrectly in the 1901 census transcription (DSF 35–36). There were female line descendants of the Broadhempston tailor William Lovecraft still living in England in 1911. For example, William's daughters Elizabeth (b. 1819) and Jane (b. 1823) had had a double wedding with George Kerby, Jr. and Bernard John Muller, respectively, at Old Church, St. Pancras, London on 31 March 1844 (DSF 2.30). Two daughters of Bernard and Jane (Lovecraft) Muller were living with their widowed father Bernard John Muller in Islington, London, at the time of the 1881 UK census. Muller's spinster sister-in-law Sarah Lovecraft (1800–1889), sister of William Lovecraft (1803–1883), was also living in his household at the time (DSF 34). The estate of George Lovecraft Kerby (1859–1918), born in Hackney, London,[62] and probably the son of George Kerby, Jr. and Elizabeth (Lovecraft) Kerby, was in probate in 1919. It is unlikely that Lovecraft corresponded with female line relatives in England; in his 1931 letter to Moe, he wrote: "If I can ever get over to Devon I may try to see what sort of cousin I can unearth there aside from those planted beneath and around the parish churches of the Newton-Abbot region" (SL 3.361).[63] He would probably not have used these

---

62. George Lovecraft Kerby was still living in Hackney, London, in 1893–95 (see the London Electoral Register for those years). He was residing in Low Leyton, Essex, by the time of the 1901 and 1911 UK censuses.

63. HPL would have struck pay dirt had he managed to visit Broadhempston parish churchyard, where William Lovecraft (1776–1850), his wife Elizabeth (Bennett) Lovecraft (1779–1835), their son Edward Ashweek Lovecraft (baptized 4 January and buried 21 April 1818, age thirteen weeks), and their grandson Hugh Montgomery (d. 21 January 1850, age twenty-one months) are all buried (DSF 33; DSF 2.30). Edward Ashweek Lovecraft was probably named in honor of his paternal grandmother Sarah (Ashweek) Lovecraft (1740–1808), who married Joshua Lovecraft (1739–1811) in Denbury on 20 October 1769 (DSF 10). George Ashweek had been the proprietor of the Church House Inn in 1764 (EVB 116), so that Joshua Lovecraft probably acquired the Church House Inn from his

words if he had already been in correspondence with a Lovecraft family informant in England.

Possible Family Informants in Australia

An Australian informant is also possible, albeit unlikely. William Lovecraft (1850–1867), the grandson of the tailor William Love-craft (1776–1855) of Broadhempston and the son of tailor John Lovecraft (1813–1875) of London, emigrated to Australia. The male Lovecraft bloodline in Australia ended when William Lovecraft died in Bankside, Bankstown, West Liverpool, New South Wales, on 24 September 1867, aged only seventeen. Tailor William Love-craft's daughters Eliza (b. 1810; married Charles Scott) and Ann (b. 1811; married [1] Hugh Montgomery and [2] Charles Scott, her sis-ter's widower) also emigrated to New South Wales, Australia (DSF 2.30). At least Ann (Lovecraft) Scott (1811–1897) had descendants.

Could Lovecraft's Informant Have Been a Family Friend in New York?

Lovecraft did have correspondents in England [e.g., Arthur Harris (1893–1966)[64]], Australia [e.g., George William Sidney Fitzpatrick (1884–1948)[65]], and New Zealand [e.g., Robert George Barr (1906–1975)[66]], so international postage was no barrier for his corre-spondence. We cannot say whence he drew his enhanced know-

wife's family in 1774. Hugh Montgomery was the son of William's daughter Ann and her first husband Hugh Montgomery.

64. Arthur Harris was the longtime publisher of the amateur magazine *Interesting Items*. HPL's letters to Harris form part of the Lovecraft Collection at the John Hay Library, Brown University.

65. George William Sydney Fitzpatrick was a pioneering Australian public rela-tions executive. He was also a book collector and corresponded with HPL about book plates. Fitzpatrick was identified by David Haden in his paper "Additions and Corrections for 'Lovecraft's 1937 Diary,'" *Lovecraft Annual* 7 (2013): 180–81. My original paper "Lovecraft's 1937 Diary" had been published in the *Lovecraft Annual* 6 (2012): 155–78. Haden succeeded in identifying many of the obscure correspondents whom I failed to identify, or identified inaccurately or incom-pletely in my paper.

66. Robert George Barr's amateur journalism collection was donated to the Na-tional Library of New Zealand in 1977.

ledge of his paternal family history by 1927. Perhaps he simply studied his 1905 copy of the Allgood chart(s) more carefully than he had done when he corresponded with Moe and Kleiner about his family history in 1915–16. Or he may have benefited from conversation or correspondence with a family source at present still unknown to us.

Langley Searles's maternal uncle Nelson William Rogers (b. 10 March 1878, d. 6 August 1951) was introduced to Whipple V. Phillips and his family in Providence when he was only six or eight months old (late 1878). He became the particular friend of Whipple's daughter Sarah Susan (Susie) Phillips, who married Winfield S. Lovecraft in June 1889. Rogers visited Susie Lovecraft in her home at 598 Angell Street in Providence on Saturday, 10 February 1912, but Susie's son Howard was too ill to awaken to greet their visitor. Susie and her son shortly thereafter wrote to Rogers to acknowledge his visit, in letters dated Saturday, 17 February and Wednesday, 21 February 1912, respectively, which Rogers's widow subsequently gave to her nephew Searles, who reproduced these letters in his magazine *The Annex* in Esoteric Order of Dagon Amateur Press Association mailing 139 for Lammas 2007 (Searles 178–83).

Rogers had spent most of his life in Mount Vernon, New York, where Susie's father-in-law George Lovecraft (1815–1895) had also lived, but lived in Peekskill, New York, by the time he married Searles's aunt Sophie in 1940. He had had an earlier marriage that produced four children and ended in divorce. Rogers and Searles's aunt Sophie met through a mutual interest in political topics. He was a graduate of Cooper Union and had lectured on scientific topics earlier in his life (Searles 182).

Rogers himself gave Searles the boyhood photograph of Lovecraft (aged six years six months) in a sailor suit (first published in *Fantasy Commentator* for Spring 1945 and reprinted as the frontispiece for *Something about Cats* [Arkham House, 1949]). Rogers's widow later gave her nephew the 1912 letters written to Rogers by Susie and Howard, a photograph of Lovecraft aged eight and one-half months (probably taken early May 1891), a photograph of his mother Susie, and a photograph of his maternal grandfather Whipple V. Phillips[67] (Searles 179).

New York City Lovecraft collector Jack Grill[68] owned an early (c. 1891–92) family group photograph containing Susie, Howard, and Winfield Lovecraft, reproduced as the frontispiece for *The Shuttered Room* (Arkham House, 1959) and a photograph (c. 1895) of the family home at 454 Angell Street including Lovecraft's grandparents, his mother,[69] and his younger aunt (reproduced in the same volume opposite page 48), both of which he may possibly have obtained from Rogers, although Lovecraft's first cousin Ida (Hill) Lyon (1874–1951) of Pelham, New York, or relatives in Rochester, New York, are other possible sources.[70]

----

67. Searles published these three photographs in *Fantasy Commentator* for Spring 1948.

68. For Grill's collection see Mark Owings and Irving Binkin, *A Catalog of Lovecraftiana: The Grill/Binkin Collection* (Baltimore: Mirage Press, 1975). The c. 1891–92 family photograph is item 532 and the c. 1895 home photograph is item 536 in this book (both page 57). Both photographs are reproduced in the photographic plate section of the book although the home photograph is mislabeled as item 534. The family photograph was earlier reproduced in *Fresco* for Spring 1958.

69. I have contended that HPL's pet cat Nigger-Man is held by his mother in this photograph, but Sean Donnelly and Donovan K. Loucks have questioned my identification.

70. As of this writing, these two photographs are owned by Florida writer, editor, designer, bookseller, and bibliophile Sean Donnelly, who has collaborated with me on two collections of the work of HPL's friend Edith Miniter (1867–1934) published by Hippocampus Press, *Dead Houses* (2010) and *The Village Green* (2013). Donnelly used an enlargement of a portion of the c. 1895 photograph of 454 Angell Street as the front cover for the paper edition of HPL's *The Case of Charles Dexter Ward* (Tampa, FL: University of Tampa Press, 2010). In his editorial capacity with University of Tampa Press, Donnelly did the design work for S. T. Joshi and David E. Schultz's edition of HPL's letters to Robert H. Barlow, *O Fortunate Floridian!* (Tampa, FL: University of Tampa Press, 2007). Donnelly has also edited two collections of the work of HPL's friend W. Paul Cook: *Willis T. Crossman's Vermont: Stories by W. Paul Cook* (Tampa, FL: University of Tampa Press, 2005) and *W. Paul Cook: The Wandering Life of a Yankee Printer* (New York: Hippocampus Press, 2007). Leland M. Hawes, Jr. (1929–2013) was Donnelly's co-editor for the first title.

Conclusion

Whether Lovecraft's informant was Nelson Rogers, Emma Jane (Lovecraft) Hill, Ida (Hill) Lyon, or some other person, or whether he simply was motivated by his friend Wilfred B. Talman to study his 1905 copy of the Allgood chart(s) more closely than he had when he corresponded with Moe and Kleiner in 1915–16, we can be grateful that Lovecraft shared his enriched (or refreshed) knowledge of his paternal ancestry with us in his 1927 letter to Long and his 1931 letter to Moe. Despite the inaccuracies undoubtedly contained in Lovecraft's accounts of his paternal ancestry, he provides a wealth of detail that has already brought forth books from Richard D. Squires (1995); Chris J. Docherty, A. Langley Searles and me (2003); and David Acord (2013). The effectiveness of Lovecraft's fiction is strongly dependent upon his carefully constructed settings and chronologies, both of which are informed by his interest in family history (QAT 14). The study of Lovecraft's ancestry will continue to influence the study of the man and his work. New resources and new technologies that become available in the future will probably provide future students with a much fuller knowledge of Lovecraft's ancestry than we have today. It is possible that future students will even have the benefit of a nearly complete Lovecraft family genealogy—something of which we can only dream today.[71] As we prepare to celebrate the one hundred twenty-fifth anniversary of Lovecraft's birth in 2015, we can rest assured that Lovecraft himself, who laboriously copied the family records borrowed from his great-aunt in 1905, would

---

71. Docherty, Searles, and I did create a draft genealogy *Lovecraft, Lovecroft and Allied Families* (DSF2) in 2004. It consists of three sections: family groups, alphabetical register of records, and chronological register of records. It is very far from a complete family genealogy, which may not be possible based upon currently available records and technology. In 2014, I donated a copy of the manuscript of this draft genealogy, along with an archive of other research materials relating to HPL's family history, including the correspondence I received from my collaborators Chris J. Docherty and A. Langley Searles, to the Lovecraft Collection at Brown University. Chris J. Docherty felt strongly that the draft genealogy needed to be enhanced with charts that would illustrate family relationships more clearly. Charts drawn by Docherty and by our correspondent Richard McWilliams form part of the archive that I donated to Brown University.

share our dreams if he were still among us. The longest verified human lifespan as of this writing was that of Jeanne Calment (1875–1997) of Arles, France, who lived 122 years 164 days.[72] Thus, by 20 August 2015 Lovecraft's generation will likely have disappeared completely from among us; the author and his contemporaries will truly belong to the ages.[73] Nevertheless, we can be confident that the legacy of the man and of his work, including our knowledge of his ancestry, will continue to grow.

Works Cited

Acord, David. *The Other Mr. Lovecraft: A True Story of Tragedy and the Supernatural from H. P. Lovecraft's Family Tree.* 2013. An electronic book available for purchase from Amazon.com.

Beckwith, Henry L. P., Jr. *Lovecraft's Providence and Adjacent Parts.* West Kingston, RI: Donald M. Grant, 2nd ed. 1986.

de Camp, L. Sprague. *Lovecraft: A Biography.* Garden City, NY: Doubleday, 1975.

Docherty, Chris J.; Searles, A. Langley; and Faig, Kenneth W., Jr. *Devonshire Ancestry of Howard Phillips Lovecraft.* Glenview, IL: Moshassuck Press, 2003. [DSF] (An electronic version of this title

---

72. For Jeanne Calment, see Michel Allard, Victor Lèbre, and Jean-Marie Robine, *Jeanne Calment: From Van Gogh's Time to Ours* (New York: W. H. Freeman, 1998).

73. I am aware that there still survive a few very young correspondents of Lovecraft, now aged ninety or more (i.e., born 1925 or earlier). Arthur L. Widner, Jr. (b. 1917–2015), is no longer among us, but I certainly hope that HPL's young correspondent Charles H. Bloomer, Jr. (b. 1915) may be when we celebrate the one hundred twenty-fifth anniversary of the author's birth on 20 August 2015. Harry Kern Brobst (1909–2010), who met HPL when he attended Brown University and worked as a psychiatric nurse in Providence in the 1930s, was probably the last surviving adult friend of HPL who met the author in person. (As far as I am aware, neither Bloomer nor Widner ever met HPL in person.) For Brobst, see Christopher M. O'Brien, "In Memoriam: Dr. Harry K. Brobst (1909–2010)," *Lovecraft Annual* 4 (2010): 166–70. HPL's kinswoman Elizabeth A. (Morrish) Drew (b. 1930), the youngest daughter of Ethel M. (Phillips) Morrish (1888–1987) and Roy A. Morrish, Jr., remembers visiting HPL and his aunt Annie E. (Phillips) Gamwell in their home at 66 College Street in Providence about 1936 (see her memoir "Some Phillips Family Memories," *The Pear Tree* [Glenview, IL: Kenneth W. Faig, Jr.] no. 3 [All Saints (i.e., 1 November) 1997]: 2).

is available on familysearch.org. Go to https://familysearch.org/ catalog-search/ and search for call number 929.273 L941.)

————. *Lovecraft, Lovecroft and Allied Families*. Unpublished manuscript (2004), John Hay Library, Brown University. [DSF 2]

Evans, Rev. H[enry] R[ichard]. "Broadhempston." *Transactions of the Devonshire Association* 90 (1958): 62–126. [EVB]

————. "Woodland." *Transactions of the Devonshire Association* 92 (1960): 158–232. [EVW]

Everts, R. Alain. "The Lovecraft Family in America." *Xenophile* [St. Louis, Missouri: Nils Hardin] 2, no. 6 (October 1975): 7, 16.

Faig, Kenneth W., Jr. *George Elliott Lovecraft: Lost Scion of the House of Lovecraft*. Glenview, IL: Moshassuck Press, 2010. [LSHL] (An electronic version of this title is available on familysearch.org. Go to https://familysearch.org/catalog-search/ and search for call number 921.73 L941.)

————. "The Impact of the Fulford Will on Lovecraft's Claims of Fulford Ancestry." *Moshassuck Review* [Glenview, IL: Kenneth W. Faig, Jr.; published for the Esoteric Order of Dagon Amateur Press Association] (August 1996): 1–3. [IFW] (Contains a reproduction and a transcription of Rev. Francis Fulford's Prerogative Court of Canterbury will [1772].)

————. *Lovecraft's Pillow and Other Strange Stories*. New York: Hippocampus Press, 2013. [LP]

————. "Quae Amamus Tuemur: Ancestors in Lovecraft's Life and Fiction."[74] In Faig's *The Unknown Lovecraft*. New York: Hippocampus Press, 2008. 14–49. [QAT] (There was an earlier separate publication of this essay in *Quae Amamus Tuemur: Ancestors in Lovecraft's Life and Fiction* [Glenview, IL: Moshassuck Press, 2008]. An electronic version of the Moshassuck Press printing of this essay is available on familysearch.org. Go to https://familysearch.org/ catalog-search/ and search for call number 929.273 L941. The page citations for [QAT] in this paper use the Hippocampus Press edition.)

Hanks, Patrick, and Paula Hodges. *A Dictionary of Surnames*. Oxford: Oxford University Press, 1988.

---

74. HPL provided the Lovecraft family motto ("Quae Amamus Tuemur") in his letter to Richard F. Searight dated 14 November 1934 (*RFS* 36). S. T. Joshi translates this motto as "We Defend the Things We Love" (QAT 14).

Joshi, S. T. *The Assaults of Chaos.* New York: Hippocampus Press, 2013.

———. *I Am Providence: The Life and Times of H. P. Lovecraft.* New York: Hippocampus Press, 2010.

Lovecraft, H. P. *Letters to Richard F. Searight.* Edited by David E. Schultz, S. T. Joshi, and Franklyn Searight. West Warwick, RI: Necronomicon Press, 1992. [*RFS*]

Mellor, Moira, *Looking Back: People and Places in Broadhempston.* Totnes, UK: Broadhempston Society, 2006.

Orme, Nicholas. *The Saints of Cornwall.* Oxford: Oxford University Press, 2002.

Searles, A. Langley. "Recollections: VIII: Family Matters." *The Annex* [Bronxville, NY: A. Langley Searles; published for the Esoteric Order of Dagon Amateur Press Association] (Summer 2007): 175–84.

Sneyd, Steve. "Hunting for Lovecraft's Ancestors." *Ibid* [Teaneck, NJ: Benjamin P. Indick; published for the Esoteric Order of Dagon Amateur Press Association] (January–March 1999): 2–3.

Squires, Richard D. *Stern Fathers 'neath the Mould: The Lovecraft Family in Rochester.* West Warwick, RI: Necronomicon Press, 1995.

Lovecraft and Houellebecq: Two Against the World

Todd Spaulding

Introduction

The acceptance of H. P. Lovecraft as an author worthy of the Library of America has been the result of a modified reception or image of Lovecraft. Once marginalized as a pulp fiction writer, he has now gained renown among his non-academic readers, and serious academic analysis of Lovecraft has yielded many insightful interpretations. There are ample academic and non-academic publications to serve as evidence. The work of American scholars has served to guide Lovecraft to other languages, bringing Anglophone interpretations based on cultural fashion (ideology and cultural norms, for example). Indeed, this should come as no surprise to anyone familiar with the basics of literary criticism. His work, and he himself, are constantly under various gazes, whether structuralist, postmodern, queer theory, or astrophysics. One interesting aspect of Anglophone, in particular American, Lovecraft studies is a lack of attention to the cultural image formation under the manipulation of the translator. Or more precisely, there is a distinct lack of the "other" in the form of foreign critical output of Lovecraft.

The history of literature is, after all, a theory of translation. Antoine Berman, a translation theorist, reflects:

> It is impossible to separate the history of translation from the history of languages, of cultures, and of literatures ... this is not a question of mixing everything up, but of showing how in each period or in each given historical setting the practice of translation is articulated in relation to the practice of literature, of language, of the several intercultural and interlinguistic exchanges. (2)

The process by which one translates is relative to cultural norms and ideologies, as well as to the socio-historical context with regard to the translating culture. At this point, the source language and the source text are no longer culturally foreign objects but objects of the translating culture. In essence, the translator is a mediator who carries meaning across the barrier of language. Lovecraft's image is therefore culturally contingent with regard to translation. The American image of HPL is well known among the Anglophone world, but what is Lovecraft's image outside of our largely monolinguistic academic field?

The purpose of this article is to reveal a glimpse at the modern image of Lovecraft in France. His French literary history is as rich and intriguing as his American literary history, yet it is largely unknown to an Anglophone reader. Anyone familiar with Lovecraft's oeuvre is keenly aware of a difference between the "Dream Cycle" and the "Cthulhu Mythos" texts.[1] The French were first fascinated with his "Dream Cycle" texts, notably "The Statement of Randolph Carter," "The Silver Key," "Through the Gates of the Silver Key," and *The Dream-Quest of Unknown Kadath*, which were translated under the title *Démons et merveilles* (*Demons and Marvels*) in 1955. Lovecraft, however, was introduced to France two years earlier, when two surrealists, Robert Benayoun and Gerard Legrand, published an article titled "H. P. Lovecraft et la lune noire" ("H. P. Lovecraft and the Black Moon") in the surrealist esoteric/supernatural–minded magazine *Médium*. For the surrealists, Lovecraft's texts served as examples of the power of the unconscious mind—indeed, in understanding the surrealist concepts of the marvelous and the uncanny, one can make the plausible argument that Lovecraft is a surrealist author, or at the very least lends himself to surrealist interpretations.

Lovecraft's surrealist image was then refracted by Jacques Bergier and Louis Pauwels's esoteric philosophical treatise *Le Matin des magiciens* (*The Morning of the Magicians*) in 1960. The authors explain that their worldview or philosophy is the exact opposite

---

1. The author is entirely aware of the history of use and implications in bifurcating HPL's oeuvre with the terms "Dream Cycle" and "Cthulhu Mythos." However, for simplicity's sake, the terms will suffice for this paper.

of surrealism: rather than looking for untapped potential and powers of the unconscious mind, it is in the supraconscious or a heightened wakened state that harbors man's potential. For Bergier and Pauwels, it is this supraconscious that unlocks man's hidden abilities such as extrasensory perception, precognition, astral projection, etc. In other words, the marvelous does not unravel itself in the depths of the unconscious mind, but in the everyday; and it is when one is fully "awake" that one can see the marvelous unravel itself in the mundane quotidian.

Le Matin des magiciens is something of an alchemy of scientific fact combined with "traditional" or mystic knowledge. Although Lovecraft is mentioned in the book only once, he was a constant feature in Bergier and Pauwels's magazine *Planète* (1961–68). Essentially, *Planète*'s 40-issue run is an extension of *Le Matin des magiciens*, where science fact and evidence appear alongside fictional work of other authors and alternate history documents. Bergier in particular shaped Lovecraft's place in the French culture in his preface of the first mass-market publication of Lovecraft's work in France, Deux-Rives's *Démons et merveilles*. "H. P. Lovecraft, ce grand génie venu d'ailleurs" ("H. P. Lovecraft, this great genius from elsewhere") was reprinted numerous times up through the 1980s and 1990s, its tendrils extending from a scholarly en vogue atmosphere of primitivism reigning in the academic sector with heavy interpretative analysis commuting from fields such as anthropology and ethnology and histories of religion, Claude-Levi Strauss and Mircea Eliade, to name a few such influential thinkers in France in the 1950s.[2] Bergier presented a Lovecraft who believed verbatim what he recounted in his tales—he was a mad poet who lived asynchronically with his cultural time-milieu. In this respect, both American and French Lovecraft studies have something in common: both were under the influence of a personage who interpreted Lovecraft's œuvre and overall worldview incorrectly. August Derleth's counterpart is none other than Jacques Bergier. One reason for Bergier's wholesale construc-

---

2. The French Lovecraftian Michel Meurger explored this topic more fully this topic in "Retrograde Anticipation: Primitivism and Occultism in the French Response to Lovecraft 1953–1957," tr. S. T. Joshi, *Lovecraft Studies* Nos. 19–20 (Fall 1989): 5–19.

tion or refraction of Lovecraft in France is that most of Lovecraft's nonfiction, what I have termed his *ars supernaturalis*, were simply unavailable in French in until 1991.[3] Lovecraft criticism in France, then, was free to develop apart from the Anglophone community, which had access to the entirety of Lovecraft's œuvre with the death of August Derleth in 1971.

As S. T. Joshi has remarked, the French hold particularly "significant and provocative views about Lovecraft" ("Preface" xiii). For the most part these views have developed largely in isolation to the cultural fashions in which Lovecraft's introduction took place. The image of Lovecraft in France has encountered a renaissance, so to speak, since the entirety of his œuvre was made available in 1991; however, only one volume of his letters has been translated. The French Lovecraft image has gradually become parallel to that of the American Lovecraft image, having evolved similarly from different cultural contexts.

This article is a look into the status of Lovecraft in France. I have chosen three modern French critical works on Lovecraft: Michel Houellebecq's *H. P. Lovecraft: Contre le monde, contre la vie*, Didier Hendrickx's *H. P. Lovecraft: Le Dieu silencieux*, and Cédric Monget's *Lovecraft: Le Dernier Puritain*. I have attempted this analysis to determine how much of the French Lovecraft has been influenced by American Lovecraft studies vis-à-vis Lovecraft's particularly unique French literary history.

In this study Houellebecq's *H. P. Lovecraft* functions as a signpost. As a marker, it is Bergian in influence, although unmistakably modern and forward-thinking enough to blaze a new trail. Through analysis of Houellebecq's book, this article explores the high points of what we will call "modern" French Lovecraft studies. This "modern" period dates from 1991 to the present day. This article seeks a response to the question: What influence has Houelle-

---

3. *Ars supernaturalis* is the term that I have designated for the group of HPL texts in which he describes his philosophy behind weird fiction. Those texts are: "Commonplace Book" (1919–36), *In Defence of Dagon* (1921), "Lord Dunsany and His Work" (1922), "Supernatural Horror in Literature" (1925–27), "Notes on Writing Weird Fiction" (1932/33), "Some Notes on Interplanetary Fiction" (1934), and "In Memoriam: Robert Ervin Howard" (1936).

becq's interpretation of Lovecraft had on Lovecraft studies in France and beyond? I maintain that Houellebecq's interpretation has had a great deal of influence for the academically minded Lovecraft reader and scholar in France. His book reveals a complex and ambiguous Lovecraft whose attitude and philosophy operate in reaction to a hostile world and life. This attitude is certainly part of the French spirit as observed in the existentialist movement that Jean-Paul Sartre and Albert Camus spearheaded. Sartre and Camus's texts explore the vacuity of meaning in the world, and from this standpoint a world hostile to mankind, indifferent at best.

Lovecraft and Houellebecq: Against Both the World and Life

It is clear that Michel Houellebecq benefited from the explosion of the scholarly and popular interest in Lovecraft that blossomed following the 1960s. His book was published in France in 1991 and in the United States in 2005. Whereas Bergier had little to go on and therefore invented Lovecraft's image as a "genius from elsewhere," Houellebecq's Lovecraft is a distilled image composed of information garnered from L. Sprague de Camp's *Lovecraft: A Biography* (1975),[4] Lovecraft's own correspondence, and various other sources, including Houellebecq's particular outlook on life. His worldview is very much influenced by his observation that the cultural revolution of May 1968 in France has led to turmoil and even further alienation between man and society in France (or even in the West). Houellebecq's literature is a fusion of cosmic indifference, existentialism, and a seething criticism of modern society. His interpretations of Lovecraft were only possible following the publication of a certain amount of scholarship in the form of articles, biographies, or books. There has been a certain time lag because of the time (roughly 1953 to 1991) it took for Lovecraft's work to be translated in its entirety into French. The availability

---

4. L. Sprague de Camp's *Lovecraft: A Biography* was published in hardcover in 1975 by Doubleday. A year later (1976) a corrected and abridged version appeared in paperback from Ballantine Books. Barnes & Noble republished the latter in hardcover in 1996.

of Lovecraft in France has irrevocably altered the image of Love-craft, and Houellebecq's book is symptomatic of that change.

There are two general images of Lovecraft in France. First, there is Jacques Bergier's Lovecraft as a mystical-madman-genius. This coexisted with Michel Houellebecq's Lovecraft as an antilife-poet-genius. The distinction is marked in the final line of Houel-lebecq's *H. P. Lovecraft:*

> Offrir une alternative à la vie sous toutes ses formes, constituer une opposition permanente, un recours permanent à la vie: telle est la plus haute mission du poète sur cette terre. Howard Phillips Lovecraft a rempli cette mission. [To offer an alternative to life in all its forms constitutes a permanent opposition, a permanent re-course to life—this is the poet's highest mission on this earth. Howard Phillips Lovecraft fulfilled this mission.] (130; tr. Dorna Khazeni 119)

This citation demonstrates Houellebecq's view of Lovecraft as a poet. While Bergier's Lovecraft was certainly a mad genius, Bergier would never have described Lovecraft as a poet. If anything, Berg-ier's Lovecraft is a kind of crackpot/madman infused with esoter-ic ideals.

H. P. Lovecraft: Contre le monde, contre la vie is split into three distinct parts: "Another Universe," "Technical Assault," and "Holo-caust." We will proceed to analyze the book in order to isolate his image of Lovecraft.

Another Universe

In this section, Houellebecq explores the philosophical atheism and materialism that underscore Lovecraft's stories and reinforce his crushing cosmic (or world) view. In the cosmic viewpoint, man's position as referent (that by which all things are measured and given meaning) is peripheral at best. Houellebecq remarks that Lovecraft's textual universe is "à ce point imprégné, transper-cé jusqu'à l'os par le néant absolu de toute aspiration humaine . . . Tout disparaîtra. Et les actions humaines sont aussi libres et dé-nuées de sens que les libres mouvements des particules élémen-taires" [so impregnated, pierced to the core, by the conviction of the absolute futility of human aspiration [and in fact,] everything will disappear. And human actions are as free and as stripped of meaning as the unfettered movement of the elementary particles] (13; tr. Khazeni 33). In this universe we are not even beyond good and evil, or other ideas driven by morality, because these do not exist outside of humanity.

Reading Lovecraft's texts should be considered an event, that is, "a change of the very frame through which we perceive the world and engage in it" (Žižek 12). Lovecraft has changed the face of horror in literature, starting with what can be considered "la littérature fantastique" and creating something entirely new, infused with scientific realism, marking the need for the new genre of weird fiction. Houellebecq notes that

> Depuis l'introduction du virus en France par Jacques Bergier, la progression du nombre de lecteurs a été considérable. Comme la plupart des contaminés, j'ai moi-même découvert HPL à l'âge de seize ans par l'intermédiaire d'un 'ami.' Pour un choc, c'en fut un. Je ne savais pas que la littérature pouvait faire ça. Et, d'ailleurs, je n'en suis toujours pas persuadé. Il y a quelque chose de *pas vraiment littéraire* chez Lovecraft.

> [Ever since [Lovecraft's] virus was first introduced into France by Jacques Bergier, the increase in the number of readers has been substantial. Like most of those contaminated, I myself discovered HPL at sixteen through the intermediary of a 'friend.' To call it a shock would be an understatement. I had not known literature was capable of this. And, what's more, I'm still not sure it is. There is something not really literary about Lovecraft's work.] (17; tr. Khazeni 34)

One can imagine a feverish Houellebecq reading *The Case of Charles Dexter Ward*, eagerly devouring the pages in much the same way that Charles Dexter Ward himself sought out arcane knowledge in forbidden books.[5] One story is simply not enough;

---

5. *The Case of Charles Dexter Ward* is essentially a story about Ward's ancestral ties to esoteric concepts such as alchemy, necromancy, and sorcery. He becomes so engrossed in his ancestry that he is eventually murdered by an ancestor whom he resurrects through occult application of esoteric knowledge.

one must read another, and another, always wanting more. One craves the experience of Lovecraft's mythology and of mankind's interaction with it. Houellebecq defines this as ritual literature. The reader rediscovers the ritual with impatience, "il [le] retrouve avec un plaisir grandissant, à chaque fois séduit par une nouvelle répétition en des termes légèrement différents, qu'il sent comme un nouvel approfondissement" [he return[s] to it] with mounting pleasure, seduced each time by a different repetition of terms, ever so imperceptibly altered to allow him to reach a new depth of experience] (19; tr. Khazeni 37). It is this experience, and the desire to reproduce the experience, that, for Houellebecq, affirms the virus-like or non-literary quality of Lovecraft's literature.

Houellebecq elegantly describes Lovecraft's "oeuvre [comme] une imposante architecture baroque, étagée par paliers larges et somptueux, comme une succession de cercles concentriques autour d'un vortex d'horreur et d'émerveillement absolus" [body of work [as] an imposing baroque structure, its towering strata rising in so many layered concentric circles, a wide and sumptuous landing around each—the whole surrounding a vortex of pure horror and absolute marvel] (24; tr. Khazeni 40). In this view, the outermost circle contains Lovecraft's correspondence and poetry; these are neither published in their entirety nor are they available in translation.[6] The second circle contains Lovecraft's ghostwritten and collaborative stories, including the tales that Derleth "finished" from Lovecraft's notes. The third circle contains Lovecraft's stories, all of which are available in French. The fourth or innermost circle contains what Houellebecq terms "the great texts." Hovering above this arrangement is Houellebecq's analysis of Lovecraft's personality. Houellebecq also names the most important "great texts" of Lovecraft's, all of which were published in the years following his return to Providence. The "great texts" are: "The Call of Cthulhu," "The Colour out of Space," "The Dunwich Horror," "The Whisperer in Darkness," *At the Mountains of Madness*, "The

---

6. In 2001 all HPL's poems were published by Night Shade Books in a volume edited by S. T. Joshi entitled *The Ancient Track: Complete Poetical Works of H. P. Lovecraft*. More recently, *The Ancient Track* was revised in 2013 and published by Hippocampus Press.

Shadow over Innsmouth," "The Dreams in the Witch House," and "The Shadow out of Time."

Houellebecq's image of Lovecraft is distinct from Bergier's in that Lovecraft's antihumanist worldview appears to resonate more with Houellebecq's own worldview as seen in his works. By this, I mean to say that many of Houellebecq's stories seem to portray a very Lovecraftian position on the meaninglessness of mankind. This worldview, as Bergier has suggested, is more poignant and more tangible once one has suffered greatly. In a kind of structuralist description of Lovecraft's oeuvre, Houellebecq envisions a vortex surrounded by four distinct circles, each of which is populated by various elements of Lovecraft's oeuvre. Above this interplay of chaos and horror floats Lovecraft's persona (cold, antihuman, antilife), the one he inhabited and the one his readers have created. In a nutshell, Lovecraft's universe opens the reader up to anything but tranquility. Houellebecq believes this universe has an "impact sur la conscience du lecteur" [impact on the reader's mind] (26; tr. Khazeni). It is "une brutalité sauvage, effrayante; et il ne se dissipe qu'avec une dangereuse lenteur" [a savage, frightening brutality, and dangerously slow to dissipate] (26; tr. Khazeni 42). While this statement was impossible before Houellebecq, it indicates a certain change in perception of Lovecraft's oeuvre as a whole in France. Here it becomes a non-literary reception. For Houellebecq, Lovecraft can be read as an *event* rather than as a literary text, in that the *event* is a unique occurrence altering the way something is perceived. Perhaps Houellebecq perceives in Lovecraft's oeuvre an expression of what Houellebecq interprets as the West's malaise in the rise in consumerism and the loss of the traditional society (i.e., the West's pre–World War II society) as well as the loss of self that the entirety of Western thought has explored.

Technical Assault

Houellebecq regards Lovecraft's "Supernatural Horror in Literature" as somehow outdated and disappointing, for the simple fact that Lovecraft did not take his own oeuvre into account.[7] As

---

7. Composed between 1925 and 1927, this essay was published just before HPL's "great texts" were unleashed onto the world. The first French translation by Berg-

Houellebecq writes, "sans doute a-t-il ressenti le besoin ... de ré-
capituler tout ce qui s'était fait dans le domaine fantastique avant
de le faire éclater en se lançant dans des voies radicalement nou-
velles" [Lovecraft must have felt a need to recapitulate all that had
been done in the domain of horror fiction before exploding its
casing and setting off on radically new paths] (34; tr. Khazeni 47).
For Houellebecq, it was as if Lovecraft needed to create a mausoleum so as to provide a resting place for what existed prior to the
catastrophe that his texts left behind, a kind of place to visit out
of morbid curiosity.

Although Lovecraft wrote for his own pleasure and for that of
his friends, his stories were also published and read by the public.
But according to Houellebecq, Lovecraft "écrit pour un public de
fanatiques; public qu'il finira par trouver, quelques années après sa
mort" [tends to pick his readers from the start. He writes for an
audience of fanatics—readers he was to finally find only years after his death] (41; tr. Khazeni 53). Who are these readers? Who are
those affected souls who have suffered greatly? It would seem
here that Houellebecq is not necessarily referring to those who
eagerly participated in the ritual of reading Lovecraft's material as
it was published in *Weird Tales*. Rather, Houellebecq seems to
imply that the generation of scholars who have analyzed his texts
in a "postmodern" world are the readers for whom he wrote. In
any case, Lovecraft's stories are meticulously precise, all of them
building up an atmosphere of dread and terror that culminate in
the last few pages of the story. Everything is treated realistically,
aside from the one weird event that, in return, casts doubt on the
whole architecture of reality. Houellebecq analyzes this effect on
Lovecraft's characters, who fare no better than Star Trek's "red
shirts" who accompany Kirk on missions—they are always the
ones who die. However, Lovecraft's characters seem to be unable
to piece together what is happening, nor do they ever arrive at the
conclusion that they should not explore a specific location in the
middle of the night because it will either cause them to go insane
or, better yet, do die.

---

ier and François Truchaud was available by 1969 as *Epouvante et surnaturel en
littérature*.

Houellebecq summarizes Lovecraft's attitude toward the world as "[u]ne haine absolue du monde en général, aggravée d'un dégoût particulier pour le monde moderne" [an absolute hatred [. . .], aggravated by an aversion to the modern world in particular] (46; tr. Khazeni 57). According to Houellebecq, Lovecraft's literature depends on this hatred toward the modern world, and this hatred is conditioned on the "[l]e rejet de toute forme de réalisme" [rejection of all forms of realism] (46; tr. Khazeni 57). In Houellebecq's own texts, sexuality and money occupy a large portion of thematic content, but for Lovecraft these are the only two realities not included. The absence of both sexuality and money is not due to "obscurs motifs psychologiques, mais à une conception esthétique nettement affirmée . . . s'il refuse dans son œuvre la moindre allusion de nature sexuelle, c'est avant tout parce qu'il sent que de telles allusions ne peuvent avoir aucune place dans son univers esthétique" [hidden psychological motives, but an aesthetic conception clearly articulated . . . if he refused all sexual allusions in his work it was first and foremost because he felt such allusions had no place in his aesthetic universe] (48–49; tr. Khazeni 58–59). Houellebecq attributes this aesthetic refusal to Lovecraft's "Victorian pruderies," which corresponds to his self-imposed genteel behavior (50; tr. Khazeni 60). The power of Houellebecq's analysis in this section can be summed up in the fact that Lovecraft's aesthetic choice, or creative limitation, is not necessarily dependent upon "un quelconque 'trafiquage' idéologique . . . Lovecraft, lui, n'essaie pas de repeindre dans une couleur différente les éléments de la réalité qui lui déplaisent; avec détermination, il les ignore" [any sort of traffic in ideology . . . Lovecraft does not try to repaint the elements of reality that displease him; he resolutely ignores them] (51; tr. Khazeni 62). This resolution is resoundingly a combination of both his own philosophy and, according to Houellebecq, a technical imperative.

The most compelling portion of this section is the way in which Houellebecq analyzes Lovecraft's oeuvre through architectural concepts; we discover architecture by moving within it, and to some degree neither a painting nor a film can quite capture Lovecraft's imagery, neither his non-Euclidean imagined structures nor the description of colors that are not quite colors. For example in "The Colour out of Space," Lovecraft relates the observable facts of a strange meteorite that landed near his fictitious New England city of Arkham: "The colour, which resembled some of the bands in the meteor's strange spectrum, was almost impossible to describe; and it was only by analogy that they called it colour at all" (*CF* 2.373). Houellebecq looks to Lovecraft's correspondence to support his theory that Lovecraft experiences "une transe esthétique violente en présence d'une belle architecture" [a trancelike state when [he] look[s] at beautiful architecture] (59; tr. Khazeni 65). Not only do his characters experience this "violent trancelike state," but readers also enter a trancelike state when confronting Lovecraft's vertiginous use of adjectives to construct his imagery. For Houellebecq, Lovecraft's architecture is sacred because it is

> comme celle des grande cathédrales, comme celle des temples hindous, l'architecture de H.P. Lovecraft est beaucoup, plus qu'un jeu mathématique de volumes. Elle est entièrement imprégnée par l'idée d'une dramaturgie essentielle, d'une dramaturgie mythique qui donne son sens à l'édifice ... C'est une architecture *vivante*, car elle repose sur une conception vivante et émotionnelle du monde.

> [like that of great cathedrals, like that of Hindu temples, is much more than a three-dimensional mathematical puzzle. It is entirely imbued with an essential dramaturgy that gives its meaning to the edifice ... It is *living* architecture because at its foundation lies a living and emotional concept of the world.] (62; tr. Khazeni 66)

For Catholics and Hindus, their places of worship are tied to the importance of mankind's place in their respective cosmology. However, Lovecraft's architectural spaces are blatantly organized around a cosmology indifferent to man. This vision resounds nicely with and even supports the contention that Lovecraft's literature is ritualistic, in that his stories themselves constitute the sacred spaces wherein the ritual is experienced.

Houellebecq next analyzes perception in Lovecraft's stories, in particular the lack of psychological depth in his characters. Lovecraft's characters are essentially void of such characteristics be-

cause "tout trait psychologique trop accusé [aurait]" [a more ob-
trusive psychological brushstroke would have] led the story from
the domain of "l'épouvante matérielle" [material horror] to
"l'épouvante psychique" [psychological horror] (65; tr. Khazeni
68). Lovecraft's characters therefore are sense receptacles, "[des
observateurs] muets, immobiles, totalement impuissant, paralysés"
[silent, motionless, utterly powerless, paralyzed observers] (66; tr.
Khazeni 69). To support such a thesis, Houellebecq resorts to textual citation that indeed reflects the disarming effects of adjectives
as they gather into an amorphous "crescendo hideux" [hideous cre-
scendo], eventually releasing the character in a malaise of fear and
panic (66; tr. Khazeni 69).

Lovecraft's particular brand of weird fiction is difficult to cate-
gorize, as S. T. Joshi also has observed.[8] Houellebecq says this is
because "en introduisant de force dans le récit fantastique le voca-
bulaire et les concepts des secteurs de la connaissance humain . . .
il vient de faire éclater son cadre" [by forcefully introducing the
language and concepts of scientific sectors . . . he has exploded the
casing of the horror story] (72; tr. Khazeni 74). Houellebecq accu-
rately describes Lovecraft's effect on the horror genre, as well as
Lovecraft's vision that weird fiction is not one genre but a blas-
phemous hybrid offspring that recounts "antilife." Lovecraft lived
in a time of extraordinary scientific advancement both in theory
and in practice. In an effort to positively describe the universe in
objective means, the sciences, according to Houellebecq,

> lui fourniront cet outil de démultiplication visionnaire dont il a
> besoin. HPL, en effet, vise à une épouvante objective. Une épou-
> vante déliée de toute connotation psychologique ou humaine . . .
> De même que Kant veut poser les fondements d'une morale va-
> lable 'non seulement pour l'homme, mais pour toute créature rai-
> sonnable en général,' Lovecraft veut créer un fantastique capable
> de terrifier toute créature douée de raison.

> [furnished him with the tools he needed to transmit his vision.
> Indeed, HPL's aim was objective terror. A terror unbound from
> any human or psychological connotations . . . Just as Kant hoped

---

8. Of note more recently is S. T. Joshi's *Unutterable Horror: A History of Supernatural Fiction* (2012).

to set the foundation of a valid ethical code 'not just for man but for all rational beings,' Lovecraft wanted to create a horror capable of tarrying all creatures endowed with reason.] (76; tr. Khazeni 77)

Never before have Lovecraft and Kant been mentioned in the same sentence, nor in such an analogous way. Houellebecq elevates Lovecraft by his association with Kant. According to Houellebecq, the commonality between the two men is "leur volonté héroïque et paradoxale de passer *par-dessus* l'humanité" [the[ir] heroic and paradoxical desire to *go beyond* humanity] (76; tr. Khazeni 77). Essentially, Houellebecq believes that Lovecraft's concept of horror is universally valid, albeit for Lovecraft what is universally valid is the eternal struggle between mankind and Cthulhu, or an indifferent universe. For Kant what is valid lies not in the epistemological differences between mankind and the world but in things in and of themselves.

Lastly, Houellebecq analyzes Lovecraft's plot technique and use of description. The plot technique is supplemented by Lovecraft's "overuse" of adjectives, but how else would the "intersection d'entités monstrueuses, situées dans des sphères inimaginables et interdites, avec le plan de notre existence ordinaire" [collision of monstrous entities hailing from unimaginable, forbidden worlds with the plane of our ordinary existence] be described (81; tr. Khazeni 81)? Lovecraft's plot line traces such a trajectory that they have the ability for the reader, while reading the tale, to suspend disbelief in paranormal phenomena. Houellebecq prefers to say that Lovecraft "emporte notre adhésion à l'inconcevable" [converts us into believers of the inconceivable] (81; tr. Khazeni 81). Thus, Lovecraft's non-literality infects us, and now through Lovecraft's philosophy and its execution via aesthetics converts us into believers in the inconceivable.

Holocaust

This section of *H. P. Lovecraft* explores Lovecraft's, shall we say, innate disdain for people who are not categorized as white Anglo-Saxon Protestants. For Houellebecq, and many scholars of Lovecraft including Bergier, Lovecraft's disgust for other races manifested itself during his two-year sojourn in New York City. Prior to this period in his life he was no more racist than was socially acceptable for a white Anglo-Saxon Protestant in the first half of the twentieth century. In New York City, he was "contraint de vivre à New York [City]; il y conna[issait] la haine, le dégoût et la peur . . . et c'est [là] que ses *opinions* racistes se transform[aient] en une authentique névrose raciale" [forced to live in New York City], whère he came to know hatred, disgust, and fear . . . and it was [here] that his racist opinions turned into a full-fledged racist neurosis] (111; tr. Khazeni 105). When his wife Sonia Greene lost her job he had to look and compete for jobs alongside immigrants, and found that his racial background and "superior" upbringing did not give him the cultural advantage he had always been told he had. Houellebecq postulates that Lovecraft's failure at finding employment was a mystery and that ultimately "il [était] inadaptable à une économie de marché" [he was inadaptable to the market economy] (106; tr. Khazeni 101). Thus, it is not so much that he was unfamiliar with the fundamental realities of American life, it is simply that he offered nothing of value to a market economy besides his writing. This in part must be the result of his personal restrictions as to what he thought were the proper activities and behaviors of a gentleman.

Houellebecq imagines that Lovecraft's socially acceptable level of racism grew into a brutality similar to the way in which two completely different caged animals might react to each other, through aversion and fear. Indeed, when one examines certain letters between Lovecraft and his friends, his descriptions of Italians, Jews, and Asians appear to directly influence his descriptions of netherworld beings and followers of Cthulhu. In "The Horror at Red Hook" (published in *Weird Tales* in January 1927), the narrator describes the denizens of Brooklyn as a "hopeless tangle and enigma; Syrian, Spanish, Italian, and negro elements impinging upon one another, and fragments of Scandinavian and American belts lying not far distant" (CF 1.484). Miscegenation plays a large role in several Lovecraft tales, such as "The Shadow over Innsmouth" and "The Rats in the Walls," and is also heavily present in "Facts concerning the Late Arthur Jermyn and His Family."

All Lovecraft's tales that Houellebecq regards as "great texts" were written after his return to Providence in 1926. As Bergier suggested, not only should one have suffered in order to be able to understand Lovecraft, but it would appear that Lovecraft himself had to suffer greatly, through unemployment and personal problems, in order to pen his greatest tales over the next ten years. According to Houellebecq, Lovecraft's protagonists generally are all WASPish victims, while the "tortionnaires, [les] servants des cultes innommables, ... sont presque toujours des métis, des mulâtres, des sang-mêlés 'de la plus basse espèce" [torturers, servants of innumerable cults, ... are almost always half-breeds, mulattos, of mixed blood, among the basest of species] (116; tr. Khazeni 109). It would be interesting to have Lovecraft's opinion about the Civil Rights movements that traversed Western Europe and North America in the second half of the twentieth century. One thing is for certain: his phobia and hatred for non-whites is a combination of his own failure in New York City and his Puritanical upbringing. Houellebecq does not criticize Lovecraft's racism in terms of morality, but he highlights the fact that Lovecraft's racism translates into his stories through fear of hybridity or miscegenation. In fact, many of the more recent critiques of Lovecraft's racism are culturally explored through miscegenation and Social Darwinism.

Houellebecq's final thoughts are that for Lovecraft,

> l'univers, qu'il conçoit intellectuellement comme indifférent, devient esthétiquement hostile ... [l]'œuvre de sa maturité est restée fidèle à la prostration physique de sa jeunesse, en la transfigurant. Là est le profond secret du génie de Lovecraft, et la source pure de sa poésie : il a réussi à transformer son dégoût de la vie en une hostilité *agissante*.

> [the universe, which intellectually he perceived as being indifferent, became hostile aesthetically ... [t]he work of his mature years remains faithful to the physical prostration of his youth, transforming it. This is the profound secret of Lovecraft's genius, and the pure source of his poetry: he succeeded in transforming his aversion for life into an *effective* hostility.] (130; tr. Khazeni 119)

This last statement seems vaguely similar to Maurice Lévy's postulation that Lovecraft exorcised himself through the act of writing.[9] There is no question that Lovecraft himself felt tied to nine-teenth-century concepts such as those of "the gentleman," "pro-gress," and racial divisions in the social sphere. Bergier's interpretation is curiously devoid of the negativity or hatred that Lovecraft has for the modern world, while Houellebecq perceives Lovecraft's texts to be in direct dialogue with the "évolution du monde moderne [qui] a rendu encore plus présentes, encore plus *vivantes* les phobies lovecraftiennes" [evolution of the modern world [which] has made Lovecraftian phobias ever more present, ever more *alive*] (125; tr. Khazeni 116). Houellebecq implies that the world Lovecraft cherished was destroyed by "[l]a mécanisation et la modernisation . . . [et] [l]es idéaux de liberté et de démocra-tie, qu'il abhorrait, se sont répandus sur la planète" [mechanization and modernization . . . [and] the reach of liberal capitalism [which] has extended over minds] (124; tr. Khazeni 115). Ultimately, the nineteenth-century measurements of the individual no longer hold value, and for Houellebecq, an individual is now measured by "ef-ficacité économique et son potentiel érotique: soit, très exacte-ment, les deux choses que Lovecraft détestait le plus fort" [economic efficiency and erotic potential—that is to say, in terms of the two things Lovecraft most despised] (125; tr. Khazeni 116).

Thus, Houellebecq's Lovecraft is more similar to a misan-thrope than to some esoteric master as Bergier portrayed him. This represents a fundamental change from Bergier's perception of Lovecraft. Perhaps, however, this new image of Lovecraft gains more through Houellebecq's own worldview.

How Much Lovecraft in Houellebecq?

It is no mystery that Houellebecq thinks highly of Lovecraft. Why else would he have written a short "biography"? Indeed, Houel-lebecq's own aesthetic and philosophy, it would seem, as extrapo-lated from his novels, reflects Lovecraft's own sensitive disgust with reality. Many of Houellebecq's characters become disenfran-chised with the materiality of life and the value system that upholds it. It is as if Houellebecq and Lovecraft are the only two people who share a genuine vision of horror in the excessive, increasingly

9. Maurice Lévy, *Lovecraft: A Study in the Fantastic*, translated by S. T. Joshi in 1988.

narcissistic materialistic nature of Western civilization. The characters of both authors are inwardly focused, Lovecraft's in the pursuit of (arcane/forbidden) knowledge, and Houellebecq's in search of the fulfillment of sexual pleasure and monetary gain.

If Lovecraft's rejection of modernization was a total abandonment of sex and money, Houellebecq's rejection comes from a deep involvement with them. The main character of *L'Extension du domaine du lutte* reflects on the analogous features of sex and money. In "a society like ours[,] sex truly represents a second system of differentiation, completely independent of money; and as a system of differentiation it functions just as mercilessly" (*Whatever* 99). In other words, wonders Houellebecq, how do middle-aged individuals react to the passing of the "prime of their life" with regard to sex and money, both of which, according to Houellebecq, are truly the privilege of the young? Houellebecq believes that reading Lovecraft is dangerous because it has the possibility of infecting (affecting) the reader in ways unseen. Equally so, Houellebecq's novels tend to create an aimlessness, a total disgust not only with how the characters react to events, but also in their realization that "the mysteries of time were banal . . . this was the way of the world: youthful optimism fades and happiness and confidence evaporate" (*Particules* 10). After such a revelation, there is nothing left but horror, fear, and disgust; the only option, suicide.

If one reads enough of Michel Houellebecq, then certain lines from *H. P. Lovecraft* will, in all honesty, come as no surprise. Or rather, one could imagine a wooden Lovecraft perched on the lap of Houellebecq the ventriloquist. How much of Houellebecq's description of Lovecraft's abject horror is really Lovecraft's, and how much is it Houellebecq's sentiments? Does it matter? In this "biography" we find the philosophical and aesthetic antilife seeds that sprout up in many of Houellebecq's later novels, such as *Extention du domaine de la lutte* (1994; translated into English in 1996 as *Whatever*), *Les Particules élémentaires* (1998; translated into English in 2000 by Frank Wynne as *Atomised* in England, and as *The Elementary Particles* in the United States), *La Possibilité d'une île* (2005; translated into English in 2006 as *The Possibility of an Island* by Gavin Boyd).

Houellebecq's *Extention du domaine de la lutte* somewhat of a cross between Albert Camus's *L'Étranger* (1942) and J. D. Salinger's *Catcher in the Rye* (1951). Briefly, the book follows its character as he travels to different locations in France in order to train employees of other companies how to use his company's software. The main character already feels indifferent to his life, but silently and openly expresses his disgust in a society that "sickens [him]; advertising sickens [him]; computers make [him] puke. [His] entire work . . . has no meaning" (*Whatever* 82). In a modern world where individual value is determined by economic efficiency and sexual potency, what do we become when we have neither? The main character perfectly isolates his relationship with the modern world: "it's not that I feel tremendously low; it's rather that the world around me appears high" (135). His hero and, indeed, all Houellebecq's characters at one time or another have that moment of self-critical awareness, where they realize that they can no longer keep up with this world and all it demands, whether through age or physicality.

Les Particules élémentaires (1998) follows half-brothers Bruno and Michel, both of whom were quickly given over to their respective grandparents by their libertine mother. In this novel, Houellebecq explores human emotion, behavior, and bodily form analogously through scientific principles and themes. It is only when the story comes to an end that there is any idea that it is set in the future, and indeed that the novel itself is written in honor of humanity. Both Bruno and Michel are unfortunate in Houellebecq's vision of sexual economy. Bruno and Michel, in their own ways, are looking for happiness, which Houellebecq describes as "une émotion intense et profonde, un sentiment de plénitude exaltante ressenti par la conscience entière ; on peut la rapprocher de l'ivresse, du ravissement, de l'extase" [an intense, all-consuming feeling of joyous fulfillment akin to inebriation, rapture or ecstasy] (*Les Particules* 15; tr. Heinemann 10). The half-brothers attempt to experience the happiness their society advertises, sex and money, but Michel soon realizes that "l'univers humain . . . était plein d'angoisse et d'amertume" [human reality . . . was a series of disappointments, bitterness and pain] (66; tr. Heinemann 55). Each half-brother, in his own way, attempts to sidestep or delay the disappointment of human reality. Bruno discovers happiness in an open relationship and Michel finds it in mathematics. Michel's pursuit of the scientific analysis of human behavior, thought, and actions is an attempt to strip away mankind's own self-aggrandizing notion of uniqueness. A Lovecraftian cosmic indifference can be seen in the crushing realization of the isolation and disappointment that Bruno and Michel experience through the course of *Les Particules elementaires*. Michel's worldview, one that reduces humanity's uniqueness, is similar in vein to Lovecraft's leitmotif whereby his characters are constantly confronted by another system, a cosmic system whose calculations, values, and fulcrums are indifferent to humanity. Rather than believe in the illusion of contemporary society and its own self-importance, Houellebecq's underlying critique is that we are "inconséquents, légers et clownesques" [inconsequential, shallow and ridiculous] (260; tr. Heinemann 214). As if to highlight this point, in the "Epilogue" we discover that Michel has been successful at creating artificial life. The ridiculous, shallow, and inconsequential nature of mankind is only transitory, meaning that man and his qualities are not at the apex of the universe.

La Possibilité d'une île explores the possibility of scientific advancements in cloning procedures and the evolution of the human experience as increasingly compartmentalized and alienating. The main narration of the story unfolds through the journal entry of Daniel1, who the reader soon realizes is the biological original of a line of clones. The narration, then, is a shift between Daniel1's life story and the subsequent life stories (and reflections on Daniel1's own story) of Daniel24 and Daniel25. The future Daniels are known as neohumans, the result of a breakthrough in genetic cloning ushered into existence through scientific research and control of a scientifically based religion/cult known as Elohimite.[10] Daniel1's life story is basically, like that of many of Houellebecq's characters, a commentary on contemporary society.

---

10. Elohim is a Hebrew term that means either god or gods. This would then have been a term that the ancient Hebrew would have used to refer to God in the Torah. The Elohimite cult is centered on cloning technology, thus, one could infer that the cult and its members have replaced the Hebrew God as creator of life.

Daniel1's narration is a self-conscious exploration of passing from the upper limits of what can be considered youth to middle age. Similar to previous observations by protagonists in *L'Extension du domaine de la lutte* and *Les Particules élémentaires*, in a society that increasingly liberates sexual identity and sexual forms of pleasure, Daniel1 remarks that "[d]ans le monde moderne on pouvait être échangiste, bi, trans, zoophile, SM, mais il était interdit d'être *vieux*" [in the modern world you could be a swinger, bi, trans, zoo, into S&M, but it was forbidden to be *old*] (*La Possibilité* 209; tr. Bowd 148). Thus, the true boundary established by society is that between the young and the old, which firmly privileges youth over old age. Daniel1's social commentary is as poignant as certain of Lovecraft's comments sown throughout his stories, although perhaps Daniel1's comments are generated from a self-conscious position of exteriority to the "promised land," whereas Lovecraft's social commentary seems indifferent to any position of social standing and more concerned with an overall myopic view of mankind. In most of Lovecraft's tales, there is a belabored search for forbidden knowledge, which in some fashion will reveal the illusory nature of the universe as humans perceive it. In *La Possibilité d'une île*, the illusory nature of the world is clearly understood by Daniel1, who is a comedian. Reflecting on his career, he remarks that "si l'on agresse le monde avec une violence suffisante, il finit par le cracher, son sale fric; mais jamais, jamais il ne vous redonne la joie" [if you attack the world with sufficient violence, it ends up spitting its filthy lucre back at you; but never, never will it give you back joy] (160; tr. Bowd 113). In this sense, Daniel1 means to say that neither money nor sexual liberation is able to provide the kind of joy that satisfies. For Daniel1 and indeed the rest of his clones, an authentic joy seems beyond the scope of possibility because the ephemeral joys of sexual pleasure and money always seem to promise more than they can deliver.

It would be absurd to claim that H. P. Lovecraft is the only influence in Houellebecq's worldview. When we understand his *H. P. Lovecraft: Contre le monde, contre la viem* we can certainly claim that Lovecraft and his texts have served as a source of inspiration. One can even go so far as to wonder whether Houellebecq is not describing his own position when he summarizes Lovecraft's attitude toward the world as "une haine absolue du monde en général, aggravée d'un dégoût particulier pour le monde moderne" [an absolute hatred of the world in general, aggravated by an aversion to the modern world in particular] (*Contre le monde* 46; tr. Khazeni 57).

"Modern" French Lovecraft Studies

"Modern" describes the period of French Lovecraft studies inaugurated by the publication in 1991 of Michel Houellebecq's *H. P. Lovecraft: Contre le monde, contre la vie*. We have briefly summarized the ways in which Bergier influenced the cultural reception of Lovecraft. Houellebecq offers an example of a shift in the image of Lovecraft.

In August 1995, in France, a group of Lovecraft scholars met to discuss their findings in the study of Lovecraft and his tales at Cerisy-la-Salle. This conference was then published in 2002 by Broché and included an addition by the American Donald R. Burleson, who is known in Lovecraft studies as a deconstructionist. This volume is important because it gives a good sample of just how much Lovecraft studies in France have changed since the famous Cahiers de l'Herne *H. P. Lovecraft* (1969). Notably, Maurice Lévy's "Lovecraft, trente ans après" ("Lovecraft, thirty years after") serves as a reminder of just how much was unknown about Lovecraft, and coincidentally how much Bergier invented.

More recently, however, Didier Hendrickx's *H. P. Lovecraft: Le Dieu silencieux* (2012) offers a regressive interpretation of Lovecraft and his philosophy as seen in his works. It is quite unfortunate, however, because Hendrickx perpetuates certain occultist interpretations such as the famous "black magic" quotation, an inaccuracy that August Derleth fostered.[11] Hendrickx's interpretation of Lovecraft texts also suffers greatly from his enthusiasm for August Derleth, in that he projects concepts such as good and evil

---

11. "All my stories, unconnected as they may be, are based on the fundamental lore or legend that this world was inhabited at one time by another race who, in practising black magic, lost their foothold and were expelled, yet live on outside ever ready to take possession of this earth again" (cited in Joshi, "The Cthulhu Mythos: Lovecraft vs. Derleth" 46).

into the "Cthulhu Mythos" and "Dream Cycle." As Robert M. Price points out, "Lovecraft would have regarded Derleth's benevolent 'Elder Gods' as an instance of childish wish-fulfillment as he did the Christian story of salvation" ("Demythologizing Cthulhu" 122). As previously explored, when Lovecraft resubmitted "The Call of Cthulhu" to *Weird Tales* in July 1927, he included a letter addressed to the editor, Farnsworth Wright, expressing his conviction that

> all my tales are based on the fundamental premise that common human laws and interests and emotions have no validity or significance in the vast cosmos-at-large. To me there is nothing but puerility in a tale in which the human form—and the local human passions and conditions and standards—are depicted as native to other worlds or other universes. To achieve the essence of real externality, whether of time or space or dimension, one must forget that such things as organic life, good and evil, love and hate, an all such local attributes of a negligible and temporary race called mankind, have any existence at all. (*SL* 2.150)

This same letter was translated and included in the 1969 Cahiers de l'Herne issue, which Hendrickx praises. It is unfortunate that the publisher of Lovecraft's oeuvre (Derleth) did not read Lovecraft's correspondence closely as he did his tales. Hendrickx's analysis is also regressive in the fact that he appears to be highly influenced by the reign of primitivism in French literary circles at the time when Lovecraft was first introduced to France, as was briefly explained earlier. Lastly, after a close reading, one can even come to the conclusion that Hendrickx's Lovecraft research is hamstrung by the fact that his reading of Lovecraft is restricted to what has been made available in the French language, and it would appear that the most recent document cited is the issue of *Phénix* devoted to Lovecraft (September 1986). His citations of Lovecraft's correspondence to support his interpretation of Lovecraft's mythology are restricted to the only volume that was translated into French. In later volumes Lovecraft directly addresses the literality of his mythology and the fact that he does not specifically believe in it.

If one can put aside these questionable associations—and this is difficult because he repeatedly reiterates the good-versus-evil dichotomy—Hendrickx's analysis can be quite lucid and, at times, even excellent. In fact, despite the somewhat regressive interpretation of Lovecraft's work, Hendrickx's critical appreciation and vision are certainly contemporary in the fact that he understands Lovecraft's regard "acéré sur la société industrielle et ce monde technomarchand en pleine éclosion et déjà grand consommateur d'humains" [sharpened on the industrial society and this technomarket world fully bloomed and already a great consumer of humans] (Hendrickx 8). Hendrickx views Lovecraft's ability to pierce the veil of his contemporary society as something that produced much anguish in him, coupled with the early deaths of two father figures (his father Winfield Scott Lovecraft died in 1898, his grandfather Whipple Van Buren Phillips in 1904). For Hendrickx, Lovecraft wrote as "un baume pour apaiser le mal-être" [balm to sooth the malaise] (9). The primary leitmotif in *Le Dieu silencieux* is that Lovecraft lucidly remarked a general degradation in interpersonal communication in the West. For Hendrickx, Lovecraft explores this degradation through three mythical structures that are present in his stories: 1) the Cthulhu Mythos, 2) Lovecraft's literary New England, and 3) his childhood. For Hendrickxs these "[t]rois époques, trois espace-temps primordiaux dont nous pourrons observer la dégradation et dégager les solutions imagine par Lovecraft pour tenter d'y remédier et donner un sens à son existence" [three time periods, three primordial space-times which we will be able to observe the degradation and discern the imagined solutions by Lovecraft so as to try and fix them and to give a sense to his existence] (25). As Hendrickx points out, this is not necessarily anything new: Robert M. Price had already noted the three mythical structures in his article "H. P. Lovecraft and the Cthulhu Mythos," first published in *Crypt of Cthulhu* no. 36 (September 1986) (which Hendrickx undoubtedly read in its translation in *Phénix* no. 36 in 1986).

The difficulty is that Hendrickx appears to reiterate Bergier's Lovecraft, the mad-poet, although this time he is very much aware of his contemporary society and is disgusted, rather than aloof and unaware. Hendrickx's notion of authorship and writing is that "[é]crire c'est ici accomplir un geste premier, sans passé, présent ni futur, c'est accéder au temps primordial, devenir un dieu" [here, to write is to accomplish a first gesture, without past, present, or future. It's to gain access to a primordial time, to become a god] (13). Lovecraft wrote to recover his lost New England, his lost childhood, and somehow to help overcome the "evil" gods. Because of the way in which Hendrickx interprets Lovecraft's mythos, he reads into it a redemptive feature that appeases Lovecraft's "troubled" mind. According to Hendrickx, then, Lovecraft's stories are representative of his own fears (foreigners, miscegenation) and anxieties with regard to politics (at times aligned with fascism) and philosophy (materialist, nihilistic, elitist). For Hendrickx, Lovecraft wrote as a means to control internally what he could not control externally. Being a man who considered himself firmly influenced by nineteenth-century customs and thought, Lovecraft clearly remarked the beginning of a different era in the first quarter of the twentieth century. It is for this reason that Lovecraft wrote, to appease his malaise, because, as Hendrickx himself wrote, "L'auteur est le maître absolu" [the author is the absolute master] (132). Didier Hendrickx's *H.P. Lovecraft: Le Dieu silencieux* is remarkably poignant and forward-thinking at times, but ultimately a book whose influence is academically dated, and largely based on inaccurate data.

Let us consider another recent study in French on Lovecraft. Cédric Monget's study *Lovecraft: Le Dernier Puritain* (2011), published by La Clef d'Argent. The difference between Hendrickx's and Monget's scholarship is clear when one compares the two Works Cited sections. Monget's bibliography comprises more than nine-tenths English-language sources, whereas Hendrickx's sources are all restricted to French. As a result, the complexity and depth with which Monget approaches Lovecraft and his philosophy is remarkably succinct and innovative. Monget's Lovecraft is no longer the mad/gifted-poet-mystic that Bergier passed on as his inheritance to future French Lovecraftian scholars, but rather more aligned with the modern image of Lovecraft that American scholars such as S. T. Joshi and Robert M. Price have been promoting since Joshi's *H. P. Lovecraft: Four Decades of Criticism* (1980) was published. Monget highlights the disparity between the images, a "faute de disposer d'écrits plus tardifs" [lack of laying out [his] writings much later] (71). This leads to the fact the

French "s[e] [sont] longtemps imaginé[s] Lovecraft comme étant un mystique décadent vivant dans la réclusion ou un occultiste laissant échapper dans ses récits les parcelles d'une connaissance secrète réservée au seul initiés" [have for a long while imagined Lovecraft as being a decadent mystic living in seclusion or an occultist having let escape in his tales the packets of secreted knowledge reserved only for initiates] (71). Whether by design or not, this statement applies perfectly to Hendrickx's approach to Lovecraft, and indeed the approach that French Lovecraft scholarship inherited from Benayoun, Legrand, Bergier, and Pauwels.

The goal of *Lovecraft: Le Dernier Puritain* is to "replacer l'athéisme de Lovecraft dans son contexte biographique et dans sa dynamique intellectuelle" [to relocate Lovecraft's atheism in its biographical context and in his dynamic intellect] (77). This allows Monget to pillage Lovecraft's correspondence and his secondary writings to portray his tales as a product not only of his aesthetics and an extension of his philosophy (materialist) but also of his atheism. This approach allows a materialist atheist, such as Lovecraft, to incorporate the structure of religion while subverting it with a denial of man's importance. This is certainly a difficult task considering the fact that the esoteric or occultist interpretation of Lovecraft denies Lovecraft's cosmic indifference to mankind. The occultist or esoteric "hijacking" of Lovecraft is blind to Lovecraft's atheism and man's overall lack of importance in the universe at large. Rather, this interpretation looks at the symbology of his texts in a specific, esoteric manner in that "[l]es extraterrestres jouent alors le même rôle que le Dieu des Chrétiens" [the extraterrestrials play the same role as the Christian's God] (73). Monget characterizes reading Lovecraft as an occultist as a "trahison, mais une trahison à laquelle il a prêté la main, non sans humour et désinvolture, par certains de ses écrits" [betrayal, but a betrayal which he himself lent, not without humor and casualness, by some of his stories] (73).

What allows for the seemingly contradictory label of "the last puritan" is the fact that Lovecraft's philosophy logically concludes in

l'absence de Dieu. Il n'y a nulle place pour Lui dans un monde où il n'y a qu'une substance et que cette substance est la matière perceptible. Il n'y a aucun rôle possible pour Lui dans un monde sans finalité régi uniquement par les lois d'airain de la causalité et où le miracle divin de la conséquence sans cause est un mensonge que l'homme fait.

[the absence of God. There is no place for Him in a world where there is only a substance and that this substance is perceptible matter. There is no possible role for Him in a world without finality reigning uniquely by bronze rules of causality and where the consequence of the divine miracle without causation is a lie that man himself created.] (69)

Despite his rejection of a god or gods, Lovecraft understood the necessity of religion but saw that "les progrès de la connaissance humaine ont rendu caduques les croyances passées" [the progress of human knowledge has worn out bygone beliefs] (69). When understood in this way, Lovecraft's philosophy and atheism underscore the lack of character development in his stories; "en effet, ce sont les phénomènes qui recèlent en leur sein l'horreur et non la psychologie des héros" [indeed, it is the events that at their heart deal in horror, not in the psychology of the heroes] (60). This again highlights Lovecraft's cosmic indifference, in that man if anything is secondary or even tertiary in the cosmos at large. This view is resoundingly different from Didier Hendrickx's, who undoubtedly sees Lovecraft's cosmic indifference and the stories he wrote as a way to recover past, and lost, mystical structures.

Conclusion

We began by studying Michel Houellebecq's 1991 *H. P. Lovecraft: Contre le monde, contre la vie*, as it appears to be a watershed moment separating the older French image of Lovecraft and the modern French image of Lovecraft. After having studied the framework through which Houellebecq explored Lovecraft and the universe he created, we wondered whether Houellebecq's interpretation, which differentiated itself from Bergier's, proved influential in modern French Lovecraft studies. To answer this question, we explored two recent works: *H. P. Lovecraft: Le Dieu silencieux* by Didier Hendrickx and Cédric Monget's *H. P. Lovecraft: Le Dernier Puritain*.

Of the two works, Hendrickx, albeit more recent, proved to be more retrogressive in its interpretation of Lovecraft, his biography, philosophy, and oeuvre in general. Hendrickx indeed brings a critical approach to Lovecraft's texts that was not necessarily available in the initial introduction of Lovecraft to France (whether that be through lack of translated works or through theoretical literary approaches). Hendrickx's interpretation suffers from a primitivist approach to Lovecraft's texts, in that the signs and symbols that dealt with the occult or the esoteric were taken to be the author's own convictions. This, coupled with the fact that Hendrickx's resources are restricted to those published in the French language, and the most recent being the *Phénix* 1986 issue devoted to Lovecraft, leads one to believe that this publication is, in reality, a manuscript that preceded the publication of Houellebecq's book.

Cédric Monget's study, in contrast, is rooted in the most recent information on Lovecraft available in English and in French. His approach to Lovecraft was certainly not available prior to any French scholar, not only because Lovecraft's correspondence was not made extensively available in English until 1976, but because much of Monget's research takes place in the English language, and in sources that have yet to be translated. This leads one to believe that modern French Lovecraft scholarship is at its apogee only when the critic has access to the plethora of fine English-language scholarship on Lovecraft. Monget's critical analysis of Lovecraft's atheism and his materialist philosophy as expressed in his tales offers an image of Lovecraft that was not possible prior to Houellebecq. Houellebecq's image of Lovecraft in France is not entirely without influence. Monget and Houellebecq agree on a few points, mostly about Lovecraft's philosophy and racism and its influence on his writing. Monget's work should be accorded its place in French Lovecraft scholarship among the finest (Maurice Lévy's *Lovecraft ou le fantastique* and Michel Houellebecq's *H. P. Lovecraft: Contre le monde, contre la vie*—both of which have been translated into English), both in its accuracy and in the possibilities it offers. One wonders, if this is the case, when Monget's study will be accessible in English.

French academic thought on Lovecraft did not influence the image of Lovecraft in America. If anything, the evidence would suggest that the majority of French academic thought on Lovecraft is the result of American Lovecraft scholarship. It was not until Lovecraft's correspondence was published in five volumes from 1965 to 1976 that American Lovecraft scholarship began to interpret Lovecraft differently, giving rise to analyses that were more aligned with Lovecraft's own philosophy and general worldview. In this sense, French Lovecraft studies' own liberation from Jacques Bergier's interpretation was a twofold process, first through the translated articles of American scholars like S. T. Joshi, Fritz Leiber, Donald R. Burleson, and Robert M. Price, among many others, and second through the translation of Lovecraft's nonfictional texts into French (the last of which appeared as late as 1991). French Lovecraft scholarship exploded exponentially over eight years in the 1990s. The most excellent French critical approaches to Lovecraft have come from bilingual scholars who have access to a set of texts that the monolingual French scholar does not. There is a certain visible level of information that a bilingual French Lovecraft scholar has over his monolingual compatriot. For a more recent example, the French Facebook group: "H. P. Lovecraft: Francophone" often discusses a variety of subjects concerning Lovecraft, from the most common "fanboy" type of question or observation to the critically informed queries showing years of academic research.[12] More often than not, justification of one's viewpoint resorts to English-language research on the part of the member. This gives the impression that those who have access to the original English texts, yet to be translated into French, are privy to information to which monolingual scholars are not.

It is my contention that although the French have been considered for a long time to be champions of Lovecraft both intellectually and pop-culturally, his fame in France (outside of the instances of an American encountering Lovecraft while abroad) has done little to affect his reception and growth in American

---

12. I discovered this group by accident after searching on Google for Jacques Bergier references. Many of the most active French scholars on HPL are members of this group: Joseph Altairac, Cédric Monget, Adam Joffrain, Bernard Bonnet, Philippe Gindre, and Christophe Till are among the most notable.

Lovecraft scholarship. Although the French image of Lovecraft has had its unique refractions and interpretations, the current image is more aligned with the American version, despite the fact that the overwhelming wealth of French translations of Lovecraft's philosophical writings and other nonfiction works are still not available in French, including most of his letters. This means that the French Lovecraftian scholar has to have access to the English-language sources.

Despite the fact that American Lovecraft scholarship is apparently more thorough than the French in that the entirety of Lovecraft's oeuvre is available without the need of translation, we cannot discount the unique ways in which Lovecraft has affected other literary systems. Since Antoine Berman has observed that differences between languages became hierarchized, we can hypothesize that cultural value and therefore cultural dominance results from direct access to the vault of original materials. In the example of the French Facebook Group, French scholars who have access to the untranslated English texts seem to have more credit with the "bank" than their French counterparts. This explains the fact that despite the literary value normally associated with the French literary system, the American literary system is particularly rich when it comes to Lovecraft (and pulp fiction magazines in general). Due to its relative dominance, the field of American Lovecraft studies has felt little need to import "significant and provocative views" from other cultures.

The value of knowledge is not always gained as a result of an answer; sometimes it is the question that is more important. In my case, I wondered whether my academic and cultural interest in Lovecraft was the result of his popularity and importance in France. I discovered that this question was not possible to answer without a proper realignment of my consideration of translation and its role within a literary polysystem. I also discovered the influence that those in positions of authority have in shaping the reception of Lovecraft, whether domestically or abroad. Many more questions have surfaced along the way, and in most cases they require an in-depth analysis much too large for the current project. For example, how will exploring the "other side" of Lovecraft benefit American Lovecraft scholars? How will the knowledge of

French Lovecraft scholarship circulate and affect its American counterpart? Ultimately, if better self-understanding comes through an interaction with the other, American Lovecraft studies can gain in understanding Lovecraft's image as a cultural "other" in France. This can only be done through a greater understanding of how translation plays an immediate role in the formation of literature, but also the greater role that translation has played in the history of literature.

Works Cited

Berman, Antoine. *The Experience of the Foreign: Culture and Translation in Romantic Germany.* Albany: State University of New York, 1992.

Hendrickx, Didier. H. P. Lovecraft: Le Dieu silencieux. Lausanne: L'Age d'Homme, 2012.

Houellebecq, Michel. *The Elementary Particles.* Tr. Frank Wynne. New York: Knopf, 2000.

———. *H. P. Lovecraft: Against the World, Against Life.* Tr. Dorna Khazeni. London: Gollancz, 2008.

———. *H. P. Lovecraft: Contre le monde, contre la vie.* 1991. Monaco: Editions Du Rocher, 1999.

———. *Les Particules élémentaires.* Paris: J'ai Lu, 2000.

———. *La Possibilité d'une île.* Paris: Fayard, 2005.

———. *The Possibility of an Island.* Tr. Gavin Bowd. New York: Vintage International, 2007.

———. *Whatever: A Novel.* Tr. Paul Hammond. London: Serpent's Tail, 1998.

Joshi, S. T. "The Cthulhu Mythos: Lovecraft vs. Derleth." In *Dissecting Cthulhu,* ed. S. T. Joshi. Lakeland, FL: Miskatonic River Press, 2011. 43–53.

Joshi, S. T., ed. *H. P. Lovecraft: Four Decades of Criticism.* Athens: Ohio University Press, 1980.

Monget, Cédric. *Lovecraft: Le Dernier Puritain.* Aiglepierre: La Clef d'Argent, 2011.

Žižek, Slavoj. *Event: A Philosophical Journey through a Concept.* Brooklyn, NY: Melville House, 2014.

Briefly Noted

Lovecraft's letters to Henry Kuttner, as edited by David E. Schultz and S. T. Joshi, will soon be republished in a special booklet to accompany the slipcased edition of Kuttner's *Terror in the House: The Early Kuttner, Volume One* (Haffner Press). In the process of preparing the letters for publication, the editors have revised their notes in light of new information.

————————————

We look forward to the publication, either late this year or early next—of Lovecraft's *Fungi from Yuggoth*, edited by David E. Schultz (Hippocampus Press). This exhaustive critical edition, on which Mr. Schultz has been working for close to forty years, illuminates the central place—both chronologically and aesthetically—that the sonnet cycle occupies in Lovecraft's work, coming as it does almost exactly at the midpoint of his brief literary career. We find not only an accurate text of the cycle, but textual variants, a facsimile of the much-revised autograph manuscript, a full listing of the individual and collective publications of the sonnets, and—most valuable of all—a wondrously detailed commentary on the poems. A lengthy commentary provides a comprehensive account of the writing and publication of the cycle, along with a critical assessment of it and an analysis of its role in Lovecraft's work; in addition, Schultz adds detailed notes on individual passages. Each poem features an original illustration by celebrated Lovecraftian artist Jason C. Eckhardt. This long-awaited edition will take its place as one of the keystone volumes of Lovecraft scholarship.

Donald A. Wollheim's
Hoax Review of the *Necronomicon*

Donovan K. Loucks

In his touching memoir about his correspondence with H. P. Love-craft, Willis Conover mentions a review of Lovecraft's fictional *Necronomicon* that Donald Wollheim submitted to a Connecticut newspaper:

> "Thank you," I said, "and here's something for you—a copy of a clipping from the *Branford Review*, a small-town newspaper, which Wollheim lent me. He says he wrote it himself and sent it to the paper as a book review."
>
> . . .
>
> "Thanks immensely for the transcript of Wollheim's spoof," said Lovecraft, "about which he had never breathed a word. If the *Necronomicon* legend continues to grow, people will end up by be-lieving in it and accusing me of faking when I point out the true origin of the thing! That's what happened to Machen in connex-ion with the legend of the 'Angels of Mons'—a legend originating with his short story 'The Bowmen,' published soon after the battle.
>
> "I must get hold of this Faraday translation," he added, "even though it is probably a fake. As you will see by the accompanying historical sketch (which please return), there is no Arabic original in existence. Other errors probably originate with the reviewer—for example, Alhazred came *after* Mohammed, and the Greek as well as the Latin text of this hellish work has been published." (*Lovecraft at Last* 102–3)

The surrounding letters in Conover's book imply that this ex-change took place somewhere between 23 September 1936 and

1 October 1936. Lovecraft goes on to mention this review to Henry Kuttner in a letter later that same year:

> Incidentally, I am told that a review of a new translation of the *Necro* recently appeared in the newspaper of a small town near New York City. (Lovecraft to Henry Kuttner, 30 November 1936; *Letters to Henry Kuttner* 27)

This limited information gave me the starting point from which I hoped to finally locate the article—nearly eighty years after its publication.

The *Branford Review and East Haven News* was a weekly newspaper (published on Thursday) that began publication on 13 April 1928 as simply the *Branford Review*. In late 1932 it changed its name to the *Branford Review and East Haven News*. It reverted to simply the *Branford Review* in May 1952 and ceased publication in December 2008. The James Blackstone Memorial Library in Branford has back issues of the newspaper on microfilm, so I went there on 29 March 2014 to examine them.

Searching through issues of the *Branford Review and East Haven News* from before 1 October 1936, I browsed three months of issues at a time. I began with July through September of 1936 and then worked my way backwards in three-month blocks. After three hours of searching—and just when I was considering giving up due to hunger—I came across a column called "Book Chats" in the 31 October 1935 issue. It provided reviews of recently published books and seemed like just the kind of column that might contain the *Necronomicon* review. With a renewed motivation, I continued searching and just fifteen minutes later discovered the *Necronomicon* review in the "Book Chats" column of the 12 September 1935 issue. In addition to Wollheim's phony review, the column included a review of an actual book, Laura Yates's *An Interior Decorating Scrap-Book*. The column in full follows this article.

There is a tantalizing ellipsis in Conover's transcription that seems to imply that there was more to the article. Unfortunately, the ellipsis also appears in the original publication. There are only a few minor textual and typographical differences between Conover's transcript and the published version of Wollheim's review. For example, in the published version, the review begins with "In the early days . . ." (rather than "years"), Olaus Wormius is "a black magician" (as opposed to simply "a magician"), and the word "dealings" is rendered as "dealing."

Donald A[llen] Wollheim (1914–1990) was a well-known science fiction fan, author, editor, and founder of DAW Books. But at the time of the publication of his review of the *Necronomicon* he was just twenty years old. He probably began corresponding with Lovecraft around the very same time. Lovecraft mentions that he met Wollheim in New York City in late December 1935 or early January 1936, only a few months after the review was published. During Lovecraft's brief remaining lifetime Wollheim published several of Lovecraft's stories, poems, and essays in his fanzine, the *Phantagraph*. Lovecraft described Wollheim as "a tremendously brilliant youth" (Lovecraft to Robert A. W. Lowndes, 20 February 1937).

Wollheim was a lifelong resident of New York City. At the time he was corresponding with Lovecraft, his address was in Manhattan's Upper West Side at 801 West End Avenue. Given that, what was his connection to Branford or to the *Branford Review and East Haven News*? I returned to Branford on 24 July 2014 to see if I could find more instances of "Book Chats" and discover what that connection might have been.

On my second trip to Branford, I only found one more instance of "Book Chats" (18 July 1935). However, I was told by one of the librarians that the entire run of the newspaper was now available on the library's online "Branford History Digital Scrapbooks." When I returned home, I wrote an application to programmatically download more than six months of issues prior to and more than six months of issues subsequent to the one containing the *Necronomicon* review. Searching through these, I located two more instances of "Book Chats." In total, I found five issues containing "Book Chats" columns, all published within a four-month window: 11 July 1935, 18 July 1935, 25 July 1935, 12 September 1935 (the article containing the *Necronomicon* review), and 31 October 1935.

The first two and the last instance of "Book Chats" have the byline "Conducted by William Roth." In addition, the 18 July 1935 column states, "Donald A. Wollheim will publish a book of short stories dealing with the future of planets, space ships etc., title not yet announced." Who was William Roth, and what was his connection to Wollheim? Unfortunately, this name is so common that even identifying the correct William Roth proved impossible. I contacted the Branford Historical Society, but it was unable to provide any definitive information on Roth. I later downloaded more than two and a half years of issues of the *Branford Review and East Haven News*, but found no additional instances of "Book Chats" and no mention of Roth or Wollheim outside of these five cases. It's my hope that bringing William Roth's name to a wider audience will prompt someone else to fill in the missing information on him.

One possible connection between Wollheim and Roth is Otis Adelbert Kline. Though Kline lived in Chicago for many years, he moved to the New York City area around the time that this review appeared. He is mentioned as summering in Branford—which is only 85 miles northeast of New York City—though some sources imply he actually lived there. Perhaps he served as the go-between for Wollheim and Roth.

I've also been told that Wollheim may have had cousins in the Branford area, so perhaps his review was submitted through them. Yet another possibility is that "William Roth" is simply one of Wollheim's many pseudonyms. Rather than submitting just the *Necronomicon* review to Roth, Wollheim may himself have written the entire series of columns. However, this seems unlikely given that Conover states that Wollheim "sent it to the paper." Again, I'm hoping that someone more familiar with Wollheim or Roth will be able to put the pieces together.

Given the nature of the *Necronomicon*, it should not be surprising that there is also *misinformation* about the *Branford Review* article. Kendrick Kerwin Chua's notoriously misleading *Necronomicon* FAQ (Frequently-Asked-Questions list) states the following:

An entry which once deserved a place among these Necronomicons has been proven to be a hoax. Apparently a man by the name of Wollheim sent to the Branford Review (a Massachusetts Newspaper) a fake review of a book called Necronomicon in 1934, supposedly edited by a W. T. Faraday. Interestingly, it was this fake book review which inspired Lovecraft to write his own History of the Necronomicon, according to Willis Conover.

Chua is correct that Donald Wollheim wrote the review and that it is a fake. However, he makes several erroneous—but possibly intentionally incorrect—statements. First, Branford is in *Connecticut*, not Massachusetts. Second, the article appeared in 1935, not 1934. Third, Lovecraft's "History of the *Necronomicon*" couldn't have been prompted by this review, since Lovecraft wrote the former in 1927.

During Lovecraft's lifetime, several of his friends contributed to the myth of the *Necronomicon*, including Frank Belknap Long, Robert E. Howard, Clark Ashton Smith, Robert Bloch, and R. H. Barlow. After his death, numerous *Necronomicon* hoaxes were perpetrated. Besides the more recent hoax editions, there were early advertisements in *Publishers' Weekly* (1945), bookseller Phillip Duschnes's catalog (1946), and *Antiquarian Bookman* (1962 and 1966). But Donald Wollheim's *Necronomicon* hoax not only took place during Lovecraft's lifetime, it was the *first*.

Book Chats

An Interior Decorating Scrap-Book by Laura Yates, Westport, Conn. Published by the author.

———

The urge to do one's own interior-decorating is being popularized by radio talks, group discussions, and through the medium of advertisements in newspapers and magazines. That urge has been strengthened by the publication of "An Interior-Decorating Scrap Book['] by Laura Yates. The author, an interior-decorator by profession has put out a book that will appeal to the amateur home designer—a busy housewife, a young bride (with ambitions of owning her own home) or a student pursuing courses in this profession.

Clever suggestions are given throughout the book, for every room in the house; from attic to basement play-room. Take for example the dining room and living room combined. What to have in each is most important. The type of furniture in a room of this kind, etc. Especially, how it blends in with the room harmony and balance. Author Yates says "Avoid sets of things, the conventional dining room furniture, six or eight chairs, serving table, sideboard and china closet.['] These and other suggestions are practical, up to date and interesting. Blank pages for notes and clippings follow, with an envelope for material from magazines, newspapers, catalogues and sample books. The scrap book is looseleaf in form thus making it possible for the owner to add more leaves of information from time to time. The beautiful cover is washable.

We extend congratulations to Miss Yates, for this her textbook homemaker-scrap book in one volume, her first published effort. It is one that should run into many editions because of the author's inspiring sincerity at the beginning of the book "Nice Living is not a question of money, but of knowing"—; and for the contents themselves which are indeed a tribute to the author.

————————

The Necronomicon as Translated and Abridged from the original Arabic of Abdul Alhazred, by W. T. Faraday. Privately printed by the author.

————————

In the early days of the Middle Ages, shortly before the advent of Mohammed, a half-mad Arab, Abdul Alhazred by name, compiled this odd book. According to the foreword this is the first English translation ever made, and the only other translation ever prepared for publication is the extremely rare Latin work of the so-called black magician Olaus Wormius; who was burned at the stake several hundred years ago for heresy. This version is a compilation from the original.

This book was not intended for sale to the public. It was printed chiefly for purchase by those students of the Occult who found it necessary to consult this work in their researches. It purports to be the account of the Spheres of the Occult and their dealing with mankind from the dawn of history. It shows very clearly the deranged mind of the writer, who was so convinced he received these facts from supernatural sources. Curiously enough, it does leave a feeling of some truth in this reviewer's mind.

If we are to judge from the foreword, this book is very much abridged. The original ran to nine hundred pages of manuscript. This edition contains three hundred pages. Dr. Faraday admits to having omitted whole chapters for safety's sake. . . . . . On the whole, this publication will live as an outstanding contribution to Occult lore. It is also the introduction to the element of Elder Gods who according to the ideas of mystics came before the Modern Demons set in. It is claimed that the late Robert W. Chambers and Ambrose Bierce both consulted this work in writing some of their earlier and more fantastic works. This is a volume that will prove invaluable to certain individuals.

Works Cited or Consulted

"Book Chats." *Branford Review and East Haven News* (Branford, CT) 8, No. 24 (Thursday, 12 September 1935): 7. (Available online at http://branford.advantage-preservation.com/sites/branford.advantage-preservation.com/files/pdfs/scan_0307a_83.pdf.)

Chua, Kendrick Kerwin. *Necronomicon FAQ.*

Lovecraft, H. P. *Letters to Henry Kuttner.* Ed. David E. Schultz and S. T. Joshi. West Warwick, RI: Necronomicon Press, 1990.

Lovecraft, H. P., and Willis Conover. *Lovecraft at Last.* Arlington, VA: Carrollton-Clark, 1975.

Harms, Daniel and John Wisdom Gonce III. *The Necronomicon Files: The Truth Behind Lovecraft's Legend.* Rev. ed. Boston, MA: Weiser Books, 2003.

Reviews

H. P. LOVECRAFT. *Collected Fiction: A Variorum Edition.* Three volumes. Edited by S. T. Joshi. New York: Hippocampus Press, 2015. Reviewed by Steven J. Mariconda.

Textual criticism is a branch of textual scholarship, philology, and literary criticism that is concerned with the identification and removal of transcription errors in texts. In the Western world, the practice may be traced back to the Hellenistic period. Originally focused on religious texts, it was later extended to classical and medieval texts in Latin and Greek. In eighteenth-century England scholarly editing and publishing extending into the realm of literature, spurred largely by the wish for a clean edition of Shakespeare. The effort was not merely to identify the various texts and their transmission, but also to collocate each variant reading—the result being a "cum notibus variorum," or "edition variorum" for short.

The history and process of textual criticism is complex and fascinating. Briefly, documents such as autograph manuscripts (A.Ms.), typed manuscripts (T.Ms.), and book/magazine publications are identified and evaluated as potential sources for the definitive text, and are arranged in a kind of family tree, or *stemma*, of textual descent. The editor then applies procedures of combinatory logic to ascertain and evaluate the textual authority of each document. This in turn leads to the establishment of a critical or "definitive" text.

Textual criticism is clearly more of an art than a science, and approaches have evolved and varied. In some schools of thought, for example, the emphasis is less on the transmission of a text than identifying a "copy text" as the basis for a scholarly critical edition. Such an "ur-text" would provide the foundation upon which editorial judgment could apply controlled changes to transform it into the definitive text.

Other approaches emphasize "the author's final wishes" for the text—so that the text last in the author's hands would serve as the most suitable basis for a scholarly edition. In addition to textual transmission, here the writer's intention would play a significant role in editorial decisions. This is not as simple as it seems: the concept of the writer's intention—that is, relative to its knowability and reconstructability—is itself somewhat problematical (see, for example, "The Editorial Problem of Final Authorial Intention," G. Thomas Tanselle, *Studies in Bibliography* 29 [1976]: 167–211).

Shortly after entering Brown University in 1976 to study classical philology, S. T. Joshi began the task of examining the textual status of H. P. Lovecraft's stories, comparing the Arkham House editions of the period (1963–65) with the manuscripts and early printed appearances housed in Brown's John Hay Library. He discovered that the printed texts of Lovecraft work were corrupt and poorly printed: some stories contained over a thousand errors, ranging from misprints in punctuation all the way up to the omission of entire passages.

Never one to shy away from a job, Joshi undertook the task of preparing corrected versions of Lovecraft's fiction. This required nearly a decade of work chasing down the source material and collating the versions word by word. It is difficult to characterize the effort involved. Back in the era of the IBM Selectric typewriter Joshi typed, and re-typed, over and over again, about 2,200 double spaced pages of text. There are about 570,000 words of text here, of which 40,000 words are textual notes and apparatus. There are nearly 10,300 annotations in total, each with one or more textual variant, which had to be considered and delineated.

This massive undertaking led to the publication of Joshi's first cut at the corrected texts in three volumes by Arkham House: *The Dunwich Horror and Others* (1984), *At the Mountains of Madness and Other Novels* (1985), and *Dagon and Other Macabre Tales* (1986). These led to the publication of three annotated editions by Penguin Classics (*The Call of Cthulhu and Other Weird Stories*, 1999; *The Thing on the Doorstep and Other Weird Stories*, 2001; *The Dreams in the Witch House and Other Weird Stories*, 2004), which in turn led to Peter Straub's edition of Lovecraft's *Tales* (2005) for the Library of America. Lovecraft's

Complete Fiction (2008) for Barnes & Noble presented the texts in chronological order of writing but had proofreading problems; a corrected edition (look for the silver page gilding) appeared in 2011 and until now constitutes the most accurate edition of Lovecraft's collected fiction.

So here we are presented with completely new and hopefully definitive edition, collated by the world's leading Lovecraft scholar and based on a goodly number of still-extant manuscripts. Joshi has continued to research and analyze the textual accuracy of Lovecraft's stories, and this new edition is the result. Basing his work on the consultation of manuscripts, first publications, and other sources, Joshi has in all identified thousands of errors in Lovecraft's fiction, allowing readers to enjoy the stories as Lovecraft wrote them. For the first time, students of Lovecraft can see at a glance all the textual variants in all pertinent versions of the story—manuscripts, magazine publications, and book appearances. This edition of the fiction should replace all those that preceded it, and will bear the standard for many years.

Lovecraft, Joshi tells us, presents a few unique challenges from a textual perspective: his handwriting was remarkably difficult to decipher, and he wrote willy-nilly all around the page margins with balloons and arrows flying everywhere; he used many unusual orthological conventions (British English, eighteenth-century style); and his work was badly printed in pulp magazines and (often hand-typeset) amateur journals. Textual errors crept in not so much as the result of any one editor, but by the process of "fossilization" and the compounding of errors across repeated publications. The fact that Lovecraft did not live to oversee an edition of his work, plus the circumstance that August Derleth and Donald Wandrei of Arkham House were ignorant of textual issues and negligent of quality, finally resulted in what Joshi (aptly) calls "textual chaos."

The challenges the editor faced ranged from simple to complex. Textual problems are individual; each one requires a special solution. Some are easier than others. Relatively small errors can accrue and create unintended consequences regarding the sense of the overall text; they are nominally not hard to fix. Fortunately the task of restoring Lovecraft's fiction is often straightforward, thanks largely to the survival of manuscripts for almost all the original stories.

There was, unfortunately, a group of stories that proved more difficult. As Joshi notes: "Lovecraft often revised many of his earlier tales for subsequent publications; hence a *double tradition* arises which makes the establishment of the text sometimes difficult, especially when a reliable manuscript for the tale is not extant." When you have a parallel series of texts that branch away from one another, a greater degree of subjectivity may come into play in terms of which reading takes precedence. In some cases, for example, Joshi had to assume the creation of manuscripts not now existing to account for all textual discrepancies. In cases where no original manuscript was to be found, he had to weigh which of the various publications seemed closer to the source. When there is no original or authoritative source, there are no clear principles for understanding the relationships among derivative (manuscript and printed) texts.

Surely we are in good hands here. S.T. Joshi not only possesses a high level of expertise in the life and work of the writer being edited, but is also versed in textual and editorial theory and practice, and in analytical bibliography. I need not rehearse all he has done with Lovecraft. He has spent more time around Lovecraft's prose than anyone else, and any value judgments he had to make are unlikely to be questionable.

As Joshi explains here, the most extreme cases of textual complexity are *At the Mountains of Madness* and "The Shadow out of Time." Readers are referred to "Textual Problems in *At the Mountains of Madness*," "Textual Problems in Lovecraft," and "A Guide to the Lovecraft Fiction Manuscripts at the John Hay Library," all in Joshi's *Lovecraft and a World in Transition* (Hippocampus Press, 2014). "The Shadow out of Time" is particularly interesting in that Lovecraft was careless in correcting both the typed manuscript and the printed magazine version he sent to friends, in the process seemingly sabotaging his original intent as indicated in the A.Ms.

So what do we find here? H. P. Lovecraft as he should be read. Many of the fixes are not of much consequence individually (punctuation, hyphenation, spelling), but they do take on power cumulatively. Some corrections are consequential to the intent or effect of the prose style. A few changes are substantive in terms of content.

A great number will amuse hardened Lovecraftian critics and Mythos trainspotters alike. Take for example the utterances of the dying "Thing on the Doorstep," originally printed as "glub . . . glub . . . glub-glub." Lovecraft had in fact written "glub-glub . . . glub-glub." This seems to support Joshi's claim elsewhere that the dead body was attempting to utter the word "Edward" ("Ed-ward"), because the spirit of the latter was trapped within the revenant. Only in Lovecraft could a "glub" be so important.

More seriously, there is a surprisingly shocking element cut from the same story—a hint about a still-born "monstrous birth" to Asenath Waite, nine months after the Witches' Sabbat. Apparently she was indeed, as another excised passage states, an "uninhibited young modern."

There are two notable revisions to "The Shadow over Innsmouth," both occurring in section-opening paragraphs. Both show how Lovecraft replaced awkward passages with much more subtle and artful wording. There is, too, this substantial deleted text:

> And when I read the grim note my self-slain uncle had left behind, that panic was close to breaking loose within me. He was shooting himself, he wrote, because he had found out something he dared not tell. He wanted to be dead before some expected disaster overtook him. His mother would understand, for she had lived in Arkham and heard stray stories of a certain kind. He advised his brother to remain unmarried as he had done, and urged my mother to tell me I had better do so when I grew up. No need of explaining, he said, but [excised; new passage begun:] The archives told of many family matters, and even brought in my long-dead great-grandmother, whose origin was still so great a puzzle in Arkham. She had had many costly and singular belongings, some of which I knew about, but others of which I had never seen. There were, in particular, some jewels which her French governess had told her never to wear in New England though she might wear them freely in Europe. My grandmother had taken over this precept and applied it to herself . . . [excised]

Like so much of Lovecraft, this is just loaded with critical subtext; in this instance, autobiographical elements that cut very close to Lovecraft's emotional pathology.

On a much lighter note, Lovecraft scholar David E. Schultz and others will be pleased to find that in "Beyond the Wall of Sleep," the narrator's mindreading device—unfortunately characterized in the final text as "my cosmic 'radio'"—was originally deemed the much cooler-sounding "ether-wave apparatus." A sort of primitive wi-fi, perhaps?

In "Through the Gates of the Silver Key" (with E. Hoffmann Price), Joshi mentions a textual choice that may prove to be more controversial. As the final text stands, the ground is said to be "festering with gigantic Dholes." In some previous appearances, it was "festering with gigantic *bholes*." Apparently "Dholes" was the original reading in the "Silver Key" source manuscript. At some point Joshi had changed the noun to "bholes," thinking Lovecraft was referring to the same creatures mentioned in *The Dream-Quest of Unknown Kadath*. Now he has decided otherwise, and he has changed it back. This will provide Mythos-oriented scholars no end of hermeneutic concern, and is bound to cause much burning of the midnight oil, not to mention flame wars on certain Internet forums. But Joshi is to be excused here, as he also has redacted many of the changes the unctuous E. Hoffman Price made to the text.

The *Collected Fiction: A Variorum Edition* is limited to 750 sets, each of three hardcovers with Smythe-sewn signatures and illustrated dust jackets. (A fourth volume, Lovecraft's *Revisions and Collaborations: A Variorum Edition*, is due to appear in 2016 and will be sold separately.) For each item, an introductory note reviews the history of the text, recounts how the presented text was constructed, and touches upon decisions regarding certain passages. Copious footnotes at the base of each page indicate changes and corrections in the text, discuss problematic readings, report cross-variant readings, and so on. The editors and publisher of Hippocampus Press have conducted meticulous proofreading at each stage of production so that the accuracy of the text is assured. The book is a beautiful production, in line with the importance and quality of its content. Congratulations are due to Mr. Joshi upon the successful conclusion of his forty-year effort.

———————

PAUL ROLAND. *The Curious Case of H. P. Lovecraft*. London: Plexus Publishing, 2014. 328 pp. £14.99 (UK), $19.95 (US) tpb. Reviewed by Darrell Schweitzer.

Now, before there is any distracting talk of pots and kettles of similar hue, let me be the first to admit that there have been bad books about H. P. Lovecraft before, among the worst of which is my own *The Dream Quest of H. P. Lovecraft* (1978), which was, I think, fairly enough dismissed by S. T. Joshi as "hardly worth the paper it's printed on." It was an attempt at a popular guide, which would condense available scholarship and present it to the beginning reader in an easily palatable form. It wasn't. The difference between 1978 and now is that a huge amount of progress has been made in Lovecraft studies, so that Paul Roland had a lot more to make a mess out of, and, I am sorry to report, he has.

L. Sprague de Camp's *Lovecraft: A Biography* (1975) assembled most of the basic factual data, but was flawed by an attempt to interpret Lovecraft in terms of de Camp's own prejudices. S. T. Joshi's several times revised, vastly superior, two-volume *I Am Providence* (2010) is the product of decades of work. It amplifies and corrects de Camp and explores Lovecraft's thought to such greater depth that it must truly be considered definitive. In the post-Joshian era, of course, more books about Lovecraft will inevitably appear, but all that remains for later commentators is to condense, popularize, or reinterpret what Joshi has done. This is of course possible. Something similar happened with Edgar Rice Burroughs. Irwin Porges's *Edgar Rice Burroughs: The Man Who Created Tarzan* (1975) is the vast and definitive tome, but this did not prevent John Taliaferro from producing a very readable and useful condensed version, *Tarzan Forever*, in 1999.

That Paul Roland is not a particularly compelling writer could be excused if his book contained any real, new insights, but, alas. . . His approach is thoroughly non-scholarly. Minimal bibliography, no index, no citations for passages quoted from stories and letters. An experienced Lovecraftian will recognize most of them, but for the new reader these quotations must seem to just pop out of the air. Candidly, the most insightful way to read this book is to do so from the perspective of a knowledge of Lovecraft superior to Roland's own. This, for anyone who has kept up at all with Lovecraftian studies, should not be hard to do.

The first enormous, gaping lack we notice is an almost total failure to address what is one of Joshi's strengths: the explication of Lovecraft's thought and how his philosophical development influenced his aesthetics. The words "mechanistic materialism" turn up on page 146, but without a good grounding in critical writings outside of this book, you might have no idea what the phrase means or why it is important.

Not necessarily with malice aforethought, but with a sinking sense of disappointment, one starts to take notes. Here are some of mine:

Page 19. HPL's grandfather was Whipple Van Buren Phillips, not Whipple Van Buren.

Page 41. Roland seems to have no idea what the amateur journalism movement was. Amateur journals with 10,000 readers nationwide? Really?

Page 70. Roland clearly does not understand the Dunsanian echoes in "The Terrible Old Man." His grasp of Dunsany and Dunsany's influence on Lovecraft seems slight.

Page 82. It seems unhelpful to compare "Ex Oblivione" with the work of Franz Kafka, since Kafka was unknown in English at the time Lovecraft was writing and Lovecraft never made any mention of him.

Page 109. Just plain bad writing gets Roland into real trouble when he writes that Farnsworth Wright "would reject several of Lovecraft's most important stories ('At the Mountains of Madness,' 'The Shadow Over Innsmouth,' and 'The Call of Cthulhu' among others), only to accept them at a later date when he was in a more amenable mood."

To a newcomer this would seem a straightforward statement that Wright rejected, then published *At the Mountains of Madness* and "The Shadow over Innsmouth"—which, as someone who knows Lovecraft better than Roland does (and their ranks will seem to be swelling as you work your way through this book) would be well aware, never happened. Only "The Call of Cthulhu," of the three stories mentioned, was first rejected, then published by *Weird Tales*. It is another matter entirely that Roland seriously underestimates the abilities and importance of Farnsworth Wright, who, despite excessive concern that overly sophisticated stories wouldn't go over well with his not-very-bright readership, was the architect of the magazine's greatness and one of the most important figures in twentieth-century weird fiction. Without Farnsworth Wright there would have been *no* market for most of the writings of Lovecraft, or Clark Ashton Smith, or Henry S. Whitehead, or Robert E. Howard (at least Howard's fantasy), or so many others.

Page 135. "Lovecraft used no maps" in his creations. Yes, he did. His maps of Arkham and Innsmouth are still extant, and have been reproduced many times.

But there is no need to go on like this. Roland begins well enough with a pretty good description of Lovecraft's childhood and adolescence, but things go downhill rapidly thereafter. This book fails in any attempt to give a clear sense of Lovecraft's personality, his outlook, or what much of his life was like. Indeed, after a while Roland seems to have forgotten he's writing a biography and goes in more and more for wannabe literary analysis, which is no better than his analysis of character.

Had he contented himself with regurgitating and condensing Joshi, he might have escaped without too much adverse notice, but disaster strikes as he attempts to introduce his own original ideas. He is in serious trouble by page 33 where he tries to apply a highly dubious diagnosis of Asperger's Syndrome to explain both Lovecraft's social behavior and the lack of conventional characterization in his stories. (Joshi explained the latter in terms of aesthetics, quoting Lovecraft's letters extensively to identify what Lovecraft thought was important in fiction.) There is an absurd statement on page 145 about Lovecraft's reluctance to write fiction "on spec." No, other than such commissioned jobs as the *Home Brew* stories and "Under the Pyramids," which was a ghostwriting job for Houdini, *every* piece of fiction Lovecraft ever wrote was "on spec," i.e., written without a guaranteed sale in front of him. Lovecraft, the ultimate gentleman amateur, *never* took such things into consideration before he sat down to write, and any would-be biographer who doesn't understand that clearly has no understanding of how Lovecraft thought or conducted his career.

On page 144 there is another absurdity, that the alien "colour" in "The Colour out of Space" is "too abstract to be threatening," to which, I should think, at least Nahum Gardner and his clan would take exception.

But enough nitpicking. I have noted on page 134: "shallow Age of Aquarius nonsense—*how* long ago was 1968?" Bit by bit we get a sinking feeling about Paul Roland, which is hideously confirmed on page 195, when the author suggests that Lovecraft did not take his dreams seriously enough:

> Had he studied theosophy or any other spiritual discipline rather than dismissing them out of hand, he would have discovered that what he assumed to be a sense of insignificance was instead an awareness of an infinitesimal but vital part of a greater reality. Vital in the sense that becoming aware of the existence of one's immortal True Self (also known in the esoteric tradition as the Higher Self) cannot but engender a positive attitude and end the illusion of "suffering"—as the Buddhists call it—which stems from our temporary separation from the divine source. It is the realization that the notorious magician Aleister Crowley expressed in the maxim: "Every man and woman a star."
>
> And the knowledge that while we may be physically separate from other sentient beings, we are at our very essence part of what Jung called the collective unconscious, or what the esotericists term the universal mind. It is this shared pool of past experience and accumulated knowledge that Lovecraft appears to have glimpsed in the deepest phase of sleep. In creating his dark pantheon of gods and monsters he gave form to his readers' fears of the unknown, both in this world and the one beyond.

Gee, that reminds me of the fan I met once who offered to "prove by logic" that all the lore in the Lovecraft stories was true and received "telepathically from another dimension."

The technical term we used to use for such persons is "New Age bozo." Here Paul Roland outdoes de Camp a thousandfold, trying to force his own (very silly, mystical) ideas onto his subject, then taking HPL to task for not being an occultist, as Roland very clearly seems to be. By the way, Lovecraft did know something about theosophy, though he remarked that its imaginings were far too cheerful for his tastes, and of course he knew that Madame

Blavatsky was a humbug. Lovecraft did not just dismiss such notions "out of hand," but concluded, through careful study and consideration, that they had no validity. The reason he did not recognize any "immortal True Self" or "soul" is that he did not believe in them. To Lovecraft, biological life was an electro-chemical phenomenon of no great consequence in the cosmos at large. His sense of insignificance was just that, a sense of insignificance. That is also the main theme or message of all Lovecraft's writings, and Roland apparently doesn't get it at all.

The whole shoddy construction of *The Curious Case of H. P. Lovecraft* comes crashing down. While the dust settles, we are surprised to learn (p. 218) that *The Outsider and Others* has always remained in print, that Ramsey Campbell is a contemporary of Lovecraft, or even (p. 188) that Lin Carter was a woman. Sorry, folks. This book is rubbish. Maybe my *Dream Quest of H. P. Lovecraft* wasn't as bad as this after all; it was merely shallow and sloppy. This is actively misleading.

There *is* a need for a short, easily readable guide to Lovecraft's life and work. I can recommend two, the foremost being Joshi's *H. P. Lovecraft: Nightmare Countries* (2012) and Peter Cannon's *H. P. Lovecraft* in Twayne's United States Authors Series (1989). But not this. The allegedly special features in the Roland volume aren't so special either. He reprints HPL's "History of the *Necronomicon*" as an appendix, but of course that is available elsewhere; and he also includes the original newspaper version of Sonia Greene's memoir of her marriage to HPL. The newspaper version may have minor textual variances, but a satisfactory version is in Cannon's *Lovecraft Remembered*. There is a brief summary of Lovecraft adaptations in movies, comics, and games, something Joshi did not attempt; but considering the source, hardly trustworthy.

Nothing of interest here. Move along.

www.ingramcontent.com/pod-product-compliance
Lightning Source LLC
Chambersburg PA
CBHW051821090426
42736CB00011B/1595